ELEMENTAL THINGS

'Here a man must shed the encumbrances that muffle
Contact with elemental things . . .'
                                        On a Raised Beach

TO MY MOTHER AND FATHER

'. . . and gladly teach'

HARVEY OXENHORN

Elemental Things

The Poetry of Hugh MacDiarmid

EDINBURGH University Press

© Harvey Oxenhorn 1984
Edinburgh University Press
22 George Square, Edinburgh

Set in Linoterm Plantin by
Speedspools, Edinburgh, and
printed in Great Britain at
The Alden Press, Oxford

This book has been published
with the financial assistance
of the Scottish Arts Council

British Library Cataloguing
    in Publication Data
Oxenhorn, Harvey
Elemental things
1. MacDiarmid, Hugh, 1892–1978—
    Criticism and interpretation
1. Title
821'.912   PR6013.R7352/
ISBN 0 85224 475 4

CONTENTS

PREFACE

NO ART IS MORE stubbornly national than poetry, as T.S. Eliot remarked, and no poet is more stubbornly national than Hugh MacDiarmid. It might thus seem inappropriate, if not foolhardy, for an American so distanced by geography and culture to attempt a full assessment of this poet's work.

On the other hand, MacDiarmid himself insisted that for modern Scottish literature to assume its rightful place among world letters, it must ask to be judged in the same breath, by the same criteria. With that end in mind, I set out to write a study that might at once avail non-Scots of the pleasures MacDiarmid's verse provides, and offer those who already know the poetry a fresh, more detailed perspective on it.

The result is this book. Given my own frame of reference, this study differs from most existing approaches (without which it could not have been attempted) in three ways:

First, while I regard the cultural issues as centrally important, I have sought by and large to separate the poetry from the tortuous polemics of Scottish nationalism. Extrinsic factors must be taken seriously. But the crucial dilemma for any writer *as writer* is not the quarrel with others, but the quarrel within, which arises from external quarrels, and the writer's work must finally be judged by how it recognizes and addresses those inner conflicts.

Second, though the poems which first expressed his dilemmas may be MacDiarmid's most beautiful and exciting – I am thinking of the early lyrics and *A Drunk Man Looks at the Thistle* – I suspect that the work which seeks to *resolve* them is his most distinctive and consequential for present-day readers.

Third, MacDiarmid's singularity among modern poets lay in his insistent effort to integrate personal and representative voices, private and public roles. Hence, a major portion of this book is devoted to less well-known work of the 1930s in which that effort takes place. The grandeur of this poet's thought and ferocity of his politics have long been known. The present book does not contest, but attempts to move beyond, the image of a fire-eater in his kilt before a microphone; to approach the more gentle, vital, visionary man portrayed on this volume's cover by a fellow American, the artist Tam MacPhail.

Because this book seeks to create an audience for MacDiarmid's poems as well as serve the existing one, its approach and level of detail vary. Some of the material in the early chapters may thus be familiar to Scottish readers; I ask them to bear with me as I lay the groundwork for the argument that follows. As for 'new' MacDiarmid readers, it is hoped that as the texture of that discussion thickens, its complexity will be relieved and justified by the value of the poetry it seeks to understand.

One last point: any attempt to 'get a fix' on such a vast, ambitious and uneven body of work necessarily entails selection, and subjective emphases with which other readers may well disagree. This is not only expected, but welcomed. If such interest leads to further study, so much the better. For the important thing at this date is not to have the last word on Hugh MacDiarmid – something that no-one ever accomplished when he was alive – but to ensure that his work becomes more readily appreciated, and more widely known.

A Note on Glossing

First occurrences of Scots words have been glossed only when the English equivalents are not readily grasped, from appearance and context. It is assumed that readers familiar with the Scots ballads or with Burns will find little difficulty with the loss of opening or final consonants, or with the majority of vowel changes. In most cases the ear will make good what the eye strains at. A short selective glossary is included, at the end of the book.

Harvey Oxenhorn
Cambridge, Massachusetts
June 1983

ACKNOWLEDGMENTS

I AM GRATEFUL to Mrs Valda Grieve, and to Michael and Deirdre Grieve, for their openness and generosity, and to others in Scotland whose hospitality and conversation made my work a pleasure: Alistair Dunnet, Hamish Henderson, Norman MacCaig, John MacQueen, Edwin Morgan, and Mr and Mrs Iain Crichton Smith. I have also talked or corresponded about MacDiarmid with Michael Alexander, Ann Boutelle, David Buchan, William Cookson, Charles W. Dunn, James Green, Brian Murphy, Robert Pinsky, James MacDonald Reid, Alexander Scott and, most helpfully, with Seamus Heaney.

My research was facilitated by a grant from the English Department at Stanford University. For putting me up (and putting up with me) in Scotland, I wish to thank John and Barbara Caughie, Chris Spears, Yvonne Baginsky and Jack Shea. Thanks are also due to Iain Ruaridh Ferguson and various MacAskills on Berneray, North Uist, in whose kind company I began to understand MacDiarmid's *Stony Limits*.

My book's shape and approach owe much to rich time spent in residence at The MacDowell Colony and Virginia Center for the Creative Arts; for their support and trust, I'm grateful.

This study relied on the facilities and collections of university libraries at Berkeley, Stanford, Harvard and Glasgow, at the National Library of Scotland and the Edinburgh City Library. I am especially indebted to the staff at the Edinburgh University Library for their patient searches through MacDiarmid's collected papers, many of which were not yet catalogued, and several of which are quoted in these pages.

A note of special thanks to Archie Turnbull of Edinburgh University Press; all authors should be blessed with such enthusiastic, discerning and accommodating publishers. For advice, encouragement and aid at various stages of this project, I am grateful to Andrew Brown, Margaret Bullitt, Peter Canby, William Chace, George Dekker, Margaretta Fulton, Michael Hattersley, Richard Liberthson, Eric Solomon, Ginny Reiser and Sheryl White; for their love and support throughout, to Mera and Harvey Flaumenhaft, and my brother, Mitchel.

Lastly, I am deeply indebted to those who advised this book in its earlier form: to Albert Gelpi and Ian Watt, who, while setting the example of their own work, found time to offer rigorous, rewarding comments on the hows and whats of mine; and above all, to Donald Davie, for the whys.

The publishers record their profound appreciation of the permission of the executors, MacDiarmid estate, to quote liberally from the poet's work; as also of the publishers of the *Complete Poems, 1920–76*, Martin Brian and O'Keeffe. Similar indebtedness and acknowledgment is recorded to the following: Jonathan Cape, London, for an extract from Robert Frost's 'West Running Brook'; Faber and Faber, for an extract from Ezra Pound's 'Δώρια' (merely the latest of many kindnesses); Macmillan, for an extract from Thomas Hardy's 'In Time of "The Breaking of Nations"'. Permission to quote from works cited in the footnotes and the bibliography is gratefully acknowledged, to the authors and to the following publishers: Akros, Carcanet Press, Bodley Head, W. and R. Chambers, Chatto and Windus, Faber and Faber, Harvard University Press, Oliver and Boyd, Open University Press, and Scottish Academic Press.

CHAPTER ONE

A Scottish Renaissance

Far aff our gentles fro their poets flew
And scorn'd to own that *Lallan* songs they knew.
A. WILSON, *Poems,* 1816

My function in Scotland during the past twenty or thirty
years has been that of the catfish that vitalizes the other
torpid denizens of the aquarium. And what a job!
HUGH MACDIARMID, *Lucky Poet,* 1943

.   .   .
.   .
.

IN A VALLEY in Dumfriesshire, eighteen miles from the English border, three small swift rivers converge. Where their waters come together, they are spanned by a footbridge, linking the town on one bank with a kirk of dank brown stone on the other side. Beyond, the terrain rises. Dense woods give way to thistle-strewn pasture, hollows and swells flecked with fat sheep and bracken, the sun-dappled, rain-soaked hills of the Scottish borders. Astride its rivers, the town which those hills enclose seems built on a liquid centre, a core of flux seen by day in the play of bright water, heard at night as a gurgle down streets to the square. The names of the rivers are Wauchope, Esk and Ewes. The town is Langholm – birthplace, on August 11, 1892, of Christopher Murray Grieve.

Langholm was known for its agricultural markets and large sheep fairs, its rural beauty and strong communal traditions. The most famous of these was the Common-Riding Day, so called because it asserted the boundaries of common lands by riding around them. On the last Friday of July, the Fair Crier (son and grandson of previous criers) stood up in front of the town hall to proclaim the ceremonies (cry the fair). Soon after, a young man elected from among all others, the Cornet, leapt on his horse. Unfurling the banner of the ancient burgh, he thundered off up a steep stone street, with dozens of other riders galloping behind. Atop Whitla Hill, outside the town, they circled a monument in silence; then, moving on, they rode circuit on the boundaries of Langholm's land. At each of the corners, the Cornet dismounted and turned the common earth with a silver spade.

Back in town, the fair would be cried again several times throughout the day. A procession wound snake-like through the streets. Among the emblems carried at its head – in addition to a crown of roses – were an eight-foot thistle, a barley bannock, and a salt herring fixed to a circle of wood with a twelvepenny nail. Children received threepenny coins as gifts, and carried heather besoms.[1] With its blend of Christian emblems and pagan agricul-tural rites, the day was – and still is – an occasion of power and pride, to be reaffirmed in poetry by Grieve:

---

[1] For a full account, see Hugh MacDiarmid, *Lucky Poet* (London: Methuen, 1943), p.222. Henceforth *LP*.

The bearer twirls the Bannock-and-Saut-Herrin',   *Oat cake*
The Croon o' Roses through the lift is farin',   *sky*

The aucht-fit thistle wallops on hie;   *eight-foot | flaps | high*
In heather besoms a' the hills gang by.   *brooms*

But noo it's a' the fish o' the sea
Nailed on the roond o' the Earth to me.

Beauty and Love that are bobbin' there;
Syne the breengin' growth that alane I bear . . .   *Then | bursting*

Drums in the Walligate, pipes in the air,
Come and hear the cryin' o' the Fair.

A' as it used to be, when I was a loon   *boy*
On Common-Ridin' Day in the Muckle Toon.   *Big Town*

The 'muckle toon' was also a mill town. The tanneries and tweed mills along the River Esk were small by the standards of Glasgow – none of the looms or dye vats stood more than a few hundred yards from woods and pasture – yet they supported most of Langholm's 2400 residents. And if rituals of rural origin celebrated what they held in common, life in the mills defined modern class distinctions. Most of the workers ('waterside folk') dwelt in damp terraces along the Esk and Ewes, whereas managers and owners occupied a hill back from the waters, well above the town.

The Grieves lived between the two on Parliament Square. Christopher Grieve's paternal grandfather and cousins worked in the textile mills. Generations of his mother's family had occupied a small farm which the poet named 'Crowdieknowe'. They were poor but not indigent; reticent, independent and fierce. As a child, Grieve was terrified by thick-whiskered, iron-willed patriarchs who commonly lived past ninety. From them he inherited a sense of the ancient 'Border character', and in subsequent years he would trace his own tenacity and mettle to the men of Crowdieknowe:

Oh to be at Crowdieknowe
When the last trumpet blaws
An' see the deid come loupin' owre   *leaping*
The auld grey wa's.

Muckle men wi' tousled beards   *great, huge*
I grat at as a bairn   *wept | child*
'll scramble frae the croodit clay   *crowded*
Wi' feck o' swearin'.   *a great deal*

An' glower at God an' a' his gang   *glare*
O' angels i' the lift
– Thae trashy bleezin' French-like folk   *blazing*
Wha gar'd them shift!   *made*

Fain the weemun-folk'll seek   *eagerly*
To mak' them haud their row   *be quiet*
– *Fegs, God's no blate gin he stirs up*   *Truly | bashful | if*
The men o' Crowdieknowe!

Grieve's youth was typical of the provincial tradesman class. His father was a postman. The family lived in the library building, from whose steps the Langholm Common Riding was proclaimed each year, and young Grieve spent much of his leisure time alone in the library above his home. Looking back, he recalls that his mother had 'genteel ideas'.[1] She was a deeply religious Presbyterian and encouraged her son's intellectual pursuits. Enrolled in Langholm Academy at age seven, he progressed to Broughton Higher Grade School and Junior Student Centre, in Edinburgh, which he attended, as 'pupil teacher', until shortly before his father's death in 1911.

Grieve's early life figured in his future work in two ways: it provided the major subject matter and settings, and it inspired a personal sense of place and class that would never fade.

The subject matter reflects his combined inheritance of life in the factories (from his father's side) and on the farm (from his mother's). However much Grieve's own thought subsequently changed, the emotions that underlay it remained grounded in the rhythms and social relations of small town life. Much of his writing seeks, implicitly, to reconcile radical political and intellectual beliefs with a highly traditional, less alienated youth; to address the tensions of the larger world in the language of boyhood, and Langholm.

Recalling the scene of that childhood, Grieve writes of

> . . . a bountifulness so inexhaustible that it has supplied all my subsequent poetry with a tremendous gratitude of reminiscence . . . of an almost tropical luxuriance of Nature – of great forests, of honey-scented heather hills, and moorlands infinitely rich in little-appreciated beauties of flowering, of animal and insect life, of strange and subtle relationships of water and light . . . and a multitude of rivers.[2]

One notes in this description a surprising absence of those

[1] *LP*, p.225.   [2] *Ibid.*, p.219.

factors that tend to erode traditional and local culture; in this context certain usages which might now sound forced or archaic to an outsider still retained currency. The great levellers of modern speech – radio and television – had yet to exert their influence. Though the average rural dweller read and wrote in English, he still spoke unselfconsciously in Scots:[1] 'When I was a boy . . . we did not speak English, but a racy Scots, with distinct variations in places only a few miles away'.[2] Scots usages prevailed most notably in descriptions of the natural landscape, the weather, tools, and intimate emotion.

But while life outside the classroom continued to employ the traditional tongue, the schools tried to enforce a discipline based on the repudiation of indigenous speech and culture. Scots was discouraged in the schools. As English was mastered, teachers strove to extirpate the 'Scottish accent'. Students were discouraged not only from speaking Scots, but were also denied most opportunities to read it. As Grieve would later write:

> Intelligent young Scots . . . might well have been excused for failing to detect any . . . great qualities in the very inferior types of Scots literature they came into contact with. Scottish children are still taught only a little Burns and a few ballads. They are not taught anything of the Auld Makars. For the most part, their attention is confined to English literature. It is not surprising, therefore, that they should regard Scottish literature as a mere sideline.[3]

As shall be seen below (p. 19ff.), the terms 'English', 'Scottish' and 'Scots' as used here may blur crucial distinctions. But the main point is certainly valid: literature in English was taught, while its equal or better in Scots was systematically ignored. To understand why, we must briefly recall the changing relation of the two tongues over time.[4]

At the start of the sixteenth century, most of the people of England spoke and wrote in English, while most of the people of Scotland

---

[1] More precisely, one of a number of regional dialects mixed with a heavily accented English.
[2] *LP*, p.17.
[3] Hugh MacDiarmid, *Albyn, or Scotland and the Future* (London: Kegan Paul, 1927), pp.50, 56, 40. Henceforth *Albyn*.
[4] Much of the material in the following section may be familiar to Scottish readers. Non-Scottish readers who wish to pursue these matters in more detail will find a balanced and thoughtful introduction in David Craig's *Scottish Literature and the Scottish People* (London: Chatto and Windus, 1961), on which my own account leans.

spoke and wrote in Scots. Each tongue was the language of a literature and people, a nation and a crown. By that century's close, however, political and social upheavals affected the independence of the northern nation. First the Reformation, with its English Bible, changed the *lingua franca* for religious discourse. Then, in 1603, came the Union of Crowns. When James VI of Scotland became James I of England, a realm became a region. The Scottish court left Edinburgh for London, and the language it left behind ceased to develop.

Of course, a language which ceases to grow does not cease to exist. The majority of Scottish people continued to employ their native tongue, and for a long time educated Scots spoke in their own way while learning to write as the English did. But within little more than another century, English had become the sole language for instruction, public speech, and even private correspondence. Most education was church related; the Confession of Faith, the Shorter Catechism and metrical versions of the psalms, as well as tracts and sermons, were all in English. Moreover, secular books were expensive, and Scotland was poor. Thus anyone who bought books or sought a wide audience for his own was required to use the southern tongue.

In the eighteenth century, Scottish men of letters looked to England not only for the opportunity of wider distribution, but also for the literary culture to be found there, from London coffee-houses to great men's country homes. With access to patronage and power, figures such as Dryden, Pope and Johnson enjoyed a central position in their own culture; as acknowledged arbiters of taste, they made letters part of the 'the province of manners'.[1] Their literary notions of decorum mirrored and shaped the polite culture in which they participated day to day, and the familiar idiom of court and salon gave actuality and bite to the written works that it occasioned. It was precisely because Pope was so at home in the idiom of those he satirized that he could make full imaginative use of it; his habitual private voice merged confidently with an accepted public role.

The situation of Scottish writers was very different. Without the sinecures of a court, or the patronage of great houses, the typical Scottish man of letters had to work for a living. He was not an arbiter but an aspirant, the perpetual poor cousin. When he did

---

[1] The phrase comes from F. R. Leavis, *Revaluation* (London: Chatto and Windus, 1936), p.112.

seek to make his literary mark, it was in a still half-foreign tongue, and 'all the time he was haunted by an uneasy feeling that even his choicest English was not free from those dreadful solecisms known as Scotticisms'.[1] David Hume was so unsure of his own English that he secured the services of friends to excise Scotticisms from his writing.[2]

The complement of insecurity toward the English was a quest for distance from one's less 'cultivated' fellow Scots, and the traditional social life of Scotland. For, as David Craig has described, the rich 'socialness' of the north was not expressed in court, salon, and ballroom, but in the old communal culture of street fairs and festivals, feasts and taverns. Even Edinburgh was still villagey, with its primitive conditions, cramped closes, and vertical distribution of social classes.[3] The polite culture to which Scottish *literati* aspired thus bore little organic relation to the daily life around them. Manners which in the south expressed a positive code became for northerners a less grounded and more rigid imitation, and entailed a purposeful denial. A desire to studiously shun 'the low' (and thereby elevate themselves) made many in the rising Anglo-Scottish class indifferent to much of the life in their own country.

In addition to its implicitly anti-democratic politics, this attitude had broader implications for the culture as a whole.

In psychological terms, the rejection of indigenous folk culture meant also rejecting the non-discursive, imaginative, 'disorderly' aspects of personality as embodied in that culture; eschewing the 'gothic' for the 'neo-classic'; identifying separate languages with separated components of the psyche, and cultivating one to the exclusion of the other.

In literary terms, the result was a precise, disembodied, cosmopolitan idiom which produced indisputable triumphs in law, economics, and political and moral philosophy, but almost no expression of personal, intimate, imaginative values. From such matters the Humanists removed themselves, just as they left 'Auld Reekie' for the geometries of Edinburgh's New Town. In recoiling

---

[1] W. A. Craigie *et al.*, *The Scottish Tongue* (London: Cassell, 1924), p.7.
[2] The awkwardness of Hume (and Adam Smith) in English is discussed by George Elder Davie in *The Democratic Intellect* (Edinburgh: The University Press, 1961), Chapter One, and by Peter Giles in 'Dialect in Literature' in Craigie, p.113.
[3] Craig, Chapter One, *passim*.

from disorder, they steered clear of the vivid mess of actuality on which imaginative literature depends.

In response to the abstract elevation and poetic diction of written work in English, writing in Scots became correspondingly self-conscious and limited. It relied more and more on 'hamely' strategies which, if less bland, were no more conducive to an integration of imaginative and intellectual needs. Moreover, as the weight and quality of printed prose imposed standard English, work in Scots was reduced to its narrowest oral basis.[1] As used by Burns and his less talented followers, work in Scots became necessarily an imitation or transcript of speech. By the time of Christopher Grieve's childhood, the vernacular, which had once defined a culture, was seen as the antithesis of 'culture' – a vehicle devoid of dignity, a telltale register of social class.

Class relations in Britain were deeply shaken by the Great War. The failure of those in command to comprehend the true nature of that conflict called into question both the code by which they justified it, and the language that embodied that code. In the 1920s, it was said that all the important words had been killed in the War. While this thought produced various effects upon writing in English – one thinks of Hemingway's reticence, Eliot's colloquialism, Dos Passos' 'newsreels' – it also led others to look beyond English, to other cultures. What new resources of language and history might they offer?

The question was raised by W. A. Craigie in a lecture to the Vernacular Circle of the London Burns Club on 10 January 1921. Discussing 'The Present State of the Scottish Tongue', Craigie, then Professor of Anglo-Saxon at Oxford, warned that loss of the Scots tongue implied denationalization, adding, 'I cannot readily imagine a more humiliating situation than for a nation to depend on a glossary for the understanding of its national poet [Burns]'. After citing the literary revivals of Frisian, Catalan, Provençal, Breton, Bohemian, Hungarian, Flemish, the Norwegian 'Landsmaal' and Faroese, he challenged his listeners:

> Can you imagine a complete grammar of Lowland Scots, written throughout in that language? The Frisians and Faroese have done that for their tongues. Can you imagine a work on Botany written throughout in the Scottish tongue? There is one in the Faroese. If anyone doubts the possibility of recreating a literary tongue, capable

[1] *Ibid.*, p.250 ff.

of expressing all the necessary ideas which must occur in dealing with literature, history, science, even philosophy, I will direct him to what has been written in the new Norwegian tongue within the past twenty years . . .[1]

The gauntlet which Craigie threw down was picked up scarcely seven months later by Christopher Grieve. Since being demobbed in 1919, Grieve had written some rather conventional verse (in English) and worked as a reporter for the *Montrose Review*.[2] From 1920 to 1922, he edited *Northern Numbers*, an annual anthology of Scottish poets, including William Soutar, Violet Jacob, Lewis Spence and Neil Munro.[3] During 1922, Grieve also published a series of anonymous articles in the *Dunfermline Press*. One of these stated, 'If there is to be a Scottish literary revival, the first essential is to get rid of our provinciality of outlook, and to avail ourselves of Continental experience. The prevalent indifference in Scotland to foreign literature is itself one of the causes of the continued domination and subversion of Scottish literature by English literature.'[4]

This was written on 5 August 1922. Three weeks later, a new monthly review called the *Scottish Chapbook* appeared. Its cover bore a rampant lion and the slogan 'Not Traditions – Precedents'. Its first page proclaimed the following programme:

The Chapbook Programme
'Il far un libro meno è che niente
Se il libro fatto non rifa la gente . . .'
To make a book is less than nothing unless the book, when made, makes people anew.

The principal aims and objects of *The Scottish Chapbook* are:

To report, support and stimulate, in particular . . . the campaign . . . for the revival of the Doric; the movement towards a Scots National Theatre; and the 'Northern Numbers' movement in contemporary Scottish poetry.

---

[1] Craigie, *op. cit.*, p.45.
[2] Grieve served with the Royal Medical Corps in Salonika as a sergeant, where he contracted malaria and was invalided out. Upon his recovery in 1917, he was assigned to hospital duty in Marseilles.
[3] A more detailed account of this 'movement's' development may be found in Duncan Glen, *Hugh MacDiarmid and the Scottish Renaissance* (Edinburgh and London: Chambers, 1964). Besides ordering many of the tangled facts in an intelligible chronology, Glen avoids the inaccuracies that mar several other accounts.
[4] 'Scottish Books and Bookmen', *Dunfermline Press*, 5 August 1922, p.6.

To encourage and publish the work of contemporary Scottish poets and dramatists, whether in English, Gaelic or Braid Scots.

To insist upon truer evaluations of the work of Scottish writers than are usually given in the present over-Anglicised condition of British literary journalism, and, in criticism, elucidate, apply, and develop the distinctively Scottish range of values.

To bring Scottish Literature into closer touch with current European tendencies in technique and ideation . . .

The Scottish Chapbook was published monthly until October 1923. Each 30-page issue contained poems and stories, book reviews, 'Modern Scottish Bibliographies', advertising, and an essay called 'Causerie: A Theory of Scottish Letters', which was unsigned but written by C. M. Grieve. The magazine featured established writers (such as those in *Northern Numbers*) as well as newcomers, notably Helen Cruikshank and Edwin Muir. As such names suggest, the movement in those early days had room for Anglo-Scots and Orkneymen; the nascent Scottish Renaissance did not yet mean a Renaissance in Scots. Still, the *Chapbook* was essentially a one-man operation – published and posted from Grieve's own home – and as his own views evolved, the tone of the publication changed.[1]

In September 1922, Grieve publicly renounced his previous opposition to the Doric revival.[2] In October, *The Scottish Chapbook* led off with a lyric in Scots – 'The Watergaw' – by a poet identified as 'Hugh M'Diarmid'. In that same issue, the editor (Grieve!) tried to account for the poem's power:

> The value of the Doric lies in the extent to which it contains lapsed or unrealized qualities which correspond to 'unconscious' elements of distinctively Scottish psychology. The recovery and application of these may make effectively communicable those unexpressed aspects of Scottish character, the absence of which makes, say, 'Kailyard' characters shallow, sentimental, humiliating travesties.[3]

The terms of this argument expanded rapidly. A half year later, Grieve wrote:

[1] As did its contents. Whether because of ego, or because Grieve himself was writing the most, and best, material in Scots, the final issue (Vol.II, No.3) is devoted almost exclusively to his own poems.
[2] Address to the Annual Conference of the Burns Federation held in Birmingham, 1-2 September 1922.
[3] 'Causerie', *Scottish Chapbook* I, 3 (October 1922), pp.62-3. For 'Kailyard' see below, p.17.

> The Scots Vernacular is a vast storehouse of just the very peculiar and subtle effects which modern European literature in general is assiduously seeking, and if the next century is to see an advance in mental science, the resumption of the Scots Vernacular in the main stream of European letters is in a fashion . . . inevitable.[1]

Within three short years, Grieve's indifference to a cultural revival had changed into impassioned support. And as his efforts coalesced around restoration of the language *per se*, his vision of the movement's modern international ramifications grew more radical. Christopher Murray Grieve became Hugh MacDiarmid.[2]

As Kenneth Buthlay has said, it was 'more of a *nom de guerre* than a *nom de plume*'.[3] In the five years that followed, MacDiarmid/Grieve published four volumes of poetry, two of prose, an edition of Burns, at least seventeen articles in periodicals, and numerous reviews and polemical pieces.[4] The latter included weekly editorials in *The Scottish Nation* (May–December 1923), articles in the *New Age* (1924–28), a series of 'Contemporary Scottish Studies' in the *Scottish Education Journal* (1925), and columns and poems in *The Glasgow Herald* and *Scots Observer* (1927–28).

Throughout the period, Grieve continued to earn his living as a reporter for the *Montrose Review*, and prospered there. He had married Peggy Skinner in 1918; they had a daughter, Christine, in 1924, and a son, Walter, five years later. By coincidence, Edwin and Willa Muir came to stay with Willa's mother in Montrose after leaving Prague in 1924. Though Grieve and Muir would break bitterly six years later, during the twenties their relationship was warm.[5]

[1] 'Causerie', *Scottish Chapbook* 1, 8 (March 1923), p.210.
[2] Except for *Annals of the Five Senses*, published in 1923, all the poetry was issued under the pseudonym. The name Grieve continued to be used for prose, although with decreasing frequency, as late as 1935.
[3] Kenneth Buthlay, *Hugh MacDiarmid* (Edinburgh: Oliver & Boyd, 1964), p.1.
[4] The most useful MacDiarmid bibliographies appear in Glen; in Buthlay; in William R. Aitken and others, *Hugh MacDiarmid: A Festschrift*, ed. K. D. Duval and Sydney Goodsir Smith (Edinburgh: Duval, 1962); and, lastly, in the Catalogue to a National Library of Scotland Exhibition (Edinburgh, 1967).
[5] Mrs Grieve dates the break as occurring in London, in 1930, and ascribes it primarily to tensions with Willa, not Edwin, Muir (personal interview, at *Brownsbank*, Biggar, 24 June 1980). In any case, relations were unalterably damaged by Muir's belief that Scotsmen 'feel in Scots but think in English', his resulting opposition to Scots – and by MacDiarmid's own vituperative responses. Muir's argument appears in full in *Scot and Scotland: The Predicament of the Scottish Writer* (London: Routledge, 1936).

As far back as 1908, Grieve had joined the Fabian Society, and in 1911, James Maxton's Independent Labour Party. While in Montrose, Grieve became increasingly involved in politics. In 1922 he was elected town councillor (as an Independent Socialist); in 1926, a Justice of the Peace. Having turned down an offer to stand for a seat in the Commons, from Banffshire (as an Independent Labourite or Socialist), Grieve co-founded, in 1928, the National Party of Scotland.

His poetic gifts aside, the sheer energy and visibility of these 'supporting roles' established Grieve/MacDiarmid as a leading figure in the hotly debated national revival. In the *Revue Anglo-Américaine* of April 1924, an earnest young French critic, Denis Seurat, numbered fifty writers among 'le groupe de "La Renaissance Ecossaise"'. After devoting half of his discussion to C.M. Grieve, 'l'âme du mouvement . . . [qui] . . . mériterait à lui seul toute une étude', and half to the poetry of Hugh MacDiarmid, Seurat concluded, 'Je me suis attardé à présenter deux écrivains qui me semblait les meilleurs'.[1] High compliment indeed – and twice the intended praise!

MacDiarmid's first book of poems in Scots, *Sangschaw*, appeared in 1925. As a reviewer for the *Times Literary Supplement* explained:

> He writes in the faith without which there can be no conquest, the belief that Scotland still has something to say to the imagination of mankind, something that she alone among the nations can say, and can say only in her native tongue.[2]

What exactly was this tongue? At first known as *Doric*, it was later more frequently called *Lallans* ('lowlands'), a term used by Burns to distinguish broad Scots from the Gaelic of the Highlands.[3] As the debate surrounding Lallans grew, the terms 'plastic' or 'synthetic' Scots also acquired currency. Used by both opponents and proponents, including MacDiarmid, 'synthetic' did *not* imply the fabrication of words or phrases; it denoted the collection of

---

[1] 'Le Groupe de la Renaissance Ecossaise', pp.301, 302, 307.
[2] 'A Scottish Renaissance', *TLS* (7 January 1926), p.8.
[3] In 'Address to the Deil' and in 'Epistle to William Simpson': 'In days when mankind were but callans . . . / But spak their thoughts in plain, braid Lallans / Like you or me.' The term 'Doric' may have been discarded because it implied an inferior relationship to 'Attic' English, or suggested archaism. The latter Burns poem contains Burns' pledge to do for his part of Scotland (Ayrshire) what Ramsay and Fergusson achieved in the speech of theirs, Fife and the Lothians.

normally discrete dialects into one comprehensive tongue. That, in turn, was augmented by literary sources. As John Buchan explained in the Preface to *Sangschaw*, 'Since there is no canon of the vernacular, he [MacDiarmid] makes his own, as Burns did, and borrows words and idioms from the old masters.'

Those whom MacDiarmid most admired included the fifteenth- and sixteenth-century Scottish poets Robert Henryson, Gavin Douglas, Alexander Montgomerie, Alexander Scott, and, above all, William Dunbar.[1] For Dunbar had in his own time synthesized a poetic language to produce what is among the finest European verse of the century after Chaucer. Borrowing from alien sources, his court poems blended the meters of Continental verse with 'aureate diction' and indigenous Scots alliteration to produce extraordinary richness.[2] His Goliardic poems played upon the tension between lines in different languages (Latin and Scots). And his comic, satiric work, such as 'The Tretis of the Twa Marriit Women and the Wedo', juxtaposed the language of romance with a Scots street vernacular to secure the triumph – in verse, at any rate – of natural instinct over false piety. Dunbar was therefore seen by MacDiarmid as a model of 'technical ability, versatility in creative effort, linguistic experiment . . .'.[3]

A second respect in which the Makars would become the young poet's models was that noted by Allan Ramsay two centuries before. In his introduction to *The Evergreen* (1724), Ramsay pointed out that, unlike much medieval verse, the older Scots poetry kept its eye on the poets' native landscape. In this way, the allegorical tableaux in medieval writing (including *The Kingis Quair*, supposedly by James I) were to some extent naturalized. The difference is most apparent in descriptions elicited by the harsh northern climate and landscape. As an example, one might compare the openings of Chaucer's *Troilus and Criseyde* and Henryson's *The Testament of Cresseid*, or the Temple of Mars in 'The Knight's Tale' (ll. 1117–92) with Henryson's Saturn (ll. 155–61):

| His face fronsit, his lyre was lyke the leid | *wrinkled / skin* |
| His teith chatterit, and cheverit with the chin | *shivered* |

[1] MacDiarmid eventually came to consider Henryson Dunbar's equal, if not his superior. See MacDiarmid, Introd., *Henryson*, Sel. Hugh MacDiarmid (Harmondsworth: Penguin, 1973), p.8.
[2] John Speirs, *The Scots Literary Tradition*, 2nd ed. (London: Faber, 1962), p.57.
[3] Introd., Hugh MacDiarmid, *Selected Poems of William Dunbar* (Edinburgh: Oliver & Boyd, 1952), p.2.

His ene drowpit, how sonkin in his heid	*drooped / hollow*
Out of his nois the meldrop fast can rin	*drip / run*
With lippis bla and cheikis leine and thin.	*livid (blue)*
The ice schoklis that fra his hair down hang	*icicles*
Was wonder greit, and as ane speir als lang.[1]	

The Scots *Aeneid* of Gavin Douglas (1475–1522) could be even more stark:

. . . The soill, ysowpit into wattir, wak;	*soaked / swampy*
The firmament, ourkest with rokis, blak	*mists*
The ground fadyt, and fauch wolx all the feildis;	*fallow, dun*
Montayne toppis, sleikit wyth snaw, ourheildes;	*hide, are hidden*
On reggit rolkis of hard harsk quhyne-stane	*ragged / rocks / rugged*
With frossyne frontis cauld clynty clewis schane;	*flinty / ravine / shone*
Beaute was lost and barrand schew the landis	
With frostis haire ourfret, the feildis standes . . .	
Sour bitter bubbis and the schouris snell	*cold, wet / gusts*
Semyt on the sward ane similitude of hell	
Redusyng to our mynd, in every steid	*recalling / place*
Goustly schaddois of eild and greissly deid.	*old age / death*

Here, in the Prologue to Book Seven, a medieval convention (the pageant of seasons) is rendered actual; Scottish winter serves as a fit introduction to the underworld. The realism, sinew and concision of such writing led Ezra Pound to prefer it to the original: 'Virgil came to life again in 1514 . . . because Gavin Douglas knew the sea better than Virgil had'.[2] In Douglas, MacDiarmid also found qualities he sought to recreate in contemporary verse. Idiosyncratic blending of diction and technique were revealed as not detrimental, but essential to the expression of Scottish sensibility. Alliteration, jammed consonants, a sculpted quality, the use of catalogue and sense of mass – all would figure largely in MacDiarmid's own writing, especially in the later 'geological' poems.[3]

Finally, the old masters had been cosmopolitan figures whose work in their native language was a respected part of the European literature of their time. For them, Scots was a suitable tongue in

---

[1] The latter comparison is suggested in Speirs, p.49.
[2] Ezra Pound, *ABC of Reading* (1934; rpt. New York: New Directions, 1960), p.45. As always with Pound, one must be wary of quoting out of context. MacDiarmid misquotes him on Douglas in several places; those who are interested in the matter are advised to see the page cited and the Douglas selections Pound placed in the 'Exhibits' section of his book.
[3] See below, p.119.

which to address supra-national issues. While the language itself expressed pride in locality, their intellectual concerns fostered on-going ties with the Continent.

Long after the religious and political alliances linking medieval Scotland and France were destroyed, intellectual affinities between the two nations persisted. During her second 'Golden Age' (1740–1830), the ethics, philosophy and law of 'metaphysical Scotland' had more in common with continental rationalism than with existing English systems.[1] Hume, Hutcheson and Hugh Blair sought to make Scotland European as much as English. They did not go to London; indeed, Hume felt much more at home in Paris.[2]

Such men, with their Select Society, represented the polite, philosophical side of eighteenth-century culture. Its other aspect, with closer ties to the anti-Whig tradition, found a voice in the Edinburgh Cape Club, and its main creative talent in Robert Fergusson (1750–74). Fergusson expressed his intellectual fervour and Jacobite allegiance in lines such as these, from 'The Ghaists':

How maun their weyms wi' secret hunger slack   *bellies*
Their deeds in targets flaff upo' their back,
When they are doom'd to keep a lasting Lent
Starving for England's weel at *three per cent* . . .

Fergusson's Scots 'was the Scots not of the rustic but of the educated classes, who made daily use of it in Edinburgh at even a later date'.[3] Blending lyrical and satirical elements in a way reminiscent of Dunbar, he attempted ambitious and thoughtful poems in the native tongue. In Edwin Muir's opinion, he succeeded

. . . better than Burns, for he was a more scrupulous artist and he used a more organic language . . . One feels, indeed, that had he lived [past age 25] he might have continued, with his genius for words, to turn dialect Scots into a literary language, for it is evident from his poetry, as from no other Scottish dialect poetry . . . that *he is thinking in the terms of the language he uses* . . .[4]

When Fergusson wrote in English, he used it to ape and mock the Augustan neo-classic style. In 'The Sow of Feeling', for in-

[1] George Elder Davie, Chapter 1, *passim*.
[2] David Daiches, *Robert Burns* (New York: Rinehart & Co., 1950), pp.28 and 25.
[3] T. F. Henderson, *Scottish Vernacular Literature* (London: Nutt, 1938).
[4] Muir, p.50.

stance, his porcine heroine laments her late mate's passing as
follows:

> Oft did his lusty head defend my tail
> From the rude whimpers of the angry gale
> While nose-refreshing puddles stream'd around
> And floating odours hail'd the dung-clad ground.

The objects of this satire were Henry MacKenzie (1745–1831),
whose novel, *The Man of Feeling* (1771), inspired the vogue of
'sentiment'.

Where Fergusson had felt contempt, Robert Burns (1759–96)
expressed unbounded admiration. Though the Preface to his Kil-
marnock poems of 1786 praises Fergusson, it begins on a note of
exaggerated humility that would certainly have displeased his predecessor:

> The following trifles are not the production of the Poet, who with all
> the advantages of learned art, and perhaps amid the elegancies and
> idlenesses of upper life, looks down for a rural theme, with an eye to
> Theocritus or Virgil. To the author of this, these and other celebrated
> names their countrymen are, in their original languages, 'a fountain
> shut up, and a book sealed'. Unacquainted with the necessary re-
> quisites for commencing Poet by rule, he sings the sentiments and
> manners, he felt and saw in himself and his rustic compeers around
> him, in his and their native language.

Whether or not Burns actually wrote this preface, he was quick to
accept praise based upon its premises. By playing the simple rustic,
he thus catered to the vogue of sentiment which Fergusson had
mocked. Soon after, Mackenzie was praising in print the sagacity
of this 'Heaven-taught ploughman'. The Burns cult had begun.

Once the *literati* (from whom the educated Fergusson remained
aloof) had adopted the 'rustic Bard', Burns would find it hard to
break free of the role by which he had gained acceptance. Whenever he wrote with one eye on the genteel Edinburgh reader, the
results were defensive joking, self-conscious exercises in stilted
English, and a broad retreat from philosophical discussion in
Scots.

It was this last development that most disturbed MacDiarmid,
leading him to charge that 'Burns betrayed the movement Ramsay
and Fergusson began'.[1] By delegating different tasks to different
languages – 'reflection' to English, and 'free expression' to Scots –

[1] *Selected Essays of Hugh MacDiarmid* (London, Jonathan Cape,
1969), p.174.

Burns confirmed the equation of the vernacular with particular subjects, and predictable attitudes toward those subjects. It is true that his sardonic common sense, reductive physicality and vulgarity were more calculated than is sometimes recognized.[1] Nevertheless, strengths exercised too narrowly turn into limitations; if Anglo-Scottish writing was often deficient in actuality and spontaneous warmth, then verse in Scots was becoming nothing *but*. Moreover, a manner so deliberately vulgar was inevitably vulgarized; when divorced from Burns' social and political concerns in the years that followed, the rustic posture became a model for generations of anti-intellectual, boozy, mawkish verse in Scots.

Throughout the 1840s, such verse was widely disseminated in the *Whistle-Binkie* anthology, published serially in Glasgow. Named for a whistle-binkie, 'one who attends a penny wedding, but without paying anything . . . a mere spectator who . . . may whistle for his own amusement',[2] these books perpetuated an image of the 'canny Scot' as provincial jester, acceding to his own irrelevance. In the century's last decades, that image became the basis of the so-called Kailyard [cabbage yard] School. 'Kailyard' describes a type of writing popular in Scotland from c. 1880. Its main exponents were 'I. McLaren' (John Watson), S.R.Crockett and J.M.Barrie, and the name was apparently suggested by the line from the Jacobite song, 'There grows a bonny brier bush in my kailyard'. The genre dealt mainly with domestic life, contained a good deal of dialect speech, and was written in a heavily sentimental vein.

[1] Though Burns was not comfortable in the role of village rake, 'he occasionally expressed his general feelings of unrest and dissatisfaction with his environment by melodramatically playing the role of one'. Daiches, p.78.
[2] John Jamieson, *An Etymological Dictionary of the Scottish Language*, 1808; New Edition, rev. and enl. by John Longmuir and David Donaldson (Paisley: Alexander Gardner, 1879-82), 4 vols. Throughout this study I shall make references to three dictionaries, of which 'Jamieson' is the oldest. The others (henceforth cited in the text) are:
Sir William A. Craigie, *A Dictionary of the Older Scottish Tongue* (London; Oxford University Press, 1931-67), 5 vols, still in progress. Henceforth 'Craigie'.
The Scottish National Dictionary, ed. William Grant (1929-46) and David D. Murison (1946-76) (Edinburgh: The Scottish National Dictionary Association Ltd, 1931-76), 10 vols. Henceforth '*SND*'.
Craigie contains words in general usage up to c.1700; the *SND* concentrates on c.1700 to the present, and includes many, but not all, usages cited in Jamieson. The *OED* can be of great help for words that retained currency in Scots after passing out of standard English.

It must be noted, in fairness, that popular Victorian writing in English could be equally cloying. But it was not the *only* work in that language; there were also Browning, Tennyson, Housman, Swinburne, Arnold. Similarly, although regional speech denoted class (and restricted opportunity) for provincial Englishmen as well as Scots, it was not, as in Scotland, so distinct as to comprise a separate language. And when it was used by English writers – from Wordsworth to George Eliot, Hardy, and Lawrence – the intention was usually serious, and sympathetic. But in Scotland, by Mac-Diarmid's time the vernacular's debasement as a literary language seemed complete. Kailyard meant Scots; Scots meant Kailyard, and transcending the one meant forsaking the other.

This widespread assumption was a serious obstacle facing anyone who sought a Scots revival. To overcome it, MacDiarmid sought from the start to distinguish Scots itself from its association with Burns and his imitators. In Dunbar, Henryson, Fergusson, *et al.*, MacDiarmid saw not just superior *traditions* – what Scots verse had been – but also *precedents* for the depth it might once again achieve. In 1927 he wrote, 'If Burns is the heart, Dunbar is the head of Scottish poetry'.[1] The motto 'Not Burns – Dunbar!' signalled efforts to restore a balance. In 1923 MacDiarmid declared

> If all that the movement is to achieve is to preserve specimens of Braid Scots, archaic, imitative, belonging to a type of life that has passed and cannot return, in a sort of museum department of our consciousness – set apart from our vital preoccupations – it is a movement which not only cannot claim our support, but compels our opposition . . .[2]

The new Scottish Renaissance was not another Celtic Twilight movement; its aims, as John Buchan said in his preface to *Sangschaw*, were 'both conservative and revolutionary'. In MacDiarmid's own words:

> Whatever the possibilities of the Doric may be . . . there cannot be a revival in the real sense of the word – a revival of spirit as distinct from a mere renewed vogue of the letter – unless these tendencies are in accord with the newest tendencies of human thought.[3]

[1] *Albyn*, p.70. For 'Scottish', see below, p.19ff.
[2] C. M. Grieve, 'Causerie', *Scottish Chapbook* 1, 7 (February 1923), p.182.
[3] C. M. Grieve, 'Causerie', *Scottish Chapbook* 1. 8 (March 1923), p.212.

In the linguistic experiments of Dunbar and Fergusson, Mac-Diarmid had found inspiration for his own new work in Scots. From their 'direct' styles, he learned techniques which he sought to adapt to modern writing – use of colloquial speech rhythms, musicality, hard outlines and concentrated images. And in the Makars' cosmopolitan range he saw models for his own lifelong involvement with French, German, Scandinavian, and (especially) Russian literatures. Such catholicity of interest made this Scots nationalist, in Donald Davie's phrase, 'the least insular of British poets'.[1]

Like most significant movements for change, the Scottish Renaissance began on a note of attack and aroused both hope and anger. In Scotland (as in Ireland) the political, cultural, economic and religious aspects of national identity overlapped in complicated ways. Given the complexity of the issues, and the historical circumstances which gave rise to them, it was plausible for a person to unite in one cause with someone whom he bitterly opposed in others. And given the passions such causes aroused, the temptation existed to belittle the contributions in one sphere by people with whom one disagreed in another; to equate a love of Scotland with the particular forms one's own love took; and to exclude or overlook non-vernacular traditions as not truly Scottish – in short, to oversimplify.

For example, in 1970 MacDiarmid concluded, 'It was the betrayal of Scottish standards by the middle and upper classes that has led to the present plight. They all wanted to be upsides with their English neighbours and thus absorbed an overdose of English schooling, English literature, and so on'.[2] Here the use of 'English' mirrors MacDiarmid's use of 'Scottish' in a statement quoted earlier (above, p.5). Though it serves his polemic to equate 'Scots literature' with 'Scottish literature', the terms are not simply interchangeable; they must now be more clearly defined.

When MacDiarmid refers to Scots literature, he means writing in lowland Scots – the language of the Makars, Fergusson and Burns. Its opposite (which schoolchildren *were* taught) is not only 'English literature' written in England, but also 'literature in

[1] Donald Davie, 'A'e Gowden Lyric', *New Statesman* (10 August 1962), p.174. The statement might well be made now about Davie himself.
[2] Hugh MacDiarmid, interviewed by Duncan Glen in *Akros* 5, 13 (April-May 1970), n.p.

English' writen by Scotsmen such as James Hogg, James Thomson, Walter Scott, Andrew Lang, John Davidson and Robert Louis Stevenson. If their work is not Scottish because they did not write in Scots, then neither is that of the Latinist George Buchanan or the Gaelic poet Duncan Ban MacIntyre. Conversely, if they *are* all Scotsmen, then all of their work is in some sense 'Scottish literature', embodying varied aspects of, and contributions to, the culture as a whole.

This point is important for several reasons. First, it reminds us that, while Scots has a proper claim to primacy, as the language of the folk, it is not the exclusive repository of national identity; that the dignity of Gaelic poetry and clarity of Anglo-Scottish prose may well be positive complements to deficiencies in the lowland tradition.[1]

Second, to acknowledge this is to shift our emphasis from the quarrel of Scotland with England to the discontinuities within Scotland which stem from that external quarrel: the equation of parts of oneself with parts of a culture; the dissociation of head and heart; the isolation of Scot from fellow Scot.

Third, this means that the *real* task of any modern Scottish writer – and that by which he or she must finally be judged – is not to extirpate one cultural strain or exalt another, not to claim exclusive rights which history has denied – but to restore some parity among traditions, and reintegrate the capacities which they came, in isolation, to embody.

Because that balance was so seriously and unjustly skewed, the first efforts to revive its neglected side were necessarily strident, and at times entailed much overstatement. Looking back a half century later, it would therefore be naive (and humourless) to take all the relevant pronouncements at face value. What is more useful – and what this study shall attempt – is to distinguish successive combative strategies from a more sustained redemptive impulse which they do, or do not, serve.

This is no easy task. For as soon as particular cases are examined, the categories start to blur. For instance, John Buchan (1875–1940) studied at Oxford, and wrote many books while pursuing an active career in publishing and government. In private life, he was a director of Nelson's and later Assistant Director of Reuters. Having entered government service in 1901 as assistant to the High

---

[1] In point of fact, MacDiarmid revered David Hume (for his anti-clerical deism, most of all) and entitled a lecture at Edinburgh University in April 1961 'David Hume: Scotland's Greatest Son'.

Commissioner for South Africa, Buchan in 1917 became Director of Information for the British Government. These details seem to fit MacDiarmid's negative portrait of the Anglophile Scot. Yet in spite of – or rather in addition to – these roles, Buchan also wrote for *The Scottish Chapbook*, compiled *The Northern Muse* (an anthology of Scots vernacular writing, 1924), and provided a flattering preface to MacDiarmid's *Sangschaw*. Historian of the massacre at Glencoe, biographer of Montrose and Walter Scott, Buchan possessed great feeling and understanding for the Scottish past.

While a political conservative such as Buchan encouraged new writing in the vernacular, R. B. Cunninghame Graham (first president of the National Party of Scotland) expressed scant interest in literary nationalism. MacDiarmid's gifted collaborator, Lewis Grassic Gibbon, used Scots beautifully in the prelude to *Sunset Song*, but as a proponent of British communism rejected Scottish nationalism out of hand.[1] John MacLean was not a literary man at all, but his belief that 'the social revolution is possible sooner in Scotland than in England' inspired MacDiarmid's own 'Red Scotland' line.[2] And Edwin and Willa Muir, who came to oppose openly the use of Scots, did perhaps more than anyone else 'to bring Scottish literature into closer touch with current European tendencies' as *The Scottish Chapbook* had proposed.

This diversity of views and interests, and the intensity with which they were put forth, made internecine argument continuous, debilitating and at times vindictive. Nevertheless, the Scottish Renaissance remained, in the broad sense, a movement, and was perceived as such by both its observers and its participants. Like most similar movements, it required a core of flux, a driving force, a guiding spirit to sustain it. In the 1920s, the core of the Scottish Renaissance was a Scots Revival whose central figure was Hugh MacDiarmid.

MacDiarmid's first task was to separate Scots from its unfortunate associations of the previous one hundred years. The second step was to use that language in his own work, to 'make it new' in poems.

[1] The two co-authored *Scottish Scene* (London: Jarrold, 1934).
[2] See *The Voice of Scotland* 1, 1 (June-August 1938), pp.7-8, in which MacDiarmid quotes freely from MacLean's Gorbals Election Address of 1923.

CHAPTER TWO

'Pure Poetry'
Sangschaw and *Penny Wheep*

We must deny the meanings which men have given to life
so that life itself shall have a meaning.

EDWIN MUIR

The object of knowledge is relation.

CLERK MAXWELL

MacDiarmid's collection of Scots lyrics, *Sangschaw*, appeared in 1925. Its opening poem functions as a sort of frontis-piece, proclaiming the concerns of those that follow:

> *The Bonnie Broukit Bairn*
>
> Mars is braw in crammasy,   *handsome*
> Venus in a green silk goun,
> The auld mune shak's her gowden feathers,
> Their starry talk's a wheen o' blethers,   *lot of nonsense*
> Nane for thee a thochtie sparin'
> Earth, thou bonnie broukit bairn!   *dirt-streaked*
> – But greet, an' in your tears ye'll droun
> The haill clanjamfrie!   *crowd*

MacDiarmid here personifies the planets in order to distinguish 'Earth' (i.e. human existence, with its needs and sorrows) from the beauty of a universe indifferent to those needs. In a sustained conceit, the earth is a neglected child; the rest of the cosmos, those proud old gossips who ignore it. At first, it is they who demand and receive our attention. But then the kind of love a suffering child requires dispels our fascination with more distant matters, makes them seem trivial and vain.

So much for English paraphrase. The Scots poem owes its resonance less to an extractable idea than to the suggestive powers and music of its language. The poem opens on a note of mythic grandeur. 'Crammasy' is an archaic word whose heraldic sound recalls the heroic past. 'Venus in a green silk goun' maintains the tone of elevated allegory, yet lowers it slightly with a touch of homeliness. Then, the balladic 'auld' mune adds further famili-arity. This effects a transition from the first two lines, which seem urban, to the language of farm and bothie, where nature is a source of values. 'Starry' now becomes an ambivalent term, ascribing fatuous irrelevance to distant glamour. 'Blethers' means idle prat-tle, nonsense.[1] From third person descriptions the poem now jumps without warning to the second person singular. The effect of introducing an intimate pronoun before its antecedent is further heightened by the diminutive 'thochtie' and the direct address to 'Earth', which makes its name sound like a term of endearment.

Then alliteration (as in nursery rhymes) completes the change of tone. Though we can translate 'broukit' simply as neglected, the Scots word principally means streaked or soiled, and originally described the sooty kettles on peasant hearths. Nothing could be more removed from 'crammasy'; that is why Earth must 'greet'.

But the very act of weeping possesses an immediacy and capacity for growth (reflected in the poem's only enjambed line) beside which conventional pride and inanimate beauty have less value. The Scots 'clanjamfrie', meaning a mob or rabble, and 'frequently used to denote the purse-proud vulgar' (Jamieson), underscores the change in affections. Characteristically, the poem closes in an unanticipated outburst which at first seems to contradict what preceded, but on careful examination can be seen to have been inherent in it.

As a whole, 'The Bonnie Broukit Bairn' suggests a reorientation of values, a progression from myth to nature, from the realm of literary gods and abstract aesthetic value to that of humane sympathy. On another level, it is a social-political statement which professes more interest in the neglected indigenous culture than in all the 'starry talk' of Anglophile Scotland. Last, and most important, it is a poem that does not discuss, but rather demonstrates the right and wrong uses of language, embodying a growth from the diction of the opening, once serviceable but now stilted, into native language which, in Ruskin's phrase, serves life.

The native language had long been acknowledged to be accurate and forceful, but (because it was so specific) suited only for descriptive tasks. However, inspired in part by modernist poetics, MacDiarmid realized that the most exact words are also potentially the most resonant; that at its most radical, metaphor becomes epistemology and metaphysics. By revealing and emphasizing the intrinsic metaphoric strengths of Scots, he could thus expand the vernacular lyric's range without abandoning its traditional base. To redeem a genre in this way was to redefine it.

Most of the lyrics that follow 'The Bonnie Broukit Bairn' confound other types of categories by related means. The typical poem in *Sangschaw* or *Penny Wheep* first sketches out paired, contrasting

[1] Is it possible that there may be a slight allusion (a mere nuance) to 'blether', a bladder, and, by extension, a bagpipe, since MacDiarmid uses the word in a verse in *Penny Wheep* (1926): 'For the bubblyjock [*turkey cock*] swallowed the bagpipes / And the blether stuck in its throat'? If so, it would mirror the preceding image of an old hen shaking her comb, and offer an example of the power of Scots to fuse diverse associations in one word.

terms or situations. Then it somehow reverses the respective values
which those terms are conventionally assigned, or denies the dichotomy altogether, by means of *lacunae*, paradoxes, radical shifts
of voice, chronology, perspective or scale. One such shift – of scale
– may be seen in 'Empty Vessel', from *Penny Wheep*. The poem's
theme resembles that of 'The Bonnie Broukit Bairn', but where the
former poem began large, this one starts out small, with a concrete
situation:

> I met ayont the cairney
> A lass wi' tousie hair   *tousled*
> Singin' till a bairnie
> That was nae langer there.

These lines quote from 'Saw Ye Jenny Nettles', a traditional
song which begins

> I met ayont the kairny
> Jenny Nettles, Jenny Nettles
> Singing till her bairny,
> Robin Rattle's bastard . . .[1]

The original is almost all plot. MacDiarmid's first stanza contains
two notable changes. For the proper name, he substitutes a physical description to enhance the realism and increase our sympathy.
For the remainder of the traditional song (which portrays Jenny
seeking out Robin and exhorting him to make an 'honest woman'
of her), MacDiarmid substitutes the simpler, more suggestive line,
'That was nae langer there'. As in the best Scots ballads, details are
thus left to the reader's imagination. Stark treatment of the tragic
intensifies our interest. Was the bairnie taken from her? Did it die,
or has she abandoned it? All are possible, and each makes us want
to find out more.

But the next stanza leaps up unpredictably to this:

> Wunds wi' warlds to swing
> Dinna sing sae sweet
> The licht that bends owre a' thing
> Is less ta'en up wi't.

As in 'The Bonnie Broukit Bairn', the entire universe is suddenly juxtaposed to a minor human incident, and in comparison,

[1] This song can be found in Ramsay's *Tea Table Miscellany* and was
later included in David Herd's anthology as well. George Bruce first
noted the connection with MacDiarmid's poem.

found wanting. (Similarly, the phrase 'tak up', which connotes church hymns as well as infatuation, may suggest that the mother's song is at least as sanctified as more formal worship.) The leap is audacious, signalled by a metric change from iambic to the stressed first syllable 'wunds'. It rests once again on the precise use of strong language. 'Bends' equally describes a mother hovering over her child and what happens to the 'licht . . . owre a' thing' as it enters our atmosphere. The metrically staggered chiming sounds of 'swing', 'sing' and 'thing' hold all parts of the poem in relation even as we learn what makes each unique.

A justly famous poem, 'The Watergaw', presents not one but two dichotomies, interwoven: external reality 'versus' inner experience; a past event and the speaker's long-delayed reaction. As in the poems already examined, MacDiarmid uses Scots words to attempt connections. But the situation of this poem is more psychologically complex, the tensions more subtly articulated and less easily resolved:

A'e weet forenicht in the yow-trummle   (vocabulary
I saw yon antrin thing,   in text that
A watergaw wi' its chitterin licht   follows)
Ayont the on-ding;
An' I thocht o' the last wild look ye gied
Afore ye deed!

There was nae reek i' the laverock's hoose
That night – an' nane i' mine;
But I hae thocht o' that foolish licht
Ever sin' syne;
An' I think that mebbe at last I ken
What your look meant then.

Commenting on this poem in the person of C. M. Grieve, MacDiarmid wrote, 'Doric economy of expressiveness is impressively illustrated in the first four lines of Mr. MacDiarmid's poem. Translate them into English. That is the test. You will find that the shortest possible translation runs something like this: "One wet afternoon in the cold weather in July after the sheep shearing I saw that rare thing – an indistinct rainbow, with its shivering light, above the heavily-falling rain".' [1] In offering so excessively literal a prose translation, the author was stacking the deck in his own favour; nevertheless, his point is well-taken.

[1] 'Causerie', *Scottish Chapbook* 1, 3 (October 1922), p.63.

Where did MacDiarmid find these words? He himself has ad-
mitted, 'I went to where the language was kept, to the dictionary. It
seemed the logical thing to do'.[1] The dictionary referred to is James
Wilson's *Lowland Scotch As Spoken in the Strathearn District of
Perthshire*. If we follow him there, we shall find on page 169, for
instance, the expressions 'waater gaw', 'yow-trummel', and 'oan-
ding'. Other pages contain 'aanterin' and 'chitterin'. As one might
expect, this approach led eventually to charges of 'ruthlessly trawl-
ing the pages of the dictionary for words and expressions of fantastic, droll and whimsical sound and appearance'.[2] But surely
comments like these put the cart before the horse. What matters is
not so much the poet's method of composition as its results, not old
usages *per se*, but whether they work in the poem at hand. Here,
they do; the accuracy and beauty of words like 'yow-trummle'
more than repay the minor difficulty that their oddity entails.

On its simplest level, 'The Watergaw' recounts how a quality
perceived by the speaker in a natural phenomenon makes him
recollect the death of someone he loved. Neither that quality in the
watergaw, nor the emotion it recalls, is ever explained. Instead,
they are simply juxtaposed by the neutral conjunction 'and' in the
fifth line of each stanza. Yet the terms in which the speaker
describes external reality suggest simultaneously his own internal
situation. Thanks to the multiple associations contained in Scots
words, MacDiarmid can convey highly personal emotion in *impersonal* terms; he can show, not tell. Moreover, words which locate
the same quality in disparate things thereby suggest an underlying
unity, as of something acting through them.[3] Language becomes
the human way of participating in (or apprehending) that unity.
In a condition of change and isolation, words remain signs of connection.

Everything in 'The Watergaw' is on the verge of becoming its
opposite. 'Forenicht' is the time between twilight and bedtime normally spent visiting and sitting around the hearth. The speaker's

[1] From a BBC broadcast quoted by Walter Keir, 'Hugh MacDiarmid
and the Scottish Renaissance', in *Hugh MacDiarmid: A Festschrift*, ed.
K. D. Duval and Sydney Goodsir Smith (Edinburgh: Duval, 1962),
p.14.
[2] Lewis Spence, 'Scots Poetry Today', *The 19th Century and After*,
106, 630 (August 1929), pp.256-7.
[3] This unity is enhanced by the luminous light that pervades the
poem. It reminds me of the light in Bellini's 'St. Francis in Ecstasy'.
My phrase 'acting through them' is suggested by a line of D. H.
Lawrence's: 'Not I, not I, but the wind that blows through me!'
in 'Song of A Man Who Has Come Through'.

loneliness is more poignant, coming at a time of day reserved for conviviality. Forenicht is also, of course, when light fades into darkness.[1] Similarly, 'yow-trummle' (the cold snap frequent in late July just after the sheep have been sheared, causing them to shiver) presages the 'death' of the year. A 'watergaw' is an indistinct rainbow; it shimmers but never quite forms a proper arc. We might note, in mentioning this, how the remarkable specificity of terms for natural phenomena – that same aspect of Scots which offers a dozen words for particular types of hills – avoids any sentimental associations that a rainbow might have in English verse. 'Chitterin' means trembling. In common usage, the word described people who 'chittered' from cold or fear, or birds 'chitterin'' in the woods. The word's use here, to describe the watergaw, links that phenomenon to the trembling ewes of line one, and to the lark (laverock) of the second stanza.

While it shares certain characteristics of the animated world, the watergaw is also a supernatural sign which exists 'ayont' (beyond, both fig. and lit.) the downpour. It conjures up the loved one's dying look. Is it thus a sign of redemption, i.e. life after death like a rainbow beyond the storm, revelation of which lit up the dying face? Or, as Iain Crichton Smith suggests, does the light of the watergaw seen through rain recall that 'wild look' on the dying person's face as seen through the speaker's own tears?[2] Was the last look wild with fear, or because it had grown as inaccessible and otherworldly as a watergaw? Its violence does not suggest a happy revelation.

In short, we find almost frightening force packed into six lines. All is transitory, uncertain, energized, kinetic. And the effect of violence is achieved without doing violence to either syntax or language. Metaphysical overtones arise naturally out of concrete physical descriptions. The understated rhythmic pattern, within which words seek to burst their metric frame, creates an increase in tension; the whole first stanza chitters.

In the second stanza, an immediate shift into the colloquial and proverbial 'mediates between the strangeness of nature and

[1] 'Forenicht' here is used much in the same way that *uht*, or first light, creates the elegiac tones of some Anglo-Saxon poems. MacDiarmid loved such times, which today are fashionably known as 'interfaces'. How much richer his evocations are than that soulless, mechanical word!

[2] 'The Golden Lyric', in Duncan Glen, ed., *Hugh MacDiarmid: A Critical Survey* (Edinburgh and London: Scottish Academic Press, 1972).

strangeness of human relations'.[1]

> There was nae reek i' the laverock's hoose
> That nicht – an' nane i' mine . . .

Literally, this means there was no smoke; figuratively, that there was no light in the sky (lark's house), that it was a dark stormy evening. In both respects the bird's plight expresses the man's; they share the same condition. In a world where nothing lasts, meanings are elusive, and judgments tentative: 'I *think* that *mebbe* at last I ken . . .'

Some critics have called the poem's ending sentimental.[2] But it seems to me that this charge implies a greater certainty about just what 'your look meant' than the poem allows. It is, after all, a 'wild' look recalled by a 'foolish' licht. As Iain Crichton Smith has written: 'There is a kind of hint of the helplessness of the animal in that use of the word wild. It is as if the being were a kind of animal dying and unable to communicate with the human being looking at it...'[3] Similarly, 'foolish' may mean meaningless, and/or deprecate the speaker, whose understanding is not equal to his experience.

What we are left with is a sense of inevitable change and, in this case, resulting sorrow. However, in coming to terms with his personal loss, the speaker discovers that the condition of change is present in varied forms throughout Creation.

MacDiarmid's search for likeness in unlike things owes much to the Blakean notion that 'Everything that lives is holy'. Once this is accepted, Calvinist moral dichotomies ('The curst conceit o' bein' richt') fall by the wayside. So does the notion of 'proper' and 'improper' subjects for poetry, as well as 'suitable' or 'unsuitable' languages in which to write. To a *Times* reviewer's complaint that 'Scots . . . has contracted associations too homely, too trivial for high [sic] poetry' or that it has 'a penchant for ugly words and subjects', MacDiarmid might reply that anything seen properly reveals more than itself.[4] Moreover, in a repressed culture, paying increased attention to neglected or proscribed themes is an ideological act.

Regarding the sources of that repression, a word of caution is in

---

[1] David Daiches, 'Hugh MacDiarmid's Early Poetry', in *ibid.*, p.62.
[2] Matthew P. MacDiarmid, for instance, in 'Hugh MacDiarmid and the Colloquial Category', *Agenda*, Vol.5, No.4, Vol.6, No.1 (Autumn-Winter 1968).
[3] Iain Crichton Smith, 'The Golden Lyric', in Glen, p.138.
[4] 'A Scottish Literary Renaissance', *TLS* 7 (January 1926), p.7.

order. As David Craig notes,[1] it was axiomatic of the Scottish Renaissance 'that what the Scottish imagination mainly suffered from after the Reformation was some suppression of profane art and worldly feelings by a Calvinist Church. But if we read that literature . . . we find that what is happening is not so much censorship or suppression as the bringing out by Calvinism, into full potency, of a native trait which itself tended to thwart imagination . . . whereby making the subject concrete, bringing it into realization, thereby reduces it to the common terms in which it can be felt as absurd'. By contrast, 'Ex Vermibus' uses common terms in a way that is neither polite nor demeaning – as a springboard for imagination. Let us not confuse *grotesquerie* (a matter of style and content) with *vulgarity* (a matter of intention). The difference between the two can be seen in the following poem:

> *Ex Vermibus*
>
> | Gape, gape, gorlin!, | *fledgling* |
> | For I ha'e a worm | |
> | That'll gi'e ye a slee and sliggy sang | *cunning* |
> | Wi' mony a whuram. | *quaver* |
>
> | Syne i' the lift | |
> | Byous spatrils you'll mak' | *notes in music* |
> | For a gorlin' wi' worms like this in its wame | *belly* |
> | Nae airels sall lack. | *notes, tones* |
>
> | But owre the tree-taps | |
> | Maun flee like a sperk, | |
> | Till it has the haill o' the Heavens alunt | *alight* |
> | Frae dawin' to derk. | |

Like the other poems we have thus far examined, 'Ex Vermibus' begins on the level of mundane physicality and proceeds to attribute the same qualities to things as disparate as worms and heaven, assimilating one aspect of reality to another by means of language. The good-natured tone of camaraderie at the poem's start seems at first to belie any serious intent. There is something comical, indeed repulsive in those greedy, gaping mouths into which worms are crammed. From then on the Scots words effect a transition from these lowly physical things to the supposedly higher realities that they make possible and are therefore intrinsic to. The progression is achieved by a series of aural and visual puns. 'Whuram' – a grace note or quaver – is both a pun on worm and a visual analogue of the

[1] 'Scottish Literature and the Scottish People' (London: Chatto, 1961), pp.74-5.

worm's wriggle. 'Spatrils' – musical notes written on a score – sustains the musical analogy but also describes the bird's turns in flight. And 'airels' – tunes – echoes 'spatril' in both sound and sense, taking up individual notes in a coherent song. Then, in the final stanza, these airels in turn acquire a life of *their* own; they too 'flee like a sperk'. Just as the worms become spatrils become airels become song, so the 'sperk' becomes part of the light of the Heavens.

This is a long way to come in twelve short lines, yet surely the transition is made. Though the words are difficult, transitions are handled with a rapidity and simplicity that avoids affectation or strain. As usual, the meaning opens incrementally from line to line; exact use of words impels that expansion while alternating line lengths keep its energy under control. Stanzas characteristically culminate in a penultimate long line, followed by an abrupt 'cut-line' closure. It is as if the experience struggles upward on a ladder of language (in sliggy fashion), and at the end of each stanza arrives, all at once, at a new level of perception.

Reviewing *Sangschaw*, Edwin Muir was struck by its 'almost fantastic economy, a crazy economy which has the effect of humour and yet conveys a kind of horror'.[1] And a more recent discussion calls this quality a 'disgust-wonder synthesis', a phrase which, though awkward, is apt.[2] For what MacDiarmid offers is indeed a synthesis, a kind of truce with horror. The wonder which subsumes revulsion never quite dissipates it; as we shall see, the constant possibility of sudden reversion to the former feeling becomes a central structural principle in *A Drunk Man*. This quality is unsettling. Yet it keeps the insight honest, so to speak, by holding sanctimoniousness at arm's length.

It may be useful in this connection to compare MacDiarmid's intentions in *Sangschaw* and *Penny Wheep* with those of Wordsworth. In his Preface to *Lyrical Ballads* (1802), Wordsworth wrote of his poems, '. . . the feeling therein developed gives importance to the action and situation, and not the action and situation to the feeling'. In other words, while restoring subjective honesty to verse, he would not slight the objective circumstances that inspire it. In fact, the Romantic choice of subject matter was often affected

---

[1] Quoted by Hugh MacDiarmid in *Lucky Poet* (London: Methuen, 1943), p.22, and by Duncan Glen, *Hugh MacDiarmid and the Scottish Renaissance* (Edinburgh and London: Chambers, 1964).
[2] Ann E. Boutelle, 'The Thistle and the Rose: A Study of the Poetry of Hugh MacDiarmid', Diss., New York University, 1972, p.38.

by an *a priori* assumption that, in Emerson's phrase, 'Nature is made to conspire with spirit to *emancipate* us' (italics mine). Wordsworth could not help but depict his 'natural' subjects in moral terms.

We may compare 'Ex Vermibus' with 'To a Skylark'. Both are twelve-line poems about birds, and both find emblematic significance in the bird's free yet necessary movement between heaven and earth. We've already seen how the former employs a full range of humour, rhythm and language to effect an expansion of meaning. By contrast, the poem that *begins* 'Ethereal minstrel . . .' hasn't very far to climb; it has already made up its mind at the onset, and the only real process remaining is mechanical composition.

The point is not so much that 'Ex Vermibus' possesses greater charm as that it earns its culminating vision. And *en route* to that vision MacDiarmid finds time to grant the bird its due. He respects what he sees enough to let it be just a bird. But for Wordsworth, the natural object bears little intrinsic interest aside from the moral meditation it occasions.[1] One need only contrast Wordsworth's use of the rainbow in 'My Heart Leaps Up' with MacDiarmid's evocation of a watergaw to realize that two different kinds of poetic intention are at work. The matter on which they differ is the place of ideas in short lyric poems.

An erroneous commonplace regarding *Sangschaw* and *Penny Wheep* is that these volumes somehow re-introduced ideas into Scottish verse. Statements by Albert Mackie are typical: 'One of MacDiarmid's revolutionary actions in his treatment of Scots was to . . . use the Northern tongue for all purposes and especially for intellectual speculation and polemics'.[2] Even aside from its factual inaccuracy – all MacDiarmid's polemics from the *Chapbook* days on were in English, and as his verse grew more polemical it too abandoned Scots – this statement is untrue, as comparison with the

---

[1] 'These lyrics are . . . secularized versions of an older devotional poetry, employed in the examination of the soul's condition as it approaches and retreats from God.' M. H. Abrams, 'The Correspondent Breeze: A Romantic Metaphor', *The Kenyon Review* 19 (1957), p.124.
  Similarly, 'Keats' "Ode . . ." is concerned with the states of mind which a nightingale's song sets going in him, and what sets them going is not the physical quality of the song but the myth of Philomela.' C. Day Lewis, *The Lyric Impulse* (Cambridge: Harvard University Press, 1965), p.21.
[2] 'Hugh MacDiarmid and the Scottish Renaissance', in Duval *et al.*, p.166.

work of a truly philosophical poet should make clear.

Wordsworth's lyrics not only stand up to intellectual discussion, but invite it. If one asks what a particular poem *means*, the answer can be found in explicit conceptual phrases such as 'half-perceive, half-create', 'keep watch o'er man's mortality', and so on. But it will get us nowhere to search for the 'idea' of 'Moonlight Among the Pines' or the phrase 'Time whuds like a flee'. On the contrary, the impact of MacDiarmid's lyrics derives precisely from what *isn't* there. It depends on refinement of style to heighten suggestive power in the absence of explanation, to achieve 'a kind of shock . . . which goes beyond logic'.[1]

Much later statements by critics, or by MacDiarmid himself, must not mislead us in this matter. It is important to insert at this early point two general cautionary notes about MacDiarmid's prose. First, because it was written in heated polemical contexts, it sometimes exaggerates and thereby coarsens positions which find more subtle expression in the poetry. Second, MacDiarmid's retrospective statements often attempt to bring preceding work into accord with incompatible subsequent positions. It is therefore a good idea to exclude these pronouncements from considerations of what was intended at the time of the original writing. For example, in 1952 he described the slogan 'Not Burns – Dunbar' as a 'call for the intellectualization of Scots poetry rather than an imitation of Dunbar's language'.[2] If by 'intellectualization' is meant a broadening of interest and expression far beyond the bounds to which kailyard verse had confined them, there can be no question that he is correct. But concern for, and sensitive evocation of, individual states of mind is *not* the same thing as elucidation of ideas, the products of mind. And in the early lyrics, it was clearly the former that concerned MacDiarmid in his better work. Indeed, most of these poems are deliberately obscure, as MacDiarmid's other writings at that time make clear.

In the *Scottish Chapbook* of November–December 1923, a foot-note to 'You Know Not Who I Am' says of Stefan George, '. . . he retires behind difficult idiom [sic] and obscure symbolism . . . . Impatient as one may be of these mannerisms, one cannot but admire the persistence with which he refuses to commercialize his art, satisfied to be read and appreciated by the few'. A further clue to what MacDiarmid was attempting at this stage can be found in

[1] 'The Golden Lyric', in Glen, p. 139.
[2] Introd., *Selected Poems of William Dunbar* (Edinburgh: Oliver & Boyd, 1952).

'Following Rebecca West in Edinburgh: A Monologue in the Vernacular'. In this rather unsophisticated imitation of *Ulysses*, irate passages in Scots (the 'monologue') alternate with narrative explanations in English. One of these reads:

> He was purposely using many obsolete words, partly to despite me for forcing him to talk of Edinburgh, and partly because they acted as a brake on his utterance. In any case, he was deliberately inconsequent, allusive, and obscure.[1]

And in the *Scottish Chapbook* of October 1923, we find Grieve saying of MacDiarmid:

> ... he is, I think, the first Scottish writer who has addressed himself to the question of the extendability ... of the vernacular ... to give it all the utmost suggestionability it lacks (compared, say, with contemporary English or French) but would have had if it had continued in general use in highly cultured circles to the present day.

It is significant that when MacDiarmid considers the resources of other languages, the quality which he singles out for praise is their 'suggestionability'. This in part reflects his immersion in the platonism of Ouspensky and the aesthetic theories of Paul Valéry, both of which will be discussed below. But there was also a simpler, more immediate reason.

These poems were introduced in the context of a culture where professed certitudes – religious, political, intellectual – had forestalled artistic innovation for a century. Before new values could be forged, it was necessary to undermine the mental set which seeks, and settles for, fixed truths. The goal at this stage was therefore not to substitute one set of meanings for another, but simply to *make people see*. To use an optical metaphor, *Sangschaw* and *Penny Wheep* replace the fixed glass of Scottish convention with a zoom lens of imagination, in whose perspective the data of quotidian life appear both more precarious and more marvellous. In a cosmos where sunbeams tremble, moonlight kelters, and the world itself 'wags' like an eemis stane,[2] human claims to universal truth can only be met with laughter:

> I lauch to see my crazy little brain
> – And ither folks' – tak'n itsel' seriously,
> And in a sudden love o' fun my saul
> Blinks dozent as the owl I ken't to be.

---

[1] *Scottish Chapbook* 2, 1 (October 1923).   [2] See below, p.51ff.

Thus, one way in which MacDiarmid's world view finds expression
is humour. Another is a style which avoids assertion, choosing
instead to suggest the nature of any individual thing in terms of
something other than itself. This can be seen in 'Au Clair de la
Lune'.

The sequence of four lyrics thus-entitled in *Sangschaw* is preceded by epigraphs, of which the second runs:

> 'They mix ye up wi' loony fowk
> Wha are o' stars the mense,   *peer, equal*
> The madness that ye bring to me,
> I wadna change't for sense.'

MacDiarmid's own poem then begins:

> Earth's littered wi' larochs o' Empires   *ruins*
> Muckle nations are dust.   *great*
> Time'll meissle it awa', it seems,   *waste, crumble*
> An' smell nae must.

This first poem is called 'Prelude to Moon Music'. In *Sangschaw,*
Penny Wheep, and especially *A Drunk Man,* moonlight represents
something like what *'l'azur'* meant to French symbolists – aspiration towards infinitude and unity of being. Hence the 'prelude' to
'moon-music' must be a passing beyond earth-music, i.e. beyond
the processes of time to which even 'muckle nations' succumb. The
clipped rhythm and severe impersonality of this stanza reflect the
process of rising above one's normal limits. The verb 'meissle' in
colloquial usage means 'to eat slowly, nibble daintily, as children
with sweets' (Jamieson). Its use here to describe the fate of Empires
conveys a touch of disdain.

The poem continues:

> But wheest! – whatna music is this,
> While the win's haud their breath?
> – *The Moon has a wunnerfu' finger*
> *For the back-lill o' Death!*

The 'back-lill' is the thumb hole of the chanter (finger pipe) in a
bagpipe. The metaphor, with its vague echoes of Aeolian harps,
may be thought too self-consciously clever and unclear. Perhaps
MacDiarmid means something like 'Death is the mother of
Beauty', that mortality is the instrument on which immortal melo-
dies are played. At any rate, the note that emerges sounds a release
from the time-bound world of 'larochs' to the imaginative realm of

the succeeding lyric, 'Moonstruck':

> When the warl's couped soon' as a peerie   *overturned | top*
> That licht-lookin' craw o' a body, the moon,
> Sits on the fower cross-win's
> Peerin' a' roon'.
>
> She's seen me – she's seen me – an' straucht
> Loupit clean on the quick o' my hert.   *leapt*
> The quhither o' cauld gowd's fairly   *quiver, warble*
> Gi'en me a stert.

The movement here closely resembles that of 'Ex Vermibus'. This poem also begins with a fanciful, light perception expressed in homely terms; the 'auld moon' which shook her gowden feathers in 'The Bonnie Broukit Bairn' is once again a 'craw o' a body'. But as usual, a powerful Scots word in the second stanza undercuts the whimsy and jolts us into more sinister maters. 'Quhither' denotes warbling in one dialect, and in another means the darting motion of a snake's tongue (Jamieson). Linked to 'cauld gowd', the description instantly dissipates any sentimentality that might accrue to moonlight. It prepares us for the typical third stanza shift from sensuous description into metaphysics:

> An' the roarin' o' oceans noo'
> Is peerieweerie to me: *faintest sound*
> Thunner's a tinklin' bell: an' Time
> Whuds like a flee.   *flits*

How much is assumed in the use of that innocent 'and'; the leap is immense! What the mind apprehends in such a state is neither supernatural nor mystical but (in the philosophical sense) metaphysical. The sudden transition here reminds one critic of Vaughan. But as he goes on to say, '. . . unlike Vaughan's experiences, the experiences described by MacDiarmid are a kind of folk emotion communicated through a language which, however eclectic and literary, draws its ultimate sustenance from a folk speech'.[1] By using that folk language to convey a metaphysical experience, MacDiarmid makes it plausible and vivid. He takes us along.

Part III continues the expansive movement where Part II left off. We have now ascended from a ground-level view of earthly ruin to a 'God's eye view' of the Universe; from 'dust' in Poem I to oceans

[1] David Daiches, 'Hugh MacDiarmid and Scottish Poetry', *Poetry* (Chicago) 72, 3 (June 1948), p.208.

in Part II, and now to 'seas of space'.

> *The Man in the Moon*
> The moonbeams kelter i' the lift,   *undulate*
> An' Earth, the bare auld stane,
> Glitters beneath the seas o' Space,
> White as a mammoth's bane.

We are now looking down from such a distance that even those
things which represent immutability on earth are themselves seen
as victims of change. In one dialect (Lanarkshire), 'kelter' describes a cart tipped backward while unyoking, so that its shafts tilt
at the sky. It thus describes, metaphorically, the slanting moonbeams. More commonly, however, the word connotes violent
struggle; eels kelter upriver, and fish kelter on the hook.[1]
Described thus, the moonbeams which represented notions of
grandeur and unity become merely one more example of muta-
bility. Even the earth itself will suffer the same extinction as the
mammoth whose 'bane' it resembles.[2] The poem then concludes:

> An', lifted owre the gowden wave,
> Peers a dumbfoun'ered Thocht,
> Wi' keethin' sicht o' a' there is,
> An' bodily sicht o' nocht.

'Keethin' sicht' is defined in Jamieson as 'the view a fisher has of
the motion of a salmon, by marks in the water, as distinguished
from what is called a "bodily sight"'. The image embodies perfectly that combination of tentativity, confessed incapacity and
wonder ('dumfoun'ered Thocht') in the face of imperfect knowledge which can be traced all through the early lyrics.

It may also be read as a statement of what poetry can and cannot
do. Throughout his career MacDiarmid liked to quote as a 'clue to
possible method' Mallarmé's notion that 'To evoke in a deliberate
shadow the unmentioned object / by allusive words, never direct
words / which may be reduced to an equal silence / That means an
attempt very near creation'.[3] Here one must be careful to distinguish between MacDiarmid's admiration for the Mallarméan

---

[1] The latter meaning prevails in Perthshire and general usage.
[2] MacDiarmid's fascination with whiteness/mammoth/death as
associated images recurs, this time with whales, in *A Drunk Man*
(ll.1467, 1659, 1786) where Melville ('a Scot') enters the poem.
[3] Hugh MacDiarmid, *In Memoriam James Joyce* (Glasgow:
MacClellan, 1955), p.42.

method, and the uses to which he himself put it. In *Sangschaw* and *Penny Wheep*, words with multiple associations are juxtaposed to suggest unstated correspondences. To this extent, the language employed is allusive.

However, 'allusive' is not the same as 'abstract', nor 'indirect' the same as 'vague'. No more in MacDiarmid than in Mallarmé, the allusion in a word like 'kelter' is not from concrete description to abstraction (either philosophical or literary), but from one natural fact to another, with which it shares some defining qualities. A given word may suggest that moonbeams wriggle like a hooked fish; however, no explicit statement limits the range of possible conclusions this allows.[1]

Several reasons have already been suggested why MacDiarmid courted ambiguities. One additional reason requires a brief digression, and has to do with the nature of abstract thought. In general parlance we tend to associate 'abstraction' with an expansion of meaning, as when one speaks of 'rising above particulars' to formulate the 'broader picture'. It is true that by generalizing one achieves distance from specific events and objects, and is thus able to discern the patterns in which they all participate. Understanding proceeds by category.

But categories have a way of turning prematurely into hierarchies; when one event supports a range of equally valid conclusions, we tend to favour those that reinforce our previous formulations. Moreover, our interest in specific things/events/ people can narrow to only those aspects of them that relate to our personal preoccupation. When this occurs, we may have the meaning we desire (*a* meaning really), but miss the full range of experience. Just so did it happen that as Wordsworth became more explicit about his own states of mind, his meters became flatter, his diction more tumid, and his images more simply descriptive. The language of rustic life – or a stylized version thereof – was employed not for specificity and physicality (such as what Pound admired in Villon), but as a vehicle for abstract meditation, 'a more permanent and far more philosophical language'. In the eagerness to point out 'beautiful and permanent *forms* of Nature', physical nature itself was betrayed, or at least neglected, by one who professed to love her.

[1] By contrast, where the correspondences *are* stated more explicitly, the results resemble Nineties mannerism (as in 'Prelude', Part IV and 'Ballad of the Five Senses') or (in 'Bombinations of a Chimaera') unsatisfactory pastiche of Blake.

Where Wordsworth sought balance and tranquillity, MacDiarmid found erratic energies and unpredictable, sometimes violent, change. Instead of explicit formulations of generalized truth, his lyrics amass and concentrate startling details. In this way the poems remain no nicer, and no less ambiguous, than Nature itself. Because the poems don't have to prove anything, the poetic voice is more impersonal. The natural world is stripped of the moral garments in which romantic poets and Calvinist preachers clothed it.

One danger faced by lyric poets (especially the most talented) is that they can be mesmerized by their own capacity to instil a swoon; that prettiness or aural roundedness will blunt more charged intentions. In MacDiarmid's case, this risk was compounded by a diction which calls attention to itself, and by his pastoral subjects. A post-War poetry given over to ewes, rainbows and fledglings treads a fine line between pure feeling and sentimental nostalgia, and inevitably oversteps that line at times. MacDiarmid was aware of this danger. To forestall it, he fashioned a musicality that could serve, but not subsume, darker perceptions. Thus in most of the poems in *Sangschaw* and *Penny Wheep* the sweetness of language is cut by the tartness of rhythm. As Edwin Morgan writes, the most striking thing about MacDiarmid's lyricism is that it is 'not lax but functional, gauged, at once economical and liberated'.[1]

This measured strength derives from cadences acquired from two sources, one traditional, and one contemporary.

The traditional source is the Scottish ballads. In an essay of 1924, Edwin Muir noted that the Scottish ballads possess, to a greater degree than their English counterparts,

> . . . terrific simplicity and intensity, an intensity which never loosens into reflection. There is nothing in the ballads but passion, terror, instinct, action: the states in which soul and body alike move most intensely; and this accounts for the impression of full and moving life which, stark and bare as they are, they leave with us . . . It is their absence of reflection which distinguishes them from English ballads. . .
>
> This sense of life and death, pleasure and sin, joy and loss, not thrown out lavishly but intensified to one point, to a breaking point where a flame springs forth: that is the sense which had inspired the greatest Scottish poetry.[2]

[1] *Hugh MacDiarmid* (Harlow, Essex: Longman, 1976), p.9.
[2] 'A Note On The Scottish Ballads', in *Latitudes* (1924; rpt. New York: Viking, 1972), pp.19, 17.

As a twentieth-century writer, MacDiarmid is more introspective than his folk antecedents. But his best short lyrics have that same stark volatility. In reading them – or better, hearing MacDiarmid read them – one gains the sense of reticence barely containing tremendous feeling. The dignity and self-restraint intensify the emotion.

The contemporary model of similar techniques was the poetry of Thomas Hardy.[1] MacDiarmid's debt will become apparent if we set 'Prelude to Moon Music' beside one of Hardy's poems:

> *In Time of 'The Breaking of Nations'*
> Only a man harrowing clods
>   In a slow, silent walk
> With an old horse that stumbles and nods
>   Half asleep as they stalk.
>
> Only their smoke without flame
>   From the heaps of couch grass;
> Yet this will go onward the same
>   Though Dynasties pass . . .   (etc.)

Turning back to MacDiarmid's text (p.36), one hears echoes of Hardy's 'clods' in MacDiarmid's 'dust', of 'though Dynasties pass' in 'larochs o' Empires', and of Hardy's subtle variations on a 4/3 accentual line. Both poets are adapting the ballad form; both alternate restrained short lines with more expansive long lines in order to enforce expressive pauses. By appending 'it seems' within commas at the end of line three, MacDiarmid achieves the same tone of irony and stoic resignation. Of course, to note similarities is not to belittle the latter poet's technique, which warrants closer examination.

'Prelude''s first stanza consists of two declarative sentences with parallel syntax; lines are laid down like bricks to achieve solidity. Stanza two, however, contains an interjection, a broken line, a question and an exclamation. The phrasing enforces a dead stop after 'wins haud their breath', and the resulting fusion of sound and sense creates a kind of blank spot or vacuum. We have seen this effect in 'The Bonnie Broukit Bairn', and shall meet it again and

---

[1] This comparison has been attacked in the past; see Kenneth Buthlay, *Hugh MacDiarmid* (Edinburgh: Oliver & Boyd, 1964), p.117, and below, p.53. For now, those who wish to consider it might set in pairs Hardy's 'The Moon Looks In' and MacDiarmid's 'Moonstruck'; 'In the Room of the Bride Elect' and 'The Frightened Bride'; 'During Wind and Rain' and 'The Eemis Stane'.

again, most notably in 'O Wha's the Bride?' from *A Drunk Man*.

The technique may relate to folk antecedents; though most Scottish ballads are free of either proverbial or metaphoric language, there exists one traditional genre in which an exchange of riddles constitutes dramatic action.[1] And the ghostly strain (emphasized here by the alliterated 'wh' sounds) runs deep in Scottish literature. The effect of mystery also reflects MacDiarmid's professed desire to adopt contemporary European 'ideation'.

In an essay of 1926, he writes, 'Comprehensibility is error. Art is beyond understanding . . . The function of art is the extension of human consciousness'.[2] The essay, 'Art and the Unknown', then proceeds to define consciousness as a 'cleared space' and art as that which extends the space in any direction: 'No artist is great (or really an artist) unless he reaches some point in the unknown outside the cleared space and then adds to the cleared space'.[3] MacDiarmid's words come, almost *verbatim*, from Ouspensky's *Tertium Organum*, first translated into English in 1920.[4] The notion of Art as a tool of psychic evolution survives and unifies all other changes in MacDiarmid's subsequent career. As shall be seen, it underlies his translations of Blok, his praise of Dostoyevsky, his quarrel with doctrinaire Communism, his 'geological' poems, and the linguistic experiments of his later life. For our immediate purpose, two points suffice.

The first is that even within the circumscribed meters of traditional form, MacDiarmid's rhythms can 'clear a space' for more radical intentions. Much of the second stanza's power to startle depends upon the equally powerful effect of regularity in the preceding stanza.

Secondly, if rhythmic discontinuity is what propels us into the second stanza, resumption of continuity at its close is what facilitates the change of focus. The final lines may *sound* like a response to what was asked. But they don't really answer the question at all, at least not on its own terms. Elsewhere, MacDiarmid writes, 'It's soon', no' sense, that faddoms the herts o' men'.[5] The trick here is to make an extraordinary change *sound* ordinary. As the sense

---

[1] David Buchan, ed. *A Scottish Ballad Book* (London: Routledge, 1973), p.4.
[2] In *At The Sign of the Thistle* (London: S. Nott, 1934), p.44.
[3] *Ibid.*, p.45.
[4] Cf. Serge Ouspensky, *Tertium Organum: The Third Canon of Thought . . .*, 2nd American ed. (New York: Knopf, 1922), pp.83, 86. For a full discussion, see Boutelle, p.25f.
[5] 'Gairmscoile', in *Penny Wheep*.

becomes more unusual, sound remains conventional; the strangeness of the italics is offset by predictable strong rhyme. The reader can share the altered perception without being overly disconcerted. We are charmed by traditional means into non-traditional ends – lulled, not bludgeoned, into vision.

There are several other kinds of poems to be found in these early volumes. One of these kinds may be exemplified by 'Country Life'.

Ootside! . . . ootside!	
There's dooks that try tae fly	*ducks*
An' bum-clocks bizzin' by,	*flying beetles*
A corn-skreich an' a cay	*corncrakes / jackdaw*
An' guissay i' the cray.	*sow / pig-sty*
Inside! . . . inside!	
There's golochs on the wa',	*earwigs*
A cradle on the ca'	*rocking*
A muckle bleeze o' cones	*great blaze*
An' mither fochin' scones.	*turning*

Whether because of the predominantly rural settings, or the harsh winters, or the close-knit nature of family life, this theme of interior/exterior contrasts runs deep throughout Scottish literature, from the beginning of Henryson's 'Testament of Cresseid' to Burns' 'Tam O' Shanter'. At first reading, 'Country Life' seems like little more than a negligible footnote to that tradition. The most that these details would seem to offer is a Burns-like celebration of the domestic ideal. But while the poem does have something of Burns' energy, it shows little of his sentiment – or any sentiment at all.

In this respect it owes less to Burns than to Fergusson, whose 'The Farmer's Ingle' Burns imitated in 'The Cotter's Saturday Night'. In the Burns version, pious interjections create a defensive, unctuous quality; they sound at points like a tour guide's narration for visiting clergy. The hearth-stone is 'clean', the 'wifie' is 'thrifty' and 'frugal', Father is as 'Priestlike' as the porritch is 'haelsome'. But Fergusson's poem affirmed without so strong a need to justify; its descriptions are more concrete and accurate:

Weel kens the *gudewife* that the pleughs require	
A heartsome *meltith*, and refreshing synd	*meal / swill*
O' nappy liquor, o'er a bleezing fire:	
Sair wark and poortith douna weel be join'd.	*want, destitution*
Wi' butter'd *bannocks* now the *girdle* reeks,	

I' the far nook the *bowie* briskly reams;
The readied *kail* stand by the chimley cheeks,   *cabbage broth*
And had the riggin het wi' welcome steams,   *warm the roof*
Whilk than the daintiest kitchen nicer seems.

One can easily spot the echoes of this in MacDiarmid's second
stanza. However, for his purposes MacDiarmid excises not only
Burns' piety (including six full stanzas of Bible reading!), but also
Fergusson's ghost stories, wisecracks, and mention of personal
relations – indeed, anything which one would expect to flesh out
the contrast and give it some interest. Either we're faced with a
very slight poem indeed, or something else is being attempted.

Surely the 'secret' of this poem lies less in what it says than how it
sounds. For within a structure that expresses dichotomy, the
syntax and meter suggest equivalency – dooks to golochs, beetles to
babies, the corncrake (which nests in fields) to people by their
hearth. The tone is good-natured and matter-of-fact, not satirical.
Beyond external differences of kind, all of which receive equal
notice and affection, the creatures share something deeper. They
buzz about, they reproduce, they nourish themselves and their
offspring. In the exaggerated mirroring of 'ootside' and 'inside'
there may be a humorous hint that, after all, such distinctions don't
amount to much; that though life forms require different names,
they nevertheless participate in common rhythms.

T. S. Eliot wrote that the intellectual appeal of music is more
closely related to structure than to content.[1] If this is so, then we
should expect lyric poetry, as the verse genre most closely allied
with music, to convince by analogous means. This is certainly the
case in 'Country Life'. If we dwell only on the prose sense of the
language, we will agree with David Daiches that 'it doesn't push
through to the vision, but is content to state the contrast with a
compelling simplicity'.[2] But as we've seen, while the words define
contrast, the sounds imply relation. We *think* distinctions, but *hear*
similarity.

If one is to demur at this poem it must be for sounding a little too
much like an exercise. Even the most vivid and accurate language
can't affect a reader unless it conveys strong feeling. In this case the
music has been clipped so drastically that its appeal is largely
intellectual in Eliot's sense, i.e. as a structure.

'Farmer's Death' is quite another matter:

[1] In 'The Music of Poetry' (1942).
[2] In Glen, p.63.

Farmer's Death
For Edwin Muir

Ke-uk, ke-uk, ke-uk, ki-kwaik
The broon hens keckle and bouk   *hiccup*
And syne wi' their yalla beaks
For the reid worms houk.   *grub, dig*

The muckle white pig at the tail
O' the midden slotters and slorps   *slobbers*
But the auld ferm hoose is lown   *hushed*
And wae as a corpse.   *woeful*

The hen's een glitter like gless
As the worms gang twirlin' in
But there's never a move in by,
And the windas are blin'.

Feathers turn fire i' the licht,
The pig's doup skinkles like siller   *buttock sparkles*
But the auld ferm hoose is waugh
Wi' the daith intill her.

Hen's cries are a panash in Heaven,   *hat plume*
And a pig has the warld at its feet;
But wae for the hoose whaur a buirdly man   *stalwart*
Crines in a windin' sheet.   *shrinks*

Though this is a poem about death, the overall impression it leaves is of teeming life. This paradox turns on the interplay of sound and structure. If we read 'Farmer's Death' as a companion piece to 'Country Life' (and the titles invite this), we shall notice a similar binary structure. However, in this poem each quatrain divides into two lines that deal with 'life' and two that pertain to dying. In terms of sense, each stanza is a unit that advances the poem's progress. But in terms of diction and grammar, we have two independent poems whose only connection is aural – through rhyme and meter. Separated, they read:

Ke-uk, ke-uk, ke-uk, ki-kwaik
The broon hens keckle and bouk
(And syne wi' their yalla beaks
For the reid worms houk.)
The muckle white pig at the tail
O' the midden slotters and slorps . . .
                                   But the auld ferm hoose is lown
                                   And wae as a corpse . . .

The hen's een glitter like gless
As the worms gang twirlin' in . . .
>   But there's never a move in by
>   And the windas are blin' . . .
Feathers turn fire i' the licht
The pig's doup skinkles like siller . . .
>   But the auld ferm hoose is waugh
>   Wi' the daith intill her . . .
Hen's cries are a panash in heaven . . .
And a pig has the warld at its feet . . .
>   But wae for the hoose whaur a buirdly man
>   Crines in a windin' sheet.

To separate the stanzas thus is to reveal two discrete realities
proceeding with equal inevitability to independent closures.
Whereas 'Country Life' offered mirrored sets of nouns, in 'Farmer's Death' verbs tell the story and create a dramatic structure. The
'left-handed poem' is relentlessly verbal; regardless of what happens on the 'right' (indented lines), those creatures continue to
keckle and slotter and skinkle with indifferent energy. (Almost all
of the barnyard verbs are intransitive; animals don't make anything, or understand what is going on; for them existence constitutes fulfilment.) Conversely, the verbs on the 'right' are all
variants of 'to be', with one exception, to shrivel.

All of the 'left-hand' lines are highly consonantal and alliterated.
This gives them a slightly primitive sound. The accented vowels
are frontal and high pitched, and the meter never deviates from its
accentual three beat line. By contrast, the 'right-hand' lines are
limpid. They contain no alliteration. Stressed vowels are low in
pitch, though longer. While the barnyard 'side' sustains its initial
energy level, culminating in a verbal flourish, the 'farmer poem'
exhibits a slow falling-off. At the end of each four-line stanza, sad
plain words neutralize the preceding verbal pyrotechnics, drawing
us back to the human reality. The two-accent line leaves a metric
'hole' which expresses absence. Its effect is like the tolling of a bell,
and is repeated three times. Then, in the final stanza, the 'right-
hand' penultimate line increases from three to four accents. This
corresponds to the emotional flare-up in 'The Watergaw'. By
suddenly switching the metrical 'balance of power' (this is the first
time a right-hand line is longer than a left-hand line), MacDiarmid
shatters the dramatic structure and turns our attention entirely to
the human situation. Simultaneously, the line collapses in a series
of falling vowels – wae, hoose, whaur, buirdly, man.

Up to this point, the farmer has never been mentioned in a poem about his death. Instead, by letting the tensions balance and build, MacDiarmid has added another perspective to the traditional outside-inside contrast. Moreover, by substituting descriptions of the house for its occupant, he has lulled us into the false comfort of euphemism. One mustn't forget, amid all the discussions of Mac-Diarmid's 'excesses', his remarkable gift for understatement. It is precisely because of the reticence maintained thus far that the closure possesses power.

When the word 'man' finally appears, it is left hanging at the end of a long line as an extra foot. Then, the final line is the first irregular one in the 'right hand' poem and also contains its first verb. Because of a reversed first iamb, stressed syllables are jammed together so that the resulting phrase ('Man crines') stands out. And in the final line an added foot combines with long vowel sounds and internal rhyme to create a keen.[1]

What makes this a better poem than 'Country Life'? First of all, the introduction of a dramatic incident yields a driving tension not present in the other poem. One might generalize so far as to say that MacDiarmid's affecting lyrics arise from particular human dramas (as in 'Wheelrig', 'Reid E'en' and 'The Frightened Bride'), while those that work less well entail merely fanciful observation (for instance, 'The Diseased Salmon', 'The Long Black Night'). This distinction becomes increasingly important as a touchstone for judging the subsequent poetry. MacDiarmid's thought is always dialectical. The dialectic becomes obtrusive in a work of art unless it is shaped into drama. A clash between different visions, or voices, or aspects of the self – any of these will do. But should the dramatic structure fail to be sustained, what remains is mere pedantry. Secondly, because MacDiarmid's verse depends so much on paradox, it works best when the paradoxical elements are kept small.

From the poems selected for discussion thus far it might be inferred that *Sangschaw* and *Penny Wheep* are wholly taken up with cosmic speculations and linguistic experiment. This is not the case. Many of the poems in these volumes have the directness of folk lyrics; they extend the 'singing line'. In these MacDiarmid eschews

[1] When reading this poem aloud, one can't help hearing 'cries' in the word 'crines', given its stress and placement. This is cheating perhaps, but only partly; in a poem that *does* combine English and Lallans, all associations seem valid. If one accepts this reading, then 'man crines' in the closure corresponds to the hen's 'ke-uk' with which the poem opens; it rounds out the structure with irony.

the ironic, self-protective toughness of much twentieth-century poetry (including his own later work). He is not yet embarrassed by simplicity. It is as song, expressing unified emotion honestly, that many of his early poems succeed.

Yet even in highly emotional poems like 'The Watergaw', intensity does not produce confessional display. Instead, the speaker's own evident vulnerability is translated into tenderness and sympathy for a wide variety of human situations. Many of these poems concern themselves with loss, neglect, and the victims of unkindness. Both books contain sensitive poems about women, such as 'The Currant Bush', or this:

> The Frightened Bride
> Seil o' yer face! The send has come.   *Fortune favour you | bride's esco*
> I ken, I ken, but awa' ye gan,
> An' dinna fash, for what's i' yer hert   *worry*
> A' weemun ken an' nae man can.
>
> Seil o' yer face! Ye needna seek
> For comfort gin ye show yer plight.
> To Gods an' men, coorse callants baith,   *lads*
> A fleggit bride's the seilfu' sicht.   *frightened | blessed*

In the hands of a less original or less scrupulous artist, these poems could have easily become a sentimental gallery of village 'types'. But MacDiarmid 'does not seek to argue, assert, explain, or advise. He holds up no hand-rails. He simply holds up pieces of reality and says "See"'.[1] At the same time, by having the subjects frequently speak in their own voices he induces the reader's sympathy, and avoids the temptation any poet faces, to intrude on his subject.

Moreover, many of these lyrics are spoken in the second person. Whether stated or implied, the 'you' in them is not the unspecified, (perhaps) self-referential pronoun of Prufrock – or Ashbery – but the speaker's fellow participant in a dramatic fiction. Voices are not disembodied; people talk to one another. As in Hardy's poems to his first wife, the speaker's isolation is made more poignant because the person addressed is or was once real.

Sangschaw and *Penny Wheep* contain lighter verse as well. There are humorous poems and poems for children ('Hungry Waters' and 'Morning') and poems like 'Wild Roses':

---

[1] MacDiarmid's own description of the painter William Johnstone in *Lucky Poet*, p. 104.

Wi' sae mony wild roses
Dancin' and daffin'   *frolicking*
It looks as tho' a'
The countryside's laffin'.

But I maun ca' canny   *go slow*
Gin I'm no' to cumber
Sic a lichtsome warld
Wi' my hert's auld lumber.

Hoo I mind noo your face
When I spiered for a kiss
'Ud gae joukin' a' airts   *dodging*
And colourin' like this!

Unfortunately, there are too many poems (especially in *Penny Wheep*) which are plagued by a mannered cuteness.[1] The 'tip-off' in most of these cases is metrical. MacDiarmid rarely succeeds with straight rhyming dimeter or trimeter; the dynamic swells and surprises which distinguish his first-rate poems from slighter ones seem to require a longer, more varied line.

One of the hallmarks of MacDiarmid's early verse is a spooky fusion of romantic love and supernatural ballad. It figures largely in *A Drunk Man*, and can also be seen in these verses from 'Moonlight Among the Pines':

Thraw oot your shaddaws
Owre the heich hillsides,
A' ye lang trees
Quhair the white mune rides . . .

Lines like these are sometimes cited to suggest MacDiarmid's debt to Valéry because they constitute 'pure' poetry. But surely the primary influence here is from Scottish sources, and rather distant ones at that. Matthew MacDiarmid states this quite well:

. . . Though this is independently perfect verse, reflection tells us that it is only its perfection that blinds us momentarily to its traditional connections . . . What has happened is that just as the Augustan and sentimental vogue for the realistic pastoral gave Scots colloquial poetry its opportunity once before, so now the current vogue of 'pure poetry' allowed the revivers of Scots to develop and refine traditional features of style . . . The early MacDiarmid writes pure poetry. Later,

[1] It would appear that MacDiarmid published what he regarded as the best lyrics first, in *Sangschaw*; and that *Penny Wheep* includes a number of poems excluded from the earlier volume.

he will wish, unfairly, to say poor poetry. So much misleading talk has been heard about *Sangschaw* and *Penny Wheep* restoring ideas to Scots poetry. Ideas were precisely at this stage, what it avoided. One can say only that he successfully brought it into line with a European fashion of sensibility that was luckily sympathetic to its genius.[1]

Whatever the similarities, the fundamental differences emerge quite clearly if 'Moonlight Among the Pines' is compared with a typical poem from Valéry's *Album de Vers Anciens*, 'Le Bois Amical'.

Both poems bear out Valéry's dictum (in *Variété*) that 'there is a fine part of the soul that can enjoy without comprehending'. In MacDiarmid this effect derives from a stark use of strong verbs and plain nouns. But Valéry is soft and adjectival; words like 'vague', 'obscure' and 'pure' set the tone. The enamelled quality of artifice in golden oars and wings and azure indicates that this is a metaphoric wood, a projection of the speaker's inner self. MacDiarmid, by contrast, is not a symbolist; his poem cites natural (actual) scenery to dramatize the human situation. The utterance, like Valéry's, is the speaker's state of mind. But unlike Valéry's, it is direct. And if we think of MacDiarmid's career as a whole, we shall find that the directness remains long after the interest in 'pure' lyrics fades.

A rather different poetic influence can be heard in 'Cloudburst and Soaring Moon', 'In the Pantry', and 'In the Hedgeback'. In their rough vigour they emulate not only the Burns of the songs, but also John Millington Synge. MacDiarmid admired his Irish predecessor's desire to naturalize poetic speech and subjects, as expressed in Synge's 'The Passing of the Shee'. One character in a prose piece declares, 'Yon mannie Synge was richt: "It may almost be said that before verse can be human again it must learn to be brutal. . . ." The like's true o' a' forms o' literature'.[2] In a speech to the Burns Federation, MacDiarmid quoted James Hogg: 'Are my verses no' as guid as Keats? They're faur better. Keats' verses are owre pretty to be as guid as mine'.[3] And, in the person of Grieve, MacDiarmid wrote of himself, '. . . He has shown a well-knit muscular figure that has not been seen in Scottish literature for many a long day'.[4]

[1] 'Hugh MacDiarmid and the Colloquial Category', pp.75-6.
[2] 'Following Rebecca West in Edinburgh . . .', *Scottish Chapbook* 1, 3 (October 1922), p.72.
[3] Address to the Annual Conference, held in Birmingham, 1-2 September 1922.
[4] 'Causerie', *Scottish Chapbook* 1, 3 (October 1922), p.63.

We may be rightly suspicious of this aggressively 'muscular' pose. And we should bear in mind what has been said of Synge: He 'is not, as he seems to think, avoiding poetic diction altogether, but only substituting one sort of diction for another. He is still refusing to use certain words, the words of romantic glamour; he has only chosen to exclude a different set of words. He is still using a poetic diction, a selection of words; he is only making his selection on a different set of principles'.[1] Nevertheless, by his adherence to, and advocacy of those principles, MacDiarmid also rendered a valuable service to modern poetry. He helped bring Scottish verse into the twentieth century.

One more short poem needs to be noticed before leaving *Sangschaw* and *Penny Wheep*. 'The Eemis Stane' resounds with that sense of isolation, memory, and loss, of man alone in history and nature; of vision and passion, that recurs again and again throughout MacDiarmid's life. This lyric is, I think, the finest in either volume, and one of the most haunting he ever wrote.

> *The Eemis Stane*
>
> I' the how-dumb-deid o' the cauld hairst nicht   *dead middle | harvest*
> The warl' like an eemis stane   *unsteady*
> Wags i' the lift;
> An' my eerie memories fa'
> Like a yowdendrift.   *gale-driven snow*
>
> Like a yowdendrift so's I couldna read
> The words cut oot i' the stane
> Had the fug o' fame   *moss*
> An' history's hazelraw   *lichen*
> No' yirdit thaim.   *buried*

The poem comprises some sort of hallucination and encompasses radical shifts of vision. Let us first establish, more or less, what is being described:

> The observer sees the earth like an unsteady, tottering stone, but is it a tombstone on which the record and significance of its own past are somehow inscribed, if only we could read the inscription, or is it more like a logan-stone whose very precariousness and seeming defiance of the laws of survival are its main attraction? The desire for knowledge and the appeal of strangeness, opposite as they are, are knit together. Subjectivity ('my eerie memories') as well as the apparently more

[1] Donald Davie, 'The Poetic Diction of John M. Synge', *Dublin Magazine*, n.s., 27, 1 (January-March 1952), p.35.

objective comments of fame and history succeeds only in adding layer
upon layer of interposition on between us and the real.[1]

As Edwin Morgan's comments indicate, this poem about the
inaccessibility of meanings is itself remarkably resistant to analysis.
Its power and (to my mind) nobility come from the way its diction
and phrasing suggest countless secondary meanings without con-
firming any. First of all, there are the connotations of the Lallans
words. 'Eemis' (variable, uncertain), related to the Old Norse
ymiss and Icelandic *yms*, is the kind of adjective retained by Scots
but lost in English. In the subtlest way possible, it likens the world
to a rocking-stone, a huge boulder borne along by the ice-sheet, to
come to rest, at last, perilously poised on a hillslope. The resulting
backdrop of extinct or vanished civilization prepares us, uncon-
sciously, for the transformation of earth to tombstone five lines
below. As George Bruce has written, the portentous Shakespearean
sound swell of the first two lines is deflated instantly by the stressed
verb, 'wags'. Once brought down to this human level, what follows
can acquire dignity and mystery.[2] Even more remarkable is the
way the opening long lines balance on the short line that begins
with 'wag'; the very structure of the verse is an image of what it
describes.

As a syntactic unit, 'warl . . . wags' is matched by 'memories fa'.
The verb sequence 'wags-fa' sticks in the mind, to imply, but not
state, an equivalent fate for the two verbs' subjects. Successive
pauses required by 'lift' and 'fa' (whose broad 'a' recreates the
windy hush of a blizzard) likens the earth's situation in interstellar
space to that of the speaker in (perhaps) a human graveyard. Then,
the silence that both inhabit is filled by the onomatopoeic 'yowdendrift' in a phrase whose pitch falls like snow.

But immediately the same phrase is repeated on a rising pitch.
Why? Because as it reaches our level the snow doesn't simply come
to rest; it is picked up again, and piled by the wind into yird-drift.
'This isn't just a fanciful comparison', MacDiarmid says, 'I want
you to think about the obliterating process'.[3] The emotional effect
of this sound swell is like that of resisting burial alive.

'Yowdendrift' is introduced in the first stanza as a simile for
subjective memories. Now, when repeated, it becomes part of an
actual setting in which new metaphors (for fame and history) arise.

[1] Morgan, p.8.
[2] 'Between Any Life and the Sun', in Duval *et al.*, p.62.
[3] Morgan, p.8.

In like manner, the 'stance' which previously described the world and its fate now becomes a tombstone marking man's own. That inscription might be like the laws God gave to Moses, perhaps, or the Logos, or 'the Word' in John. No matter; even if man weren't blinded by his own drifting memories, objective circumstance would thwart his understanding. The sense of doom is reinforced as the two alliterative pairings ring – like a chisel on stone.

In utilizing the language of a countryman, MacDiarmid risked throwing into high relief the sophisticated technical effects he favoured. In poems like 'The Eemis Stane' and the equally accomplished 'Reid E'en' he solved this problem, paradoxically, by refining those techniques still more, to a point where they don't obtrude. The technique of 'mirror' stanzas is much less mechanical than in 'Country Life'. Note how when line seven's 'words . . . stane' echoes line two's 'warl! . . . stane', the extra stress in 'cut oot' suits the transition from drift into fixed doom. Similarly, in each stanza an assonantal end rhyme (nicht-lift, stane-fame) ossifies into standard masculine rhyme at the close.

We have already noted the effect of 'wags' in line three. If one looks at the poem as a structure alone, one sees a progression from a very long opening line to short lines, to a moderately long line to a very short one. In dynamic terms, it moves from *forte* to *piano* to *mezzo forte* to *pianissimo*. Metrically, one is forced to observe an *accelerando* at the start of each stanza; a *ritardando* in the middle.[1] In meticulous modulation, 'The Eemis Stane' sways, falls, drifts upward, and then settles, very slowly, down. The cosmic bang with which the poem begins becomes, in the end, a human whimper.

Kenneth Buthlay has objected to 'tendentious linking of Mac-Diarmid to English writers', along the lines I have suggested above (p.41). Yet it would be hard to read 'The Eemis Stane', let alone write it in 1924, without feeling the influence of Hardy. Even if we refuse to acknowledge any correspondence in the architectonics, the reliance on psalm and ballad forms, the handling of metre and stanzas, or the tone (of dignity that does not moralize); even denying all these, surely there is some echo simply in subject matter. One immediately thinks of 'During Wind and Rain' and other graveyard poems, of Jude and his chisels, of 'starlit Stonehenge'. To suggest the influence is certainly not to belittle Mac-Diarmid's achievement or Scottish poetry. Indeed, one could do

---

[1] I remind anyone who might object to my use of musical terms that some of these lyrics were written for music.

worse than be grouped with Hardy! MacDiarmid stands in no
danger of eclipse; the originality and greatness of these poems are
unmistakably his own. As Buthlay rightly points out:

> 'The Eemis Stane' has style, in a distinctive sense. This is one of the
> many things that cannot be learned from a dictionary. And as one
> reads the best of the Scots lyrics one realizes that the style has been
> hall-marked by MacDiarmid. One has the sensation of a great talent
> finding itself in a medium. [1]

This discussion of *Sangschaw* and *Penny Wheep* has been largely
(though I hope not inordinately) taken up with textual analysis.
The intention has been to try to show that these apparently simple
poems often require and reward close reading. It may be useful
now to summarize what this kind of writing can and cannot do.

These poems possess great musicality and richness. They are
energetic, active poems; this is verse in which things *happen*. It
relies heavily on individual words, which '. . . by their very
unfamiliarity . . . sharpen our perceptions of verbal qualities to
which we habitually pay too little attention, and invite a more
positive response from our imagination'. [2] The effects of suggestion
and concentration obtained by largely traditional means coincide
with modernist practice. MacDiarmid's ability to use natural
scenery to express a human situation, and to do it by simple
juxtaposition, resembles the economy of Japanese *haiku* and Classical Chinese verse. At the same time, his poetry's phanopoeic
qualities point forward, toward the art of film. One sees cinemato-
graphic 'panning' in 'Overinzievar'; 'jump-cuts' in 'Somersault'
and 'Morning'; 'dissolves' in 'The Watergaw' and 'Trompe L'Oeil'.

Despite his interest in Valéry and Mallarmé, MacDiarmid's
intentions are less in accord with French symbolist verse (or with
Eliot) than with those of 'objectivists' like Pound. 'A number of his
Scots poems . . . could be used to illustrate the imagist principles of
having "an actually realised visual object" in mind, of observing a
drastic economy in the use of words, and of concentrating upon
hard, clear, dry qualities in order to avoid emotional slither'. [3]
These poems are not self-referential, hermetic structures, not
forms commenting on a form. They are ways of exploring the
objective world and one's own place in it, of discovering the 'ferlies
[marvels] in a bensil o' bleeze', the drama in ordinary things.

[1] Buthlay, p.44.
[2] *Ibid.*, p.29.
[3] *Ibid.*, p.32.

The limitations of this style arise directly from its strengths. MacDiarmid's advocacy of synthetic Scots ignores a necessary distinction between *vernacular* and *colloquial* speech. When Burns mixed literary sources with dialects of his day, he was fusing the past to an active present. And the success of Wergeland's Norwegian *Landsmaal* resulted from widespread popular participation. But however much Scots usages were retained in MacDiarmid's youth, they had ceased to grow, and for a language, this is the first step towards dying. The success of his own efforts proved the value of Lallans as a literary tongue, but could not restore it to common parlance on a scale that would nurture future works of art. Denied vital interaction with a vital popular speech, work in Scots was bound to remain a specialized and idiosyncratic genre.[1] This by no means detracts from the poems MacDiarmid did write. The point is simply that effects dependent on lexical surprise won't bear too much repetition.

Like the imagism with which it has much in common, this style was conceived as a corrective to Swinburnian pseudo-decadence, on the one hand, and Georgian politeness on the other. It succeeded on both counts. Thus,

> Reading such verse one does not have to concern himself unduly with thoughts of the poet being Scots, with a Scots theme in a Scots context. It is simply great verse; it is free mind, free expression. . . .
>
> Yet even this perfection can be thought limited. . . . There is . . . too little mind in it. We are being asked excessively to think with our senses, and though this is freedom on one side, it is restriction on another. . . .[2]

'Too little mind'. Is it heretical to say the same about the number on a fire engine, or the petals on that wet black bough? I think not. For, once having made their revolutionary mark, almost all the original imagists moved on. They did not (with a few exceptions) reject their earlier methods, but attempted to incorporate them into larger forms, forms capable of greater statement.

MacDiarmid too attempted this. His first, and most famous long poem, *A Drunk Man Looks at the Thistle*, appeared in 1926. Whether it coheres as one poem; whether it represents an exten-

[1] Even in the successful imaginative prose of Lewis Grassic Gibbon's 'A Scots Quair', or MacDiarmid's lovely 'Shetland Lyrics', published in 1939 (see below, p.165). As for the Scots verse by a later generation, very little of its feels unselfconscious.

[2] Matthew P. MacDiarmid, in *Agenda*, Vol.5, No.4, Vol.6, No.1 (Autumn 1967-Winter 1968), p.75.

sion of Scots or a piecemeal desertion of it; whether it is mere
'gallimaufry' or a major twentieth-century work; these are some of
the questions we must address in the following pages.

CHAPTER THREE

'Where Extremes Meet'
A Drunk Man Looks at the Thistle

I have not been very sensitive about our free songs. I have not excluded all that is over-free and glowing. I wished to preserve an image of the livelier moments of the lyric Muse, when she sang without fear, without scruple, and without sin.

ALLAN CUNNINGHAME to Sir Walter Scott

It is the glory of man, and something more than his glory, to waste his powers on the void. . . . The role of the non-existent exists; the function of the imaginary is real; and we learn from strict logic that *the false implies the true*. Thus it would seem that the history of thought can be summarized in these words: *It is absurd by what it seeks; great by what it finds*.

VALÉRY, Fragment from 'On Poe's Eureka'

IN DECEMBER 1925, Hugh MacDiarmid advertised a major work-in-progress in the *Glasgow Herald*:

> It is interesting news that Mr. Hugh M'Diarmid has now composed a gallimaufry in braid Scots verse, entitled 'A Drunk Man Looks At the Thistle'. It is, in fact, a long poem of over a thousand lines split up into several sections, but the forms within the sections range from ballad measure to *vers libre*. The matter includes satire, amphigouri, lyrics, parodies of Mr. T. S. Eliot and other poets, and translations from the Russians, French and Germans. The whole poem is in braid Scots, except a few quatrains which are in the nature of a skit on Mr. Eliot's 'Sweeney' poems, and it has been expressly resigned [sic] to show that braid Scots can be effectively applied to all manner of subjects and measures.[1]

Readers who encountered this notice barely three months after the appearance of *Sangschaw* might well have wondered whether writers in full command of their learning feel obliged to advertise it. In this case, the poet's recourse to such puffery led him to make claims which the finished work cannot bear out.

It is not 'a long poem split into several sections', but a sequence of fragments which cohere loosely by means of image and symbol. Some were written independently, in other contexts.[2] As Kenneth Buthlay first noted, the 'translations' from French and Russian are in fact adaptations of existing English versions.[3] *Some* of the poem is in braid Scots, but in parts of *A Drunk Man* (as not in *Sangschaw*) a good deal of the Scots quality derives from orthography as much as from native diction.[4] Finally, though the forms do 'range from ballad measure to *vers libre*', most of the poem is in couplets or

[1] *The Glasgow Herald*, 17 December 1925. An 'amphigory' is a nonsense verse or composition, a rigmarole with apparent meaning which proves to be meaningless. A 'gallimaufry' is a medley, mixture, hodgepodge.
[2] Sections of the final poem had appeared in *The Glasgow Herald* in February 1926: 'Love' and what became 'The Ballad of the General Strike' were composed in 1925.
[3] Kenneth Buthlay, *Hugh MacDiarmid* (Edinburgh and London: Oliver & Boyd, 1964), p.74.
[4] For a helpful discussion, see John C. Weston, 'Preface', *A Drunk Man Looks at the Thistle* (Amherst, MA: University of Massachusetts Press, 1971), pp.vii-xiv.

rhymed tetrameter. Only 127 lines – less than five per cent of the total – are free verse, and even these are not true *'vers libre'*.[1] [For those who might wish to pursue this issue, the poem's actual distribution of forms breaks down as follows: 1140 lines (roughly 42 per cent) are quatrains, whether ballad measure, iambic tetrameter or pentameter; this includes quatrains fused into verse blocks of 12 or 16 lines (1219ff.) (1727–34). 363 lines (roughly 13 per cent of the poem) are couplets; 270 lines (roughly 10 per cent) are 'Skeltonic' tercets; and the remaining verse is in various rhymed stanzas often reminiscent of the modified Spenserian MacDiarmid had used in 'Gairmscoile', a poem in *Penny Wheep*.] Taken together, MacDiarmid's claims are half-truths which call attention to the insecurity they were intended to conceal. They also underscore the author's need to be thought cosmopolitan and avant-garde, and point towards increasingly ambitious goals.

We have noted in relation to *Sangschaw* and *Penny Wheep* how the purity that comprised their great virtue also defined their limitations. The poet sang not as himself, the private man, but as anonymous voice of a class. However well that folk persona served MacDiarmid the Scots reviver and lyricist, it imposed restrictions on MacDiarmid the twentieth-century intellectual. On the one hand, it drastically curtailed the range of permissible reference; on the other, it ruled out free-ranging discourse about ideas. In order to pass beyond these 'wee bit sangs', he settled on a larger form which would retain the flavour of that early work, yet permit abstract, intellectual insertions that would expand its range. The resulting poem is from first to last an anomaly.

If this were all, we should be forced to conclude straight off that this is the sign of a hack writer whose high-falutin' goals far exceeded his talents. The crucial difference, as may become clear, is that MacDiarmid *knows* that his task is somewhat anomalous – or at least that we will perceive it as such. He therefore uses that sense of incongruity, indeed exaggerates and draws upon it as a source of disconcerting humour, energy and tension. What he says, in effect, is: 'The contradictions that I face, as a modern Scot, a writer and an intellectual, are even more extreme than you, the reader, could imagine'. To demonstrate this is at once to enlist the reader's sym-

---

[1] Lines 2056-183, while 'free', are technically *'vers libéré'* because of the consistent recurrence of incorporated blank verse (iambic pentameter) lines. Similarly, lines 1230-441 and 1451-631, which *look* like free verse, are in fact unrhymed iambic tetrameter, with little variation in the handling of syntax and caesurae.

pathy and to make the writer's efforts all the more impressive
should he succeed in somehow transcending and uniting this 'routh
[plenty] o' contraries'.

In short, it is as *tour de force* that *A Drunk Man* is offered, and
asks to be judged. The ceaseless contradictions in tone, mood and
creed are reconciled, if at all, by sheer force of personality, holding
them all in relation.

Given this, is it 'idle to attempt a coherent account of a poem so
deliberately and provocatively incoherent', as a *TLS* reviewer
wrote?[1] Not, perhaps, if one takes the anomalies as given, and
instead devotes attention to the ways in which the poem changes,
the means by which its thoughts do cohere. Behind this shall rest
two basic questions: Does the poem move forward? What does the
speaker learn?

The first words of this long dramatic poem are spoken by a
drunk man alone on a barren hill in 1925. After another night's
boozing with old cronies, he is staggering homeward to his wife,
through moonlit fields. In the quiet night his head still reels from
the noise and fumes of the public house:

I amna fou' sae muckle as tired – deid dune.	*drunk / as much*
It's gey and hard wark coupin' gless for gless	*very / upending*
Wi' Cruivie and Gilsanquhar and the like,	
And I'm no' juist as bauld as aince I wes.	

The elbuck fankles in the coorse o' time,	*elbow / becomes clumsy*
The sheckle's no' sae souple, and the thrapple	*wrist / gullet*
Grows deef and dour: nae langer up and doun	*unimpressionable / stiff*
Gleg as a squirrel speils the Adam's apple.	*lively / climbs*

The opening phrase recalls Burns' well-known drinking song
('We are na' fou', we're nae that fou' / But just a drappie in our e'e
. . .').[2] The speaker himself, however, is now ageing; his old
routine brings not exhilaration, but exhaustion. Stopping to rest,
he mutters predictable complaints about the rising cost and falling
quality of whisky. He worries 'what the wife'll say' when he gets
home. Such statements, along with the casual reference to Cruivie,
Gilsanquhar 'and the like', suggest a conventional range of concerns in a social milieu that is taken for granted. The figure we
bump into, emerging from his pub, appears frustrated – cantan-
kerous perhaps – yet very much at home in the speech, locale and
culture that define him.

[1] 22 September 1927, pp.650-2.
[2] 'Willie Brew'd a Peck o' Maut'.

Then, without warning, gripes about liquor turn into something
more serious:

> And a' that's Scotch aboot it is the name,
> Like a' thing else ca'd Scottish nooadays
> – A' destitute o' speerit juist the same.
> (17–20)

And lest we mistake his anger merely for the unselfconscious,
comic ramblings of a Tam O'Shanter (as many readers are likely to
do at this point), he reveals where these complaints are tending:

> (To prove my saul is Scots I maun begin
> Wi' what's still deemed Scots and the folk expect,
> And spire up syne by visible degrees   *soar*
> To heichts whereo' the fules ha'e never recked.
>
> But aince I get them there I'll whummle them   *overturn*
> And souse the craturs in the nether deeps,
> – For it's nae choice, and ony man s'ud wish
> To dree the goat's weird tae as weel's the sheep's!)   *endure | fate*
> (21–8)

No element of the Scots legacy, not even the hateful Kailyard
tradition, will be rejected; rather, it will be subsumed in larger
concerns. All speculations will be faithful to – but not confined by –
local circumstances.

Having hinted at his ultimate intentions, the Drunk Man returns
to 'what the folk expect' – a broad satire on the state of Scottish
culture:

> You canna gang to a Burns supper even
> Wi'oot some wizened scrunt o' a knock-knee   *mite*
> Chinese turns roon to say, 'Him Haggis – velly goot!'
> And ten to wan the piper is a Cockney. . . .
>
> Croose London Scotties wi' their braw shirt fronts   *conceited*
> And a' their fancy freen's, rejoicin'
> That similah gatherings in Timbuctoo,
> Bagdad – and Hell, nae doot – are voicin'
>
> Burns' sentiments o' universal love,
> In pidgin English or in wild-fowl Scots,
> And toastin' ane wha's nocht to them but an
> Excuse for faitherin' Genius wi' *their* thochts.
> (37–40; 45–52)

Like all good satire, this helps the reader feel comfortably superior to the objects of his disdain. The Drunk Man's proprietary attitude towards Burns, complete with sentimental personal addresses ('I'm haverin', Rabbie, but ye understaun'') is likely to appeal to professional Scots and to reinforce their own complacency.

But MacDiarmid's true plan is not to chastise some but to implicate all; any who respond to the Drunk Man's complaints too smugly will soon be 'whummled' as forewarned:

> I'se warrant you'd [Burns] shy clear o' a' the hunner   *I'll | hundred*
>
> Odd Burns Clubs tae, or ninety-nine o' them,
> And haud your birthday in a different kip   *lodging*
> Whaur your name isna ta'en in vain – as Christ
> Gied a' Jerusalem's Pharisees the slip
>
> – Christ wha'd ha'e been Chief Rabbi gin he'd lik't ! –
> Wi' publicans and sinners to forgether,   *meet*
> But, losh! the publicans noo are Pharisees,
> And I'm no' shair o' maist the sinners either.
>   (84–93)
>
> As Kirks wi' Christianity ha'e dune,
> Burns Clubs wi' Burns – wi' a'thing it's the same,
> The core o' ocht is only for the few,   *aught*
> Scorned by the mony, thrang wi'ts empty name.   *busy*
>   (109–12)

The Drunk Man reveres both Christ and Burns as moral nonconformists who acted in anti-institutional, anarchic capacities. Institutions such as the Church and Burns Clubs shelter their members from precisely the sort of creative doubt which the objects of their veneration sought, and that is why the 'mony' join. But for the 'few' the only admissible response is imitation; admiration for specific heroes inspires heroic action. In the course of his monologue, the speaker will compare himself with Christ, Burns, Ulysses, Melville, and Dostoyevsky. At various points the thistle he is forced to contemplate becomes a crown of thorns, the moonlit hillside his Gethsemane:

> Aye, this is Calvary – to bear
> Your Cross wi'in you frae the seed,
> And feel it grow by slow degrees
> Until it rends your flesh apairt,
> And turn, and see your fellow-men
> In similar case but sufferin' less
> Thro' bein' mair wudden frae the stert! . . .   *wooden*

Though the imagery is derived from Christian dogma, specific matters of religion and location count less ('What tho'ts Montrose or Nazareth?') than the courage to pursue an unconforming way.

Thus, unlike his cronies, the Drunk Man leaves the pub. He trades the facetious 'hard wark coupin' [upending] gless fer gless' (l.2) for the real 'hard wark Haud'n' [holding] by a thocht worth hae'n [having]' (105). Comparing his lot with that of others, his responses range from contempt to jealousy, from self hatred to fierce pride:

> Wad I were them – they've chosen a better pairt,
> The couthie craturs, than the ane I've ta'en,   *smug creatures*
> Tyauvin' wi' this root-hewn Scottis soul;   *struggling*
> A fer, fer better pairt – except for men.
>
> Nae doot they're sober, as a Scot ne'er was,
> Each tethered to a punctual-snorin' missus,
> Whilst I, puir fule, owre continents unkent   *unknown*
> And wine-dark oceans waunder like Ulysses. . . .
>   (393–400)

Ironically, it is the Drunk Man's loyalty to the true collective past that makes the false exhibitions of others so painful, and warps his passion into isolation. In a similar state of mind, Burns cried out (in 'Epistle to James Smith'):

> O ye douce folk, that live by rule
> Grave, tide-less blooded, calm and cool
> Compar'd wi you – O fool! fool! fool!
>   How much unlike!
> Your hearts are just a standing pool
>   Your lives, a dyke!

The Drunk Man echoes Burns' language, and transforms the exile's complaint into a rebel's creed:

> I doot I'm geylies mixed, like Life itsel',   *suspect | very much*
> But I was never ane that thocht to pit
> An ocean in a mutchkin. As the haill's   *bottle, measure | whole's*
> Mair than the pairt sae I than reason yet . . .
>
> I'll ha'e nae hauf-way hoose, but aye be whaur'
> 'Extremes meet – it's the only way I ken
> To dodge the curst conceit o' bein' richt
> That damns the vast majority o' men.
>   (129–32; 141–5)

Several things should be said about this declaration. First of all, it is not an attack on reason, only a reminder of its limitations. For even when logically valid, truths that precede full experience are like verdicts passed when evidence has been withheld. 'Bein' richt' is viewed as a conceit because knowledge is always incomplete. It is 'curst' because those who state 'truths' tend to impose their certitude on others (as in the Kirk) and also 'bury heids like ostriches'; that is, lose their ability to learn from the external world.[1]

The scepticism with which the Drunk Man treats others' conclusions extends to his own as well. And while he rejects *a priori* or merely logical knowledge, he does not on the other hand espouse a crude materialism based exclusively on sense perceptions:

> I'll bury nae heid like an ostrich's,
> Nor yet believe my een and naething else.
> My senses may advise me, but I'll be
> Mysel' nae maitter what they tell's. . . .
>
> I ha'e nae doot some foreign philosopher
> Has wrocht a system oot to justify
> A' this: but I'm a Scot wha blin'ly follows
> Auld Scottish instincts, and I winna try.
>
> For I've nae faith in ocht I can explain,
> And stert whaur the philosophers leave aff,
> Content to glimpse its loops I dinna ettle   *aspire*
> To land the sea serpent's sel' wi' ony gaff.
>
> Like staundin' water in a pocket o'
> Impervious clay I pray I'll never be,
> Cut aff and self-sufficient, but let reenge   *range*
> Heichts o' the lift and benmaist deeps o' sea.   *utmost*
>   (145–60)

Having posed the two poles of a philosophical debate, the Drunk Man winds up rejecting both sides' attempts to resolve it. The emphasis on 'instincts' and the professed desire to 'reenge' – a word originally used for animals – declare a distrust of analysis, a preference for raw experience. They replace the need to be right with the will to find out more, to go, and, in Pound's phrase, 'sail after knowledge'.

In passages such as those just examined, the Drunk Man pre-

---

[1] MacDiarmid's phrase is an abbreviated version of Joubert's 'the cursed conceit of being right which kills all noble feeling' (i.e. thwarts the heroic impulse to explore). It was first quoted by MacDiarmid in *Annals of the Five Senses*, p.14.

sents himself as a realist. Reality exists – with a capital R; it can be described with confidence, through use of appropriate abstractions. The task of understanding becomes by implication almost quantitative: to encounter and then describe as much as possible. That the language at his disposal may be arbitrary, in itself 'unreal', seems as far from the speaker's thoughts as is the attitude of passivity and self-effacement such concerns can give rise to. Thus it is doubly surprising to find various self-assertive declarations followed by Scots renderings of the Russian Symbolist poet and mystic, Alexander Blok. One such rendering reads:

> But ilka evenin' fey and fremt   fated / lonely
> (Is it a dream nae wauk'nin' proves?)   waking
> As to a trystin'-place undreamt,
> A silken leddy darkly moves.
>
> I seek, in this captivity,
> To pierce the veils that darklin' fa'
> – See white clints slidin' to the sea,   cliffs
> And hear the horns o' Elfland blaw.
>   (193–6; 205–8)

To some, the supernatural note may seem dishonest. One may well ask what the 'horns o' Elfland' have to do with that heady brew of common sense and bravado just put forth in 'A Vision of Myself'.[1] And in what conceivable way does the hymn to a Platonic world soul that follows (241–52) accord with the Byronic satire of the opening section? If we cannot account for this shift at some point, we shall be forced to reject not just the lines from Blok, and successive translations, but *all* the succeeding metaphysical passages through which they echo.

To conclude thus would be to misunderstand the poem's structural rationale. MacDiarmid's consistent end, in all he wrote, was to expand the reader's sense of possibility, to challenge preconceptions that preclude growth. In *A Drunk Man Looks at the Thistle*, he attempts this in two ways. First, there are the reductive, naturalistic passages, among them the discourse on Burns Clubs, 'Outward Bound', 'Tussle With the Philistines', and 'The Splore'.[2] Like the jabs at established religion, the vulgarity and scurrility of

[1] Throughout this chapter, line references will be numbered and keyed to the 1971 University of Massachusetts edition, although MacDiarmid's original orthography is retained. For convenience, however, entire lyrics will at times be referred to by the subtitles MacDiarmid supplied for the *Collected Poems*, 1962.
[2] Lines 37-92; 545-57; 770-810; 811-44.

these sections function as *weapons*. MacDiarmid brings to bear all
the reductive power of reason upon irrational restraints. He at-
tacks, on the conscious level, from without.

Simultaneously, while thus eroding such restraints, he also seeks
to release and express subconscious, imaginative powers that the
objects of his conscious wrath constrain. This, then, is the function
of the Blok translations, of 'O Wha's the Bride' (ll.612-35) and the
lyric evocations based on whiteness and moonlight. Thus two types
of poetry which at first glance might seem incompatible in fact
work together toward one end. One addresses the conscious; the
other expresses the subconscious, and it is this poem's great virtue
to accept and make use of both. To see how this process works, we
may trace one of many instances through its various resonances in
the poem.

An early use of Christian reference comes in 'Outward Bound'
(ll.545–57) beginning,

> We're ootward boond frae Scotland
> Guid-bye, fare-ye-weel, guid-bye, fare-ye-weel . . .

Typically, it blends bad taste with bad humour, deliberately insult-
ing both Christian sensibilities and the popular Scots song it echoes.
The poetry itself is bad – the sort of thing one attributes to a
drunk's unfunny humour, and seeks to pass over quickly. The
Drunk Man himself can take it nowhere; he trails off with an
ellipsis. . . .

In the fashion of a true drunk, he immediately forgets the
extraneous conceit, yet returns a little later to the component that
really does interest him, namely how to reconcile his own abject,
ridiculous physical state with a sense of spiritual promise:

> Said my body to my mind,
> 'I've been startled whiles to find,   *sometimes*
> When Jean has been in bed wi' me,
> A kind o' Christianity!'

> To my body said my mind,
> 'But your benmaist thocht you'll find
> Was "Bother what I think I feel
> – Jean kens the set o' my bluid owre weel,
> And lauchs to see me in the creel   *frenzy* (lit. *basket*)
> O' my courage-bag confined."'. . .   *scrotum*
>   (571–80)

What began as an idle joke has now captured the speaker's full attention. He has found something that really matters to him, and as the intensity of his concern surpasses its original waggish expression, his thoughts become simpler, more direct:

> I wish I kent the physical basis
> O' a' life's seemin' airs and graces.
>
> It's queer the thochts a kittled cull   *tickled testicle*
> Can lowse or splairgin' glit annul.   *loosen | splattering slime*
>
> Man's spreit is wi' his ingangs twined   *spirit | entrails*
> In ways that he can ne'er unwind.
>   (581–6)

These words reinforce the tension at this point between what the speaker is thinking and what he is doing. Even as his speculation grows more exalted, he is exciting himself sexually, and even as he seeks to reconcile intellectually the split between flesh and spirit, the gap is growing wider.[1]

We should note, in this context, the serious puns on seemin' (582) and spreit (585); the latter echoes his old accusation, 'A' desitute o' speerit juist the same' (20). Not that the Drunk Man is consciously punning, but that in his choice of language there begins to emerge a subconscious element that may reconcile what the conscious keeps asunder.

Up to this point, the verses I have been quoting all fall into the first, 'naturalistic' category. The strains they address in naturalistic fashion reach a climax[2] in these lines:

> A luvin' wumman is a licht
> That shows a man his waefu' plicht,
> Bleezin' steady on ilka bane,   *every bone*
> Wrigglin' sinnen an' twinin' vein,   *sinew*
> Or fleerin' quick an' gane again,   *flaring*
> And the mair scunnersome the sicht   *repulsive*
> The mair for love and licht he's fain
> Till clear and chitterin' and nesh   *trembling | nervous*
> Move a' the miseries o' his flesh. . . .
>   (595–603)

[1] References to his own arousal in lines 578-94 are echoed in the 'cloudy blash o' sperm' (1250), wasted semen that dries and powders (1260ff.) and 'loppert slime' (1335). When speculating, the Drunk Man habitually incorporates images from whatever he's doing or observing at the moment.

[2] My double meaning is intended. If one accepts the previous note, the lines quoted fit both senses of the word. They also anticipate the poem 'Harry Semen' (see pp. 171-80).

'Scunnersome' . . . 'chitterin'' . . . 'nesh' – it would seem that, in what began as a joke, the flesh has outstripped and degraded spiritual pretensions.

Only one thing is 'wrong with this picture' – the Lass's response:

> O lass, wha see'est me
> As I daur hardly see,
> I marvel that your bonny een
> Are as they hadna seen.
>   (604–7)

After the conclusive self-hate of the lines just preceding, this tentative note sounds like a reprieve. From the actual, or naturalistic, Jean, we have suddenly arrived at a transcendent, Beatrice-like figure in the poem's most famous lyric, 'O Wha's the Bride':

> O wha's the bride that cairries the bunch
> O' thistles blinterin' white?   *gleaming*
> Her cuckold bridegroom little dreids
> What he sall ken this nicht.
>
> For closer than gudeman can come   *husband*
> And closer to'r than hersel',   *to her*
> Wha didna need her maidenheid
> Has wrocht his purpose fell.
>
> O wha's been here afore me, lass,
> And hoo did he get in?
>   – *A man that deed or I was born*   *ere*
>   *This evil thing has din.*   *done*
>
> And left, as it were on a corpse,
> Your maidenheid to me?
>   – *Nae lass, gudeman, sin' Time began*
>   *'S hed ony mair to gi'e.*   *Has had any more to give*
>
> *But I can gi'e ye kindness, lad,*
> *And a pair o' willin' hands,*
> *And you sall ha'e my breists like stars,*
> *My limbs like willow wands,*
>
> *And on my lips ye'll heed nae mair,*
> *And in my hair forget,*
> *The seed o' a' the men that in*
> *My virgin womb ha'e met. . . .*
>   (612–35)

It is not hard to see why that lyric is widely quoted, or what in it led Yeats to exclaim, 'Lord God the man's a poet'.[1] Yet it remains difficult, if not impossible, to say just what these verses mean. Like the Drunk Man himself, the 'gudeman' is obsessed with unattainable perfection. He expects ideal (non-human) purity in his bride, and therefore feels betrayed – 'cuckolded' – by the knowledge of less-than-pure reality she brings him. To his literal, either-or mind, whatever admits corruption must be spiritually deficient, or dead; hence the accusation,

> And left, as it were on a corpse
> Your maidenheid to me?

To this the bride replies:

> *Nae lass, gudeman, sin' Time began*
> *'S hed ony mair to gi'e.*

'Time began' with Adam. By introducing this phrase, MacDiarmid here links the concept of original sin to that of the Immaculate Conception, which has already been echoed above. This brings to mind the doctrine of *felix culpa*, the fortunate fall in which Christ is the 'second Adam'. The sin of the first made possible redemption by the second. Similarly, by accepting what others might construe to be corruption, Mary brought God in Man; she became the agent of grace. Here, by substituting mercy for the gudeman's law, 'kindness' for obsessive and literal purity, the 'bride' plays a similar role.

What is intriguing is how MacDiarmid plays on the traditional references in a way that both confirms and inverts their values. For while the motive for mercy sounds Christian, the solace offered is erotic:

> *But I can gi'e ye kindness, lad,*
> *And a pair o' willin' hands,*
> *And you sall ha'e my breists like stars,*
> *My limbs like willow wands,*
>
> *And on my lips ye'll heed nae mair,*
> *And in my hair forget,*
> *The seed o' a' the men that in*
> *My virgin womb ha'e met. . . .*

These, then, are the consolations of the flesh. But they are more than that. If we think back to the lines with which this discussion

---

[1] 'Gog' [pseud. Oliver St John Gogarty], 'Literature and Life: A Drunk Man Looks at the Thistle', *The Irish Statesman* 7, 18 (8 January 1927), p.432.

began ('. . . when Jean has been in bed wi' me / A kind o'
Christianity!'), we see that what first found expression as a joke, in
bad taste, has now stumbled into a vision of truth. The flesh, which
seemed a prison, can become an expression of spirit ('breists like
stars'). Those who share kindness exercise a transcendent virtue – a
'*kind* o' Christianity'; the flesh is no longer a barrier to spirit, but a
means of participating in it.

A second paradox in 'O Wha's the Bride' concerns the bride
herself. She appears like an emblematic figure in a medieval dream
poem, carrying Scotland's national flower. What do these thistles
signify? The plight of Scotland? The crown of thorns?[1] This
mystery is heightened by a riddle: Who *is* she? Throughout *A
Drunk Man*, whiteness signifies the supernatural; thus, the bride's
'blinterin' white thistles suggest a connection with the Silken
Leddy, or Divine Wisdom, or the Female Principle (Sophia)
celebrated in preceding lyrics. Similarly, the bride's speech is in
italics, which the sequence generally reserves for timeless supernatural pronouncements.

However, her words themselves could not be more homely: the
terms of endearment – 'lad', 'gudeman' – are those that any 'quean'
might use to console the 'carle' who loves her. The result (as in all
MacDiarmid's strongest lyrics) is to physicalize an abstraction –
not to discard the supernatural nor to denigrate the actual, but to
discover one in the other: 'Sex *reveals* life, faith'.[2] God (as Joyce
wrote) is a shout in the street; Sophia has 'willin' hands', and one
way to know what one can't see is to love what one can.

I have risked belabouring these first few lyrics in order to
demonstrate three points which, when grasped, may open up an
otherwise unmanageable text to further study:

1. *A Drunk Man Looks at the Thistle* contains types of writing
that are formally and logically incompatible. When attempting
explication, it is as fruitless to assert a non-existent congruity as to
bemoan its absence. Each passage is true *only to its moment*. The
first thousand lines in particular offer not a common denominator
of meaning, but a sum of conflicting postures and perceptions,
embodied in various styles.

---

[1] Usually in *A Drunk Man*, the thistle symbolizes torment and complexity of thought, whereas moonlight and whiteness connote wholeness and supernatural vision. Given what we've just discussed
regarding corruption and forgiveness, her carrying thistles, rather
than some softer bloom, is an affecting touch.
[2] Line 988, italics mine; note the full meaning of *reveals*.

2. By thus sustaining unresolved contradictions, MacDiarmid makes many stances possible, but no particular one obligatory. He emphasizes processes of mind over its changing products, valuing particular answers less than the new questions they inspire. We might note, in this respect, that the sequence from 'Outward Bound' through 'O Wha's the Bride', which begins with torment expressed in definite statements, is subsumed (and temporarily resolved) into questions – indeed, a dialogue of questions.[1]

3. Throughout *A Drunk Man*, passages which clash in terms of subject, tone, and statement simultaneously cohere through imagery and language. As the poem progresses, the very terms which are enlisted to lament disharmony imply, through their adaptability, relation.

In a story written four years earlier, MacDiarmid described the protagonist (who is writing a column on 'The Scottish Element in Ibsen'!) in these terms:

> . . . myriad-faceted existences and his own extraordinarily vivid pictorial sense of his own cranial geography and anatomical activities were all co-visible to him. . . . Nor were any of the elements permanent or passive. . . . As one thing receded into unreality, the reality of other things became newly apparent (albeit oddly familiar and repetitive) taking him like trumpets. . . . The transfusing vitality of his interest never failed to discharge to the tiniest detail the demands of that versatility of sensation and speculation. He was athrill with the miracle of sentience.[2]

From this thinly veiled self-portrait, two phrases stand out: 'cranial geography' and 'sentience'. In the former, the mind itself becomes a *terra incognita*. And just as the external world must be confronted in direct experience, so must the internal geography. What links the two is *sentience*, that is, undifferentiated consciousness preceding the selecting and integrating activity of intellect. Though eventually, as the Drunk Man sobers up, his formulations will become more extended and coherent, most of the poem's first thousand lines function chiefly as a romp of the sensuous imagination. We are asked, no less than in *Sangschaw*, to think with our senses.

[1] One of the speakers is Sophia, and the form of this lyric resembles that of other wisdom poetry, such as paired rabbinical questions and Zen koans. A minor genre of Scottish ballad is also based on the exchange of riddles.

[2] 'Cerebral', in *Annals of the Five Senses*, pp.6-7.

Being so heavily grounded in, and dependent on, sensation, MacDiarmid's method reflects a basic fact of physiology: we can perceive only difference.[1] Thus, opposition becomes the poet's source of definition. Ocean and standing pool, sunlight and moonlight, thistle and rose – these defining oppositions shape the larger poem. Yet the primary pattern of 'pairt and counterpairt' is itself unstable, and gives way unpredictably to secondary and tertiary couplings (thistle and moonlight, water and whisky, whisky and moonlight, thistle and monster, monster and moonlight, and so forth). One also finds pairs of women, paired dances, paired flowers. I would concur with Burns Singer when he likens this to watching the change of partners in a complex reel, but would add 'under a strobe light' – for, as there are no transitions, we see only discontinuous tableaux. Various technical devices reinforce the incongruities.

Comic reality intrudes continually upon the meditative strain associated with moonlight. For instance, heroic declarations ('Let reenge / Heichts o' the lift, and benmaist deeps o' sea') can turn instantly to 'Water, water, there was owre muckle o't / In yonder whisky, sae I'm in deep water . . .' (161–2). Immediately after seeing the 'Silken Leddy' (169–220), the Drunk Man gets the hiccups. Similarly, 'O Wha's the Bride' is followed at once by this:

> Millions o' wimmen bring forth in pain
> Millions o' bairns that are no' worth hae'n.   *having*
>   (636–7)

and later, in still cruder form:

> Auld bag o' tricks, ye needna come
> And think to stap me in your womb.   *stuff*
>
> You needna fash to rax and strain.   *trouble / stretch*
> Carline, I'll *no'* be born again   *Hag*
>
> In ony brat you can produce.
>   (821–5)

In the same vein, comments to an undressing barmaid ('Less than a' there is to see / 'll never be owre muckle for me') (837–8) mock similar language applied earlier to the Ulysses-like hunger for experience.

[1] See Gregory Bateson, *Mind and Nature* (New York: E. P. Dutton, 1979), pp.70, 94-100. Also Barbara Gillam, 'Geometrical Illusions', *Scientific American* 242, 1 (January 1980), pp.102-12.

Closely allied to the comic strain is a liberal, perhaps excessive dose of 'scunner': vomit (127), hiccups (233), fantasized necrophilia (905), a pickled foetus, dried sperm (1260), the Trinity as a *ménage à trois*. Elsewhere, MacDiarmid wrote, 'They do not love liberty who fear license'.[1] Like Burns in 'The Jolly Beggars', he uses vulgarity as an expression of freedom, as a sort of guerilla raid on sanctioned proprieties. Faced with the 'dog hank of the flesh and soul', mankind is 'torn in twa / And glorious in the lift and grisly in the sod'. By offering plentiful evidence of this, MacDiarmid demands that our most elevated speculations take account of the opposite extremes, that the flesh be granted its due.

At times the Drunk Man uses the same image to support contradictory statements, without acknowledging the contradiction:

> But I was never ane that thocht to pit
> An ocean in a mutchkin.
> (130)

> We 'bood to ha'e a thimblefu' first   *intend to have*
> And syne we'll toom an ocean!
> (817)   *empty*

> O ilka man alive is like   *every*
> A quart that's squeezed into a pint.
> (1231)

Sometimes paired images, one serious and one playful, emerge in series:

> Am I a thingum mebbe that is kept
> Preserved in spirits in a muckle bottle
> Long centuries efter sin' wi' Jean I slept?   *after the time that*
> – Mounted on a hillside . . .
> (282–5)

> *Or* am I juist a figure in a scene
> O' Scottish life A D one-nine-two-five?
> (289–91)

> *Or* is this Heaven, this yalla licht?
> (667, my italics)

Occasionally, as signified by an ellipsis, the Drunk Man's expression of his own bewilderment effects the transition between sections (for example, lines 93ff.). This method has been usefully compared to the film technique of 'dissolves' in which an image

---

[1] *The Voice of Scotland*, p.95.

blurs and then returns to focus someplace else.[1]

At other times, when the Drunk Man grows excited, images come so fast that he can't control them:

> As the worms'll breed in my corpse until
> It's like a rice-puddin', the thistle
> Has made an eel-ark o' the lift   *breeding ground*
> Whaur elvers like skirl-in-the-pan sizzle,   *fried oatmeal*
>
> Like a thunder-plump on the sunlicht,   *downpour*
> Or the slounge o' daith on my dreams,   *surfacing (as of fish)*
> Or as to a fair forfochen man   *very exhausted*
> A breedin' wife's beddiness seems,   *sexual importunity*
>
> Sargossa Sea, St. Vitus' Dance,
> A *cafard* in a brain's despite,
> Or lunacy that thinks a' else
> Is loony – and is dootless richt! . . .
> (885–92)

Here, as in the preceding examples, the hypothetical construction 'Or . . . or . . . or' reinforces the sense of images as costumes one tries on and discards in rapid succession. In this, MacDiarmid's overflowing imagery is reminiscent of that in the volcanic early prose of his Scottish predecessor, Thomas Carlyle. Both display a gluttony for the particular; both revel in scurrility and flytings interspersed with exalted flights. As Frederick J. Nicholson writes, 'Dramatic in form, each proliferates from an absurd, original, and potent metaphor: spiritual nakedness in *Sartor* [*Resartus*] and "divine inebriety" in *The Drunk Man* . . . . It is this so-called intemperance, this astonishing unpredictability, this repeated administration of shock, that links our two authors to the Scottishness of Dunbar and Douglas, Burns and Robert Fergusson'.[2]

The reliance on shock in *A Drunk Man* may also reflect MacDiarmid's interest in German Expressionism.[3] In this poem, as in

---

[1] David Daiches, 'Hugh MacDiarmid's Early Poetry', in Duncan Glen, ed., *Hugh MacDiarmid: A Critical Survey* (Edinburgh and London: Scottish Academic Press, 1972), p.75.

[2] 'Thomas Carlyle and Hugh MacDiarmid', Occasional Paper No.6 (Edinburgh: The Carlyle Society, 1974). For other points of comparison, see *A Drunk Man*, ll.196, 296 and 670.

[3] MacDiarmid's initial exposure to Expressionist theory (as to many other foreign literary influences) came from his association with A. R. Orage and his circle. MacDiarmid's views on contemporary continental literature appeared in a series of columns – 'Mannigfaltig' and 'Abracadabra Plus X' – which he wrote for the *New Age* in 1923-5. In a passage in *To Circumjack Cencrastus* (1930) he adds the German

expressionist drama, one leading character serves as the author's alter ego. In both, language is stressed in long elliptical monologues that imitate thought and speech and frame a spiritual *schrei* (cry). Both protest, in the strongest terms, against the social structure. Similarly, the expressionist musical device of rendering intense emotion through polyphony, atonality and distortion may have inspired MacDiarmid to attempt similar effects. At one point in *A Drunk Man*, the thistle strikes the speaker as being 'a brain laid bare, a nervous system' (2160). This recalls the description of a character in *Annals of the Five Senses*, written four years before:

> It was necessary that she . . . make the coldest effort to regard her own organism as merely one among others. Her physical-intellectual being was the sensorium of Nature, but it was also one thing among natural things whose number was legion. It was the mirror in which she viewed the world, the part most necessary for her to know and work upon, and its value to her depended upon her knowledge of its natural distortions.[1]

When these thoughts are borne in mind, we are moving beyond mere sentience to psychology. And it is in the thistle itself that theories of perception merge with a theory of personality.

The thistle is, first of all, a literal plant. Standing at night on an uncultivated hillside, it arrests a solitary person's interest. By periodically returning our attention to the physical reality – 'this thistle', 'that yella licht' – MacDiarmid anchors the ensuing ruminations, endowing the long poem with rhythm of embarkation and return.

Yet the longer the Drunk Man looks at the thistle 'sae intimately' at 'sic an 'oor' (300), the more its plight seems to express his own:

> The roots that wi' the worms compete
> Hauf-publish me upon the air
> The struggle that divides me still
> Is seen fu' plainly there.
>   (671–4)

Metamorphosing variously into an octopus (328), a serpent (353–4), a leviathan (486), and a dragon (508), the thistle also represents entrapment in one's mortal part. It is 'the skeleton at a tea meetin''

Expressionists one by one, by name (complete list p. 189f.). Later on, MacDiarmid was deeply drawn to Brecht (for both political and aesthetic reasons) and produced (with the help of Norman MacCaig) a a translation of *Three Penny Opera*.
[1] *Annals*, 154–5.

(371), something of which the speaker longs to 'win clear' (525).
But one can no more 'win clear' of what the thistle represents than
do without the skeleton it so resembles:

> *Thistleless fule*
> *You'll ha'e nocht left*
> *But the hole frae which*
> *Life's struggle is reft!*   torn
>   (529–32)

The cost of the thistle's hardihood is its ungainliness. If 'ilka
windin' has its counterpairt / Without which it couldna' be' then to
accept life one must not resent complexity. The roots that clutch
are also 'roots that feed' (495).

In *A Drunk Man,* both the natural world and the observing personality are in a state of constant change. Everything is forever on
the verge of becoming its opposite. Even the self is an infinite series
of 'selves'. This view is, of course, romantic. Romantic, too, is the
way in which, in the process of perception, boundaries between
observer and observed become obscured through the external
agency of moonlight and the internal influence of drink. Extending
the 'zoom lens' technique first employed in *Sangschaw,* MacDiarmid creates frequent, radical alterations of perspective. As a symbol, the thistle accommodates everything from internal states – the
speaker's nervous system (2161) to a phallus (592), from Ygdrasil,
the tree of life (1457) to the entire world (2079). In so doing, it
reinforces the lust for experience professed early on, and sets the
tone of infinite, expanding possibility – something like the psychological equivalent of quasars.

Now whatever the thrills and pleasures of such a stance – and
they are many – it also poses serious dangers. One who feels obliged
to flaunt apparent freedoms may become the victim of his own
bravado; he may fail to take ordinary needs and fears quite seriously, and never (as Eliot says) 'learn to sit still'. At what point does
the lust for raw experience constitute evasion? We might note, in
this context, that while MacDiarmid shares the (typically post-
Renaissance) admiration for Ulysses, he has none of the counter-
vailing view (for instance, Dante's) of Ulysses' wanderings as flight
from commitment, and hence a dereliction.

So unqualified a philosophical position has the potential for
disastrous formal consequences. If, instead of being selective, the
poet tries to be exhaustive, the poem may change from a micro-

cosm into a filing cabinet. And if this is so, where does it end? Why stop at 2600 lines, or at 10,000?[1]

MacDiarmid himself was aware of the problem, and addressed it in correspondence from the major period of *A Drunk Man*'s composition. Most telling is a letter of August 6, 1926, in which he writes:

> There are poems in the book (which is really one whole although many parts are detachable) of extraordinary power, I know – longer and far more powerful and unique in kind than anything in 'Sangschaw' or 'Penny Wheep'; but that's not what I'm after. It's the thing *as a whole* that I'm mainly concerned with.[2]

In other words, the coherence that MacDiarmid desired mandated some sort of structural progression, the nature of which he identified earlier in the same letter:

> . . . the section I've been re-writing – which comes about midway in the book and should represent the high-water mark, the peaks of highest intensity, and could be improved by being . . . made, instead of a succession of merely verbal and pictorial verses, into a series of metaphysical pictures with a definitive progression, a cumulative effect – and that is what I've been so busy with. . . .

To decide whether he succeeded, we must now turn our attention from *A Drunk Man*'s lyrics to its discursive content, from the 'merely verbal and pictorial verses' to the 'argument' that frames and extends them. In what follows, the poem will therefore be considered as if it were a philosophical discourse, with reference to sources on which its argument draws. Then, having looked at both the lyric expression of personality and the intellectual effort to transcend it, we shall be better able to perceive how – or if – the two cohere.

The section referred to in MacDiarmid's letter occurs in lines 1004 following of the finished poem. Up to this point, *A Drunk Man* is given over largely to wounded explorations of how thistle-like and contradictory reality is. In the opening sections, the speaker establishes a context, both historical and temporal, and the grounds for his own alienation from it. That is followed by a series

[1] This is not begging the question; MacDiarmid did extend his massive later poems *ad infinitum*, and left several massive projects uncompleted for this reason.
[2] Letter to George Ogilvie, quoted in J. K. Annand, Introd., *Early Lyrics By Hugh MacDiarmid* (Preston, Lancashire: Akros Press, 1968), p.15.

of lyrics, culminating in 'O Wha's the Bride', which both expand
the sense of possibility and demonstrate how hard it is to formulate
an appropriate response to the complexities perceived. In both
respects, the first thousand lines reflect the influence of a man
whom MacDiarmid called his 'master', Leon Shestov.[1]

Shestov's *All Things Are Possible*, written in 1905, appeared in
English translation in 1920 with a foreword by D. H. Lawrence and
an epigraph from Heine: '*Zu fragmentarisch ist Welt und Leben*'.[2] To
a large extent, *A Drunk Man* begins as an exploration of ideas which
MacDiarmid discovered in this book. They include:

1) *distrust of causal explanations:*

SHESTOV:

> In the interest of *knowing* we should sacrifice, and gladly, *understand-
> ing*, since understanding is, in any case, a secondary affair.   (p.130)
>
> 'Why?' laughs at all possible 'becauses'.   (p.77)

MACDIARMID:

> For I've nae faith in ocht I can explain
> And stert whaur the philosophers leave aff.
> Content to glimpse its loops I dinna ettle
> To land the sea serpent's sel wi' ony gaff.
>   (153–6)[3]

2) *a thirst for the miraculous:*

SHESTOV:

> There arose in him [Dostoyevsky] the Russian, the elemental man,
> with a thirst for the miraculous. Compared with what he wanted, the
> fruits of European civilization seemed to him trivial, flat, insipid. The
> agelong civilization of his neighbours [MacDiarmid's Cruivie and
> Gilsanquhar] told him that there had never been a miracle and never
> would be. But all his being, not yet broken in by civilization, craved
> for the stupendous unknown.   (p.86)

MACDIARMID:

> *O Scotland is*
> *THE barren fig.*
> *Up, carles, up*
> *And roond it jig . . .*

---

[1] 'In Direadh': 'Suddenly (my master Shestov's suddenly!) . . .'
[2] *All Things Are Possible* (New York: McBride, 1920).
[3] Here the visual image is complemented by a pun on 'gaff', which also
signifies loose talk, impertinence (Jamieson), as spoken by a gaffer, or
babbler (*SND*). Perhaps this is oblique praise of Scottish reticence.

Auld Moses took
A dry stick and
Instantly it
Floo'ered in his hand . . .

A miracle's
Oor only chance.
Up, carles, up
And let us dance!
(707–14; 719–23)

3) *preference for 'life' over 'reason'*:

SHESTOV:

Laws – all of them – have only a regulating value, and are necessary
only to those who want rest and security. But the first and essential
condition of life is lawlessness. (p.127)

We should doubt so that doubt becomes a continuous creative force.
(p.90)

MACDIARMID:

Love often wuns free
In lust to be strangled
Or love, o' lust free
In law's sairly tangled.
(992–5)

Reason sers nae end but pleasure   *serves*
Truth's no' an end but a means
To a wider knowledge o' life
And a keener interest in't.
(533–6)

All of these strains may be seen to come together in two final
quotations from Shestov:

We know nothing of the ultimate realities of our existence, nor shall
we ever know anything. Let that be agreed. But it does not follow that
therefore we must accept some or other dogmatic theory as a *modus
vivendi*, no, not even positivism, which has such a sceptical face on it.
It only follows that man is free to change his conception of the
universe as often as he changes his boots or gloves, and that constancy
of principle belongs only to one's relationships with other people, in
order that they may know where and to what extent they may depend
on us. Therefore in principle man should respect order in the external
world and complete chaos in the inner. (pp.22–3)

A thinker is one who has lost his balance, in the vulgar, not the tragic
sense. (p.139)

This 'loss of balance' complemented an idea derived from elsewhere, which was of critical importance to MacDiarmid's work as a whole, and to *A Drunk Man* in particular. This is the concept of the Scottish Muse advanced by G. Gregory Smith in *Scottish Literature: Character and Influence* (1919). Indeed, *A Drunk Man* can be usefully read as a celebration of that book's central thesis:

> [Scottish literature] becomes, under the stress of foreign influence and native division and reaction, almost a zigzag of contradictions. The antitheses need not, however, disconcert us. Perhaps in the very combination of opposites – what either of the two Sir Thomases, of Norwich and Cromarty, might have been willing to call the Caledonian Antisyzygy – we have a reflection of the contrasts which the Scot shows at every turn in his political and ecclesiastical history, in his polemical restlessness, in his adaptability . . . .
>
> If a formula is to be found it must explain this strange combination of things unlike . . . . This mingling, even of the most eccentric kind, is an indication to us that the Scot, in that medieval fashion which takes all things as granted, is at his ease in both 'rooms of life', and turns to fun, and even profanity, with no misgivings. For Scottish literature is more medieval in habit than criticism has suspected, and owes some part of its picturesque strength to this freedom in passing from one mood to another . . . .
>
> There is more in the Scottish antithesis of the real and fantastic than is to be explained by the familiar rules of rhetoric. The sudden jostling of contraries seems to preclude any relationship by literary suggestion. The one invades the other without warning. They are the 'polar twins' of the Scottish Muse.[1]

In *A Drunk Man Looks at the Thistle*, there are lines – 'Grinning gargoyle by a saint', 'routh of contraries' – which come straight out of Gregory Smith. Moreover, MacDiarmid himself cited the Caledonian Antisyzygy constantly in prose defences of his literary goals.[2] Not surprisingly, responses to *A Drunk Man* have depended heavily on evaluations of Gregory Smith's theory. It is not necessary here to enter into a controversy that has been protracted and by now (one hopes) exhausted.[3] Whether or not the notion of

[1] G. Gregory Smith, *Scottish Literature* (London: Macmillan, 1919), pp.4, 35, 20.
[2] For instance, 'The Caledonian Antisyzygy and the Gaelic Idea', in *The Modern Scot* (1931-2), rpt. in *Selected Essays of Hugh MacDiarmid* (London: Jonathan Cape, 1969), pp.56-74.
[3] The most thoughtful objections to Gregory Smith/MacDiarmid are those posed by Edwin Muir in *Scot and Scotland: The Predicament of the Scottish Writer* (London: Routledge, 1936), rpt. 1971, pp.91-118;

antisyzygy holds water, it does serve to advance the poem's 'argument' as we are currently pursuing it. By recasting the speaker's personal dissociation in cultural terms, MacDiarmid characteristically forces the inquiry beyond what is individual to what is collective, from the conscious to the unconscious – indeed, to the 'collective unconscious' of C. G. Jung.

MacDiarmid's interest in Jung dated from the early *Scottish Chapbook* period (1922–3). According to MacDiarmid's theories, Lallans was the language spoken as a child, 'the one in which the poet is least likely to mistake what he thinks he feels, or what he ought to feel, for what he really feels'. Since 'childhood is the period during which people live closest to the "collective unconscious", to the soul of the people',[1] and since 'creative works proceed from below the threshold of consciousness',[2] poetry in Scots – so the argument went – was particularly suited to release unconscious and creative energies.

According to Jungian theory, each person displays a libido, a fundamental striving that is creative and purposive, and of which there is evidence in the symbolic language of dreams. In *A Drunk Man Looks at the Thistle*, the renderings of Blok, Hippius, and others function as just such symbolic dreams, in which a speaker for whom 'all things are possible' encounters the libidinous unknown. These passages have been treated, above, as a supernatural counterpoint to the realist declarations. They can also be viewed as constituting a *sexual* counterpoint – 'female' to 'male'.

This intention is apparent in the way the writing moves from the opening section's satire into the second lyric, 'from the Russian of Alexander Blok'. The Deutsch and Yarmolinsky English translation from which MacDiarmid was working reads:

> Of evenings hangs above the restaurant
> A humid, wild and heavy air.

Sydney Goodsir Smith, *A Short Introduction to Scottish Literature* (Edinburgh: Serif Books, 1951); Kurt Wittig, *Scottish Tradition in Literature* (Edinburgh: Oliver & Boyd, 1958); Maurice Lindsay, *History of Scottish Literature* (London: Hale, 1977), pp.57, 380.

[1] *TLS*, 8 January 1954. By changing 'people' to 'the people', MacDiarmid imbues the 'collective unconscious' with an implied national character. This distorts the concept; in Jung archetypes are thought of as universal, and therefore should not vary between cultures. If this is true, they should not be more accessible in any one language than in others.

[2] 'Burns Today and Tomorrow' (Edinburgh: Castle Wynd Printers, 1959), p.12.

The Springtime spirit, brooding, pestilent
Commands the drunken outcries there.[1]

MacDiarmid substitutes:

At darknin' hings abune the howff	*hangs above / tavern*
A weet and wild and eisenin' air.	*lusting*
Spring's spirit wi' its waesome sough	*woeful sigh*
Rules owre the drucken stramash there.	*drunken uproar*
(169–73)	

In terms of sound and evocation, 'eisenin'' (lustful) is an obvious
improvement over 'heavy'. But it's more than that: the Scots verb
'eisen' means, specifically, 'to desire the male, as a cow desires the
bull' (*SND*). Its connotations, reinforced by moaning in the line
that follows, effect a transition from coarse male camaraderie (the
pub, Burns Clubs, 'inside') to female mystery, seductive darkness,
'ootside'. This initiates a protracted series of alternating 'male' and
'female' poems.

The section that follows the 'silken leddy' is once again jocular
and sceptical. In it, only men are mentioned; the speaker tells the
thistle that they both are sorely in need of a shave, and adds that
'mony a man's been that afore'. What comes next, as if in response,
is another movement toward the female, in Blok's 'The Unknown
Goddess':

I ha'e forekent ye! O I ha'e forekent,	foreknown
The years forecast your face afore they went.	
A licht I canna thole is in the lift.	endure
I bide in silence your slow-comin' pace.	
The ends o' space are bricht: at last – oh swift!	
While terror clings to me – an unkent face!	unknown
Ill-faith stirs in me as she comes at last,	
The features lang forekent . . . are unforecast.	
O it gangs hard wi' me, I am forspent.	
Deid dreams ha'e beaten me and a face unkent	
And generations that I thocht unborn	
Hail the strange Goddess frae my hert's-hert torn! . . .	

This lyric is followed by another section which enquires, '. . . Dost
thou mak' a thistle o me, wumman?' (253) and refers to the 'erect'
thistle's 'rigid virtue' (309, 315), and that in turn by a 'female'
section adapted from Else Laske-Schuller (401–10). The alter-

[1] Babette Deutsch and Avraam Yarmolinsky, eds. and trans.,
This Modern Poetry (London: Faber, 1936), p.133.

nation of sexual reference continues through *A Drunk Man*'s first thousand lines.

This suggests that in both language and reference such 'female' sections play a role akin to *anima* in Jungian theory. The women in these italicized lyrics are like dream symbols emanating from, and beckoning towards, the collective unconscious. A refusal to foreclose possibility (inspired by Shestov) makes the Drunk Man receptive to such visitations and primordial images as the unconscious groups and regroups its latent contents: the notion of 'antisyzygy' prevails. In the words of Jung:

> Obviously it is a fundamental mistake to think that when we recognize the non-value in a value, or the falsehood in a truth, the value or the truth then ceases to exist. It has only become relative. Everything human is relative, because everything depends on a condition of inner anti-thesis, without which there could be no energy. All life is energy and therefore depends on forces held in opposition . . . . The solution lies not in a conversion into the opposite, but in the retaining of the former values together with a recognition of their opposites.[1]

Elsewhere Jung refers to the opposition as a Heracleitan 'enantiodromia' or 'running contrary ways'. This notion can help explain why the oppositions that pervade the first movement of *A Drunk Man*, including what we've called the 'male' and 'female' aspects, cannot at this point in the poem be reconciled.

Where Jung differs from Shestov (and I think warrants more consideration) is in his warning that, beyond its necessary function – releasing repressed energies – drift that proceeds unabated may become destructive and self-destructive. To forestall that possibility, Jung argues that at some point, what has been released must in turn be *restructured*:

> The only person who escapes the gruesome law of enantiodromia is the man who knows how to *separate himself from the unconscious*, not by repressing it, for then it merely lays hold of him from behind, but by making clear to himself that *it is something different from himself*.[2]

In its first sixteen lyrics, *A Drunk Man* has set out to release and embrace the unforeseen, and this goal is well-served by the technique of jangling parataxis. At the same time, however, so complete an embrace of the unknown has cost the speaker his stability, his judgment, even his sense of self. Having, in the poem's first

[1] C. G. Jung, *Two Essays in Analytical Psychiatry* (New York: Dodd Mead, 1929), p.79.
[2] *Ibid.*, p.75.

movement, let the unconscious out, so to speak, he must now
shape the unconscious elements into the forms and structures of
conscious realization. In the first thousand lines, everything and
anything is encouraged to root and sprout; thereafter, the Drunk
Man begins to prune.

This change is signalled by the cry, 'Yank oot your orra boughs,
my hert!', repeated five times with increasing urgency between
lines 1005 and 1070. 'Superfluous branches we do lop away, that
bearing boughs may live', say Shakespeare's gardeners; as the
Drunk Man starts to 'lop away' the tone and style of the sequence
change.

From here on, there are no more translations of foreign verse.
The length of individual sections increases notably, and transitions
between sections become less violent. The element of physical
disgust drops out, and the garrulous tone grows more reflective.
The proportion of Lallans to English diminishes (see below,
p.93). Peaks of vision and exuberance still occur, but at wider
intervals, separated by prosaic valleys. Moreover, the high points
now comprise sustained crescendos rather than spontaneous dis-
sonant outbursts. All of these changes are meant to reflect the
changing condition of the speaker as he sobers up, dehydrates, and
tires.[1]

Up to the point of change, the Drunk Man has attempted to be
all things. Resenting 'the need to wark, the need to think', even
'the need to *be*' (265) as unacceptable limitations, he has set out to
internalize all reality, to comprehend it in terms of individual
personality:

> Animals, vegetables, what are they a'
> But as thochts that a man has ha'en?
> (913–14)

Ironically, the more one's self includes, the less personal progress
is possible; ubiquity is static and precludes self definition. But with
'Yank Oot Your Orra Boughs' (repeated so often because so difficult), we find movement that is not just lateral, associative and
random, but forward and controlled:

---

[1] As previously noted, moonlight, whisky and water each symbolize
(in their own way) transcendence and release. As the moon sets, and
the Drunk Man grows more sober and dehydrated, it is thus appropriate that the argument itself wind down; metaphysical and physical
reality continue to run parallel.

> Mebbe we're in a vicious circle cast
> Mebbe there's limits we can ne'er get past
> Mebbe we're sentrices that at the last   *scaffolding*
> Are flung aside, and no' the pillars and props
> O' Heaven foraye as in oor hopes . . .
>   (1026–30)

As with the steps of progression in a Scottish country dance one
senses careful concentration, a deliberate 'casting off' that facilitates movement 'upward' in the set. And with this admission of
limits, so different from what has preceded, the Drunk Man begins
to define a more durable single self.

Accordingly, the second movement of the poem – from 1005 to
1900 – is largely given over to admissions of waste and personal
defeat, 'this hopeless airgh' [gap] twixt a' we can and should'
(1022). Frustrations that must be acknowledged are political
(1119–218), intellectual (1219–30), sexual (1260–71), spiritual
(1272–333). Coming in series as they do, these have a severely
reductive effect; the impulse towards omniscience which was previously deemed heroic now is seen as vanity. The Drunk Man's
thoughts proceed from this:

> He's no a man ava'   *at all*
> And lacks a proper pride
> Gin less than a' the warld
> Can ser' him for a bride!
>   (973–6)

to this:

> A'thing that any man can be's
> A mockery o' his soul at last.
>   (1415–16)

Significantly, the surrender of pride these lines suggest is accom-
panied by a reversal of those images that earlier signified heroic
aspiration. The Melvillian white whale of line 485 now has 'rived
the line awa'; the ocean's 'sperklin tide rins oot / and leaves a
wreath of rubbish there'; the man who earlier defied any personal
limits is now forced, in despair, to admit them:

> *Nae man can ken his hert until*
> *The tide o' life uncovers it*
> *And horror-struck, he sees a pit*
> *Returnin' life can never fill! . . .*
>   (1447–50)

This image may owe something to another of MacDiarmid's sources, P. E. Ouspensky, who had called for a 'transitional logic' rooted in awareness of 'the bottomless pit'.[1] As in Ouspensky, the crucial notion here is transition. For once he acknowledges that the pit is indeed bottomless, that it cannot be plumbed by individual experience or knowledge, one need no longer judge one's own efforts by a standard of omniscience nor berate oneself for failing to attain it. This, then, is the lesson of what may be called *A Drunk Man*'s second movement.

The limits of personal vision are bound up with the rejection of a personal deity, and of a belief in individual enlightenment – the knowledge of final causes – that such a Being could bestow. In MacDiarmid's view, there is a Force or Destiny that governs human history (1962–7; 2284). But the belief that human beings can specify either its attributes or its intentions is just one more assertion of false certitude. And as such the Christian revelation is viewed as false promise, the sort of comfort one longs to believe in, but cannot:

> O Hard it is for man to ken
> He's no creation's goal nor yet
> A benefitter by't at last –
>   (1470–3)

For MacDiarmid, the essence of divinity is its inscrutability and remoteness from human concerns. Thus a major strain in all his work is the assertion that we are, in Wallace Stevens' word, unsponsored, and must relocate divinity in man:

> *Sae God retracts in endless stage*
> *Through angel, devil, age on age*
> *Until at last his infinite natur'*
> *Walks on earth a human cratur . . .*
> *Sae man returns in endless growth*
> *Till God in him again has scouth.*   scope
>   (1990–7)

This concept of God owes something to a theory of world history propounded by Vladimir Solovyev (1853–1900) in works such as *Beauty In Nature* and *The Meaning of Love*. 'Assuming the ultimate unity of Absolute Being . . . Solovyev proposed that the diverse

[1] Petr Emianovich Ouspensky, *Tertium Organum (The Third Organ of Thought)* (Rochester, NY: Manas Press, 1920), pp.243-4.

multiplicity in a world originating from a single source is undergoing a process of re-integration with that source . . . . [He] asserted by his concept of Godmanhood that the unique intermediary between the world and God can only be man, who alone is the vital part of nature capable of knowing and expressing the divine idea of 'absolute unitotality' in the chaotic multiplicity of real experience. Consequently, the perfect revelation of God is Christ's incarnation in human nature, whose theandric (God-man) action integrated man's history with God'.[1]

Given the rejection of Christian dogma which has just been noted, it may seem odd to find MacDiarmid drawing on yet another, still more esoteric variant of Russian mysticism. What this represents, I think, is one more case of his ability to select congenial aspects of various philosophies while rejecting other aspects that do not serve his own intentions. As John Weston has said, 'This eclecticism results not . . . from a systematic selection from an exhaustive reading in each of the authors in question, but from a more casual use by a busy journalist of congenial ideas found in a vast but spotty and permiscuous [sic] reading'.[2] Dostoyevsky, for example, is revered for his nationalist fervour, his ability to entertain contradictory thoughts at the same time, and his belief in the moral value of self-abasement (1745–2033 *passim*), yet the orthodoxy in which those values coalesced for Dostoyevsky is ignored.

Similarly, throughout *A Drunk Man* the Christology must be read largely as figure and symbol, not as an expression of dogma. For MacDiarmid, the primary attraction of the Christ story rests in the incarnation, not the ascension. The convergence of flesh and spirit that was encountered before in intimate experience ('The Bonnie Broukit Bairn', 'O Wha's the Bride') is now formulated in conceptual terms.

'Retraction', or relocation of divinity within the sphere of human intercourse, is stressed by the terms in which the speaker contemplates God in *A Drunk Man*'s final movement. Whenever we find mention of 'God' – as distinct from Christ Child or Mary, earlier – the tone becomes negative, even derisive. God is 'helpless' (2439), fights little wars in which He takes both sides helplessly (2468–71), has defective vision (2472), and can't understand man's own silences (2678).

Of course, such jabs do not lend themselves to straightforward

[1] 'Solovyev, Vladimir', *Encyclopaedia Britannica: Micropaedia*, 1978 ed., Vol.9, p.340.
[2] Weston, in Glen, p.91.

theological discussion. What they do attempt, albeit in far different style, is the same relegation of a Christian God to the realm of successive, serviceable fictions that Wallace Stevens contemplates in the second stanza of 'Sunday Morning'. Stevens goes on to depict his alternative in a conceit of light, the 'old dependency of day and night'. MacDiarmid's interests are not so much epistemological as metaphysical; still, he too enlists the imagery of light:

> 'Let there be licht', said God, and there was
> A little: but He lacked the poo'er
> To licht up mair than pairt o' space at aince
> And there is lots o' darkness that's the same
> As gin He'd never spoken . . .
>   (2101–5)

> Licht cheenges naething
> And gin there is a God wha made the licht
> We are adapted to receive
> *He* changed naething
> And hesna kythed Hissel!   *revealed Himself*
> Save in this licht that fa's whar the Auld Nicht was
> Showin' naething that the Darkness didna hide.
>   (2148–54)

Earlier on, the Drunk Man noted that 'Man canna look on nakit licht' (1932). Taken with the lines just quoted, this observation leads away from light – individual enlightenment in either this or an after-life, either by one's own efforts or through the agency of a personal deity – to darkness: the collective dumb experience of mankind that will issue in an evolution whose details we cannot foresee. The unconscious, resisted earlier and feared, becomes the '*conscious dark*'. It offers a redemption that may be called 'transpersonal', that is, which allows fulfilment of the individual in a reality that transcends and encompasses any one person.

That this darkness represents acceptance, not negation, can be seen in the changing meaning of the thistle. Rooted securely in the 'entire dark' (2086), 'blind root to bleezin' rose' (1951), the thistle ceases to stand for merely individual torment:

> Nae mair I see
> As aince I saw
> Mysel' in the thistle
> Harth and haw!   *Lean / hollow*
>   (2305–8)

Rather, like Ygdrasil (the Celtic tree of life, 1457), or 'a web in which the warld squats like a spider' (2212), or Dante's celestial rose (2284–91), it encompasses, symbolically, the Universe. Thus man's own thistle nature becomes not an aberration from, but a part of the universal scheme.

As expressed in the 'Farewell to Dostoyevsky', this vision of man unsponsored in immensity is both moving and profoundly lonely:

The wan leafs shak' atour us like the snaw.	around
Here is the cavaburd in which Earth's tint.	snowstorm / is lost
There's naebody but Oblivion and us,	
Puir gangrel buddies, waunderin' hameless in't.	vagrant persons
The stars are larochs o' auld cottages,	
And a' Time's glen is fu' o' blinnin' stew.	blinding dust
Nae freen'ly lozen skimmers: and the wund	window glimmers
Rises and separates even me and you.	
I ken nae Russian and you ken nae Scots.	
We canna tell oor voices frae the wund.	
The snaw is seekin' everywhere: oor herts	
At last like roofless ingles it has f'und,	hearths
And gethers there in drift on endless drift,	
Oor broken herts that it can never fill;	
And still – its leafs like snaw, its growth like wund –	
The thistle rises and forever will! . . .	
(2216–31)	

Nevertheless, this darkness in which the thistle roots and the Great Wheel of history turns (2425f.), and in which any one man seems insignificant, has its positive aspects. Even in darkness the instinct for light remains, indeed grows more acute (2141). And once one stops trying to be or see the *source* of light, he learns the value of *reflection*; it is only in the 'conscious Dark' that his own 'conscious gleids' (sparks, 2501) acquire importance:

For gin the sun and mune at last	
Are as a neebor's lintel passed,	
The wheel'll tine its stature fast,	lose
And birl in time inside oor heids	spin
Till we can thraw oot conscious gleids	sparks
That draw an answer to oor needs,	
Or if nae answer still we find	
Brichten till a' thing is defined	
In the huge licht-beams o' oor kind, . . .	

And we may aiblins swing content   *perhaps*
Upon the wheel in which we're pent
In adequate enlightenment.
   (2497–505 ; 2509–11)

God retracts; mankind slowly, almost imperceptibly, advances.

This is all quite abstract – perhaps excessively so – in the tradition of 'Scotch metaphysics'. Yet the crucial point about these speculations is that they are worked *through*, that they ultimately issue not in rigid abstraction but in a refreshed commitment to one's own place and kind. If individuals 'canna look on nakit licht', if darkness 'comes closer to us than the licht, and is our natural element' (2109), then our efforts to overcome it must become collective.[1] Within that darkness, the 'peculiar light of love' is that which human beings *reflect* upon each other:

E'en as the moonlicht's borrowed frae the sun
I ha'e my knowledge o' mysel' frae thee.
And much that nane but thee can e'er mak' clear
Save my licht's frae the source, is dark to me.   *except as*
   (921–4)

Expressed thus in metaphors of light, this still sounds much like the Ouspenskian mysticism from which it was adapted.[2] But just as MacDiarmid adapted the Immaculate Conception in 'O Wha's The Bride', so he here substitutes a flesh and blood woman for Sophia, making sexual relations a sort of proxy for spiritual union:

O Jean, in whom my spirit sees,
Clearer than through whisky or disease,
Its dernin' nature, wad the searchin' licht   hidden
Oor union raises poor'd owre me the nicht.
. . . that sheer licht o' life that when we're joint
Loups through me like a fire a' else t' aroint.   to expel

Clear my lourd flesh, and let me move   heavy
In the peculiar licht o' love,
Be thou the licht in which I stand
Entire . . .

---

[1] For a discussion of how MacDiarmid's notions of the individual and the collective bear on his politics and psychology, see chapter 4.
[2] 'Only he who can see considerably beyond the facts discerns love's real meaning, and it is possible to illuminate these very facts by the light of that which lies behind them', Ouspensky, p.177. In the *Collected Poems*, the *Drunk Man* lines just quoted are subtitled, 'The Spur of Love', a phrase that appears in Ouspensky, p.161.

Syne liberate me frae this tree,
As wha had there imprisoned me,   as if you
   (2024–37 *passim*)

In the course of this consummation, it is as if Christ's role – 'the second Adam' – has been taken over by Jean, acting as a 'second Eve' who, in helping the Drunk Man renounce the Tree of Knowledge, restores him to the Tree of Life.

Some readers might object to this depiction of woman's role as merely a change from malevolent to benevolent passivity. The charge is, surely, unfair. For in addition to making his theoretical point in borrowed terms, MacDiarmid takes care to stress the *mutuality* of the relation in his own way. The feeling behind the theory emerges, as so often, in a memorable image from Scottish country life:

> *I'm fu' o' a stickit God.*   frustrated, stuck
> THAT'S *what's the maitter wi' me,*
> *Jean has stuck sic a fork in the wa'*
> *That I row in agonie.*   roll
>
> *Mary never let dab.*   let on
> SHE *was a canny wumman.*   cunning
> *She hedna a gaw in Joseph at a'*   hold, claim on
> *But, wow, this seecund comin' ! . . .*
>   (1632–9)

In a letter, MacDiarmid explains:

> We have a popular phrase 'the stickit minister', meaning a student who hasn't been able to qualify as a minister or alternatively has qualified but is so unfortunate that no church will call him to a ministry. 'A stickit God' simply means the feeling that one has a conception of the Divine that one cannot effectively formulate but is always grappling with. 'A fork in the wa'' is an old Scottish idiom for the practice in many countries by divers means of transferring a woman's labour pains to her husband or at least ensuring that he shares the agony when her time comes. Mary, the mother of Christ, did not invoke any such sharing of her travail by Joseph. She was a gentle woman ('canny' has several meanings, including not only quiet and gentle, but also cunning). She hadn't a hold on Joseph at all, i.e., she didn't pierce him with the prongs of the fork or force him to share her pangs. My outcry about the Second Coming means that Jean's travail is being shared by me and that the difficult birth with which I am coping is 'the second coming' in the sense that Christ's birth was the first and that a successful deliverance of a new conception of the

Divine comes chronologically second to that, i.e., is not a Second
Coming of Christ but of my own unknown personal God.[1]

This desire for a shared delivery brings to a close, at last, the circle
within which *A Drunk Man*'s argument began. In describing the
alternation of 'male' and 'female', it was suggested that no resolution could occur until the former accepted the latter, and learned
to accept the latter in itself. By means of the long immersion in
darkness, this has now become possible:

> I'm faced wi aspects of mysel
> At last whas portent nocht can tell . . .
>   (2028–9)

Change within the individual reconciles him to the partial knowledge and mutual relations by which life is sustained and evolves.
    At one point the Drunk Man has cried out

> And O! I canna thole   *endure*
> Aye yabblin' o' my soul   *gabbling*
> And fain I wad be free
> O' my eternal me.
>   (1895–8)

By the poem's end he has learned that one way to find relief from
the incessant looking over one's shoulder, from the 'yabblin of the
soul' and the *eternal* me is to accept one's *mortal* me – a limited being
with specific race, nationality, sexuality and class. And it is thus,
after the drunkenness, the speculations issuing in silence, that he
goes *home*. He must return, both philosophically and literally, to
Jean:

> I hae Silence left
> – 'And weel ye micht'
> Sae Jean'll say, 'efter sic a nicht!'

This jest rounds off the poem delightfully; he can talk all night,
but she gets the last word! At the same time, Jean's anticipated and
(when all is said and done) *desired* response completes the poem's
larger statement. For if the process of human evolution potential in
collective experience is imperceptible in any individual, then any
attempt to control, will, or rationalize its contradictory progress
will only serve to exclude the individual from it. On the other hand,

---

[1] Letter to Norman McCaig, 21 August 1968. Printed in John C.
Weston, *Hugh MacDiarmid's A Drunk Man Looks at the Thistle*
(Preston, Lancashire: Akros, 1970), p.36.

by surrendering to it, renouncing the claim to rationalize what cannot be understood, one is freed to participate in a process that transcends one's self. At that point, the personal and the impersonal, the individual and the collective, converge.

And finally, the acts which transcend personality (as a lover, a father, a thinker) constitute one's contribution to the evolutionary change he longs for, but could never *will*. Viewed in this light, the return to Jean is more than the renunciation of a quest. It is emerging from speculative isolation into social connection. An engagement whose terms we cannot dictate is ultimately preferable to the 'not done', to 'the diffidence that falters'. The way not to foreclose what might be is to open ourselves to what is.

Considering the 'argument' of *A Drunk Man* in relative isolation from its technique means, of course, accepting an artificial distinction in order to underscore and clarify *intentions*. Having taken the time to do so, we are now better prepared to judge matters of *execution*. The old questions remain: Does method serve meaning in the poem? Do the parts cohere? A plausible answer is: *not enough*. To see why, one may begin, as MacDiarmid did, with the language.

It has already been noted that, contrary to the author's claims, *A Drunk Man* is not composed entirely in Scots (*supra*, p.58). In fact, the diction varies from thick Lallans in some sections to dressed-up standard English in others. This inconsistency arises in part from the method of composition. Constituent lyrics were written at different times with different purposes in mind, and in assembling the sequence MacDiarmid took less care than he might have to regularize his use of the two tongues. His failure to do so points to a serious difficulty. If indeed braid Scots 'could be effectively applied to all manner of subjects and measures', we should expect the proportion of Scots to English words to remain more or less constant, irrespective of changes in subject and mood. Yet this is conspicuously not the case, as a comparison of several passages will make clear.

In 'The Crying of the Fair' (455f.), the poetic form – muscular closed couplets, roughly accentual with a sprinkling of trisyllabic feet – expresses the country dance rhythm. Words like 'loun', 'aucht-fit', 'breengan', and 'wallopin' help convey emotion. On another level, the young man who bears the emblem of Scotland before a ceremonial procession prefigures the mature poet who will some day lead a Scots revival. Moreover, by recalling the Fair here

(and later in 'Cattle Show', 1934), the poet offers his own contribution to a traditional subject of Scottish poetry that reaches back
from Burns' 'The Holy Fair' through Fergusson's 'Leith Races' to
'Christes Kirk On the Green'.

This passage is among the most comfortable in *A Drunk Man*:
one notes with relief the absence of that distancing (and sometimes
excessive) self-consciousness that mars long stretches of the full
poem. In recreating a time when he used Lallans unselfconsciously,
the speaker himself relaxes into Scots.

However, as this occurs, language becomes correspondingly
relaxed and ceremonial. In this particular lyric, the thistle is no
'Heracleitan image', no vortex or modernist 'node'. Rather, it
functions in the same way as on the occasion described – as a
symbol, or even pre-symbolically, as an emblem with fixed associations:

> The bearer twirls the Bannock-and-Saut-Herrin',
> The Croon o' Roses through the lift is farin',
>
> The aucht-fit thistle wallops on hie;
> In heather besoms a' the hills gang by . . .
>
> Beauty and Love that are bobbin' there;
> Syne the breengin' growth that alane I bear;
>
> And Scotland followin' on ahint
>   (459–62; 465–7)

Even when the lines that follow move beyond description of a
fixed scene, the language retains its nostalgic simplicity. We learn,
for instance, that the thistle is 'swippert and with wi' virr' (active/
quick with vigour) and that 'its uttermaist motion / can still set
roses alight'. The lyric then concludes:

Here is the root that feeds	
The shank wi' the blindin' wings	*stem*
Dwinin' abuneheid to gleids	*dwindling overhead / sparks*
Like stars in their keethin' rings,	
And blooms in sunrise and sunset	
Inowre Eternity's yett.	*Above / gate*
Lay haud o' my hert and feel	
Fountains ootloupin' the starns	*stars*
Or see the Universe reel	
Set gaen' by my eident harns,	*going / eager brains*
Or test the strength o' my spauld	*backbone*
The wecht o' a' thing to hauld!	*weight*

> – The howes o' Man's hert are bare,
> The Dragon's left them for good,
> There's nocht but naethingness there,
> The hole whaur the Thistle stood,
> That rootless and radiant flies
> A Phoenix in Paradise! . . .
>   (495–512)

These lines bring us back to the questions on which the previous chapter concluded: At what point do lexical surprise and *trompe d'oeil* become counterproductive to a poet's serious ends? We have already seen sparks meeting heaven in 'Ex Vermibus', 'keethin' rings' in 'Au Clair de la Lune'. And the second stanza here says nothing that was not phrased more concisely and movingly in 'The Bonnie Broukit Bairn'. Repeated in the present context for its melopoeic value, the Lallans exacts a price – an imprecision that forestalls the kind of evaluative statements one has been led to expect by MacDiarmid's prose. When he finally does move toward statement in the last six lines (above), the Scots disappears *entirely*: from fourteen words in twelve lines to just one – 'howe' – which is itself merely an archaic variant of hollow. While the Scots intensifies emotion, and that emotion itself augments the impact of succeeding 'ideation', the ideas themselves are phrased consistently in English. It would seem that, in practice, the two tongues are complementary, *not* interchangeable.

To test this hypothesis another way, we may see what happens when MacDiarmid uses only Scots to convey both tone and statement. Lines 811ff. lean heavily on Robert Burns. Their subtitle in the *Collected Poems*, 'The Splore', recalls Burns' 'The Jolly Beggars':

> Ae night at e'en a merry core
>   O' rondie, gangrel bodies
> In Poosie Nandies' held the splore . . .

Use of the first person address by MacDiarmid (845ff.) echoes the various songs in Burns' cantata. The Drunk Man's 'belly', 'barrel', 'freaths', 'faem', and 'barleyhood' can all be traced to Burns' 'Scotch Drink'. Add to this lines 815–16, which quote 'The Holy Fair', and the reference to Cutty Sark and Tam, and there can be little doubt what MacDiarmid intends. It works extremely well, both as Drunk Man recalling pleasures in Burns' terms, and as MacDiarmid rendering a fellow poet the praise of imitation:

My belly on the gantrees there,	*wooden stand*
The spigot frae my cullage,	*genitals*
And wow but how the fizzin' yill	*ale*
In spilth increased the ullage!	*wastage*

I was an anxious barrel, lad,	
When first they tapped my bung.	
They whistled me up, yet thro' the lift	
My freaths like rainbows swung.	*froth*

Waesucks, a pride for ony bar,	*Alas*
The boast o' barleyhood,	
Like Noah's Ark abune the faem	*foam*
Maun float, a gantin' cude,	*gaping barrel*

For I was thrawn fu' cock owre sune,	*thrown full cock*
And wi' a single jaw	*spurt*
I made the pub a blindin' swelth,	*gulf, whirlpool*
And how'd the warld awa'! . . .	*washed*
(845–60)	

These lines are a pleasure to read, and unimaginable without the Scots component. Still, the Scots here succeeds for the same reasons it works in *The Jolly Beggars*, and in the same manner.

When the lyric next moves to express ideas, still in Scots, the verse's quality falls off sharply:

Abordage o' this toom houk's nae mowse.	*Embarking / empty hulk / joke*
It munks and's ill to lay haud o',	*swings away*
As gin a man ettled to ride	*tried*
On the shouders o' his ain shadow.	

I canna biel't; tho' steekin' an e'e,	*secure it / hooking one eye*
Tither's munkie wi' munebeam for knool in't,	*The other is a rope-loop / peg*
For there's nae sta'-tree and the brute's awa'	*tethering pole*
Wi' me kinkin' like foundrie ahint. . . .	*twisting / lightning*
(873–80)	

What has gone wrong? The answer, perhaps, can be found in Ezra Pound's comment (in *How to Read*) that any attempt to be consciously poetic is ultimately self-defeating, for it distracts from the central emotion to be conveyed. MacDiarmid's advocacy of Scots was based on the claim that, for Scotsmen, that tongue constitutes the most natural, spontaneous vehicle of expression. But in this case, the diction is anything *but* at ease; the words call much too much attention to themselves. In packing an already difficult metaphor with unfamiliar language, MacDiarmid sacrifices all natural virtues of that diction; he transforms a robust folk idiom into a highly artificial, literary language. It may be quite different from the poetic diction of some English Edwardians, but its effect is the same.[1]

To conclude, MacDiarmid's Scots works best – in *Sangschaw*, *Penny Wheep*, *A Drunk Man*'s opening satire, 'O Wha's The Bride', 'The Spur of Love', and so on – when he trusts it, when he lets it be itself. It works least well when he strains it beyond evoking states of mind, 'my thochts that circle *like* hobby horses' (896) to expressing thoughts themselves. To treat the latter adequately requires English.

Ironically, this follows a pattern in Burns, of which neither poet seems to have been fully aware. *The Jolly Beggars*, for instance, a masterpiece of Lallans, concludes in a purely English chorus laced with latinate abstractions:

> Life is all a variorum
> We regard not how it goes
> Let them cant about decorum
> Who have character to lose.

Considering what precedes it, this is a singularly decorous pronouncement! Now, MacDiarmid's intentions certainly differ from those of Burns. Yet I would argue that in *A Drunk Man* the way that different tasks are delegated to the respective tongues does not differ all that much. Moreover, MacDiarmid's Scots is most often successful when used as Burns used it – to express high spirits and deepen emotion, or to deflate intellectual presumption; not to supplant, but to counterbalance English.[2]

Burns himself wrote less self-consciously in Lallans than in English, whereas with MacDiarmid the balance often seems to have swung in the other direction. The reason for this, which MacDiarmid could not will away, is that cultures and languages exist not only in place but also in time. So long as we are kept

---

[1] In such places MacDiarmid's Scots makes one recall what the French are purported to have said of Mallarmé – that his language is so peculiar that it can be understood only by foreigners! (T. S. Eliot, 'The Music of Poetry', in *On Poetry and Poets* [New York: Farrar Strauss & Cudahy, 1957], p.22.)

[2] This pattern can be observed from yet another angle in a highly theoretical passage, lines 1313-70. Once again, the argument is advanced in standard English. Where Scots does come in – 'rumple-fyke in Heaven's doup', 'loppert slime', 'dog hank' – it is deliberately vulgar, in order to undercut the pretensions it addresses.

careening through a busy text, we may overlook the results of a twentieth-century intelligence expressing concepts of recent origin in words of an earlier age. But if the reader slows down, the strains will be seen to emerge in collocations such as: 'bonny idiosyncratic' (776), 'incongruous to ane anither' (1319), 'or sic like vulgar gaffe o' life / *sub specie aeternitatis*' (1433), 'its empty airms through a' th'Inane' (2096), 'Impersonality sall blaw / through me as 'twere a bluffert o' snaw' (2549), and so forth. When used by, or for, a Scottish self-educated intellectual, these expressions may not all be untenable. But to the non-Scottish ear they sound forced.

Similarly, the very unfamiliarity of some Scots words, which makes them poetically effective on a first encounter, makes them *too* memorable; when repeated, they obtrude. One can't help hearing 'The Frightened Bride' in 'needna' fash' (1584), 'Wild Roses' in 'fidge fu' fain' (1210), 'Au Clair de la Lune' in 'larochs' (2220) and 'keethin' (498). In parts of *A Drunk Man*, the Scots usage is so forced, so obviously artificial, that it nearly turns the verse into a game. This can be part of its charm – as in the dedication to F. G. Scott – but at other times it creates a preposterous gap between sound and intended sense:

Or in whose loins the mapamound	*world map*
Wrunkles in strawns o' bubos whaur	*chains of swellings*
The generations gravel.	*collect in confusion*
(1302–4)	

Is this language *really* closer to the modern Scottish sensibility than English would be?

One critic writes of MacDiarmid, 'If his poetry often seems to begin with words, at other times words seem to be in his way, and he simply pushes past them toward the total rhythm of his meaning, oblivious of any incidental bathos or meaninglessness . . .'[1] Though intended as praise, this observation points out a serious weakness in the poem. The motivation for all that speed, that earnestness, that 'pushing past' is a commendable intention to make language express what lies beyond language – and form. The poetic cost of this oracular intention is an overall decline (with notable exceptions) in the quality of language. Encountering banal or forced usages that would have been unthinkable in *Sangschaw*, one misses that sense of craft-as-discovery which illuminates the early poems.

[1] David Daiches, Review of *Collected Poems*, *New York Times Book Review*, 25 February 1962, p.6.

Verbal lapses are not limited to Lallans passages. MacDiarmid sometimes wanders into Elizabethan and Miltonic English – 'bodkin', 'mortal coils', 'creeds malign', 'a fools fit diadem', 'while on brute needs our souls attend' – and attempts to use these phrases not allusively, but colloquially. Being closer to the time of Chaucer, Henryson, Dunbar and Gower, this diction may sound more 'Scottish' – but in truth is no less archaic for that. And while we may *wish* that the possibilities such language offers had survived – what current poet doesn't love the richness of Dunbar's, or Shakespeare's, tongues? – in fact, they have not. Language is a living thing; the effects of history upon it, even if erosive, cannot be ignored.

The same historical problem arises in relation to *A Drunk Man*'s predominant metric and stanzaic forms. For metre, stanzas and rhyme schemes, no less than language, bear connotations independent of the statements they contain. Such associations arise in part from literary precedent, and in part from intrinsic properties of form. One would not cast an elegy in trisyllabic feet, or a war poem in limericks. Yet this is the sort of thing MacDiarmid attempts, albeit less crudely, in sections of his poem.

For instance, in 'The Ballad of the Crucified Rose' (1119–28), he recalls the General Strike of 1926 in Biblical diction and ballad metre. This characteristic redirection does convey the speaker's personal passion, yet the manner in which it does so betrays the ostensible political subject. That complex event – in which the Trades Unions were manoeuvered into premature action for which they were unprepared and they themselves wished to put off – proved a fiasco. As such, it would seem to demand a sceptical, complex political evaluation. But the ballad form, by contrast, carries with it a weight of historic and cultural association tending toward romance, instinct, and lyric simplicity. In this case, the intrinsic nature of the form undercuts the poet's own political stance, and turns a volatile topical subject into timeless Literature. The 'waefu' clay' and 'Deils' that 'rejoice' and 'gang round' in this lyric have more to do with Dunbar than with Ramsay MacDonald.[1]

A gap between form and statement also emerges in the poem's more philosophical passages. Lines 1451–624 contain some extra-

---

[1] By way of experiment, I read a section of the poem in quatrains to a group of graduate students without identifying the source. Though the passage contained references that marked it as twentieth-century writing, they were led by the *metre* to guess 'Burns'.

ordinary speculation regarding evolution. Unfortunately, even as
the imagery becomes more supple and surprising, the iambic
tetrameter line – hundreds in succession! – remains almost entirely
unvaried. The result is a pedantic tum-de-tum rhythm. In his
urgent desire to persuade, MacDiarmid forsakes verse's greatest
means of persuasion; we lose not only the music of poetry, but also
the natural rhythms of spoken prose.

In the poem's penultimate section (2395–650) the long stretches
of triple rhyme *are* musical, and produce some welcome howlers:

I felt it turn, and syne I saw	*then*
John Knox and Clavers in the raw	*(Graham of Claverhouse) / rou*
And Mary Queen o Scots anaa,	*as well*
And Rabbie Burns and Weelum Wallace	
And Carlyle lookan unco gallus	*very reckless*
And Harry Lauder (to enthrall us) . . .	
But in this huge ineducable	
Heterogeneous hotch and rabble	*swarm*
Why am *I* condemned to squabble?	
(2605–10; 2635–8)	

This is all great fun. But what in the world are such lines doing in a
section called 'The Great Wheel'? And what are we to make of a
Dantesque/Ezekiel-like vision which pauses at its culmination to
crack pawky jokes? However coherent the philosophy – and I have
sought to demonstrate that it does cohere – the mis-chosen form
reduces content to self-parody.

We have encountered this problem earlier, where the poem's
pivotal definition of God was interrupted for a dance-hall style quip
on Aberdeen (1994). It is also present in these lines: 'I'm amused to
see the plicht / O Licht as't in the black tide drouns' (1975–6).
Elsewhere, in still more inappropriate metre, one reads:

Sae I in turn maun gi'e	
My soul to misery,	
Daidle disease	*dandle*
Upon my knees,	
And welcome madness	
Wi' exceedin' gladness . . .	
(1821–6)	

Daidle disease? Welcome madness? Try to imagine Baudelaire
saying this, and the problem becomes clear at once. What the
speaker 'daidles', in such lapses, is not disease, but the idea of it. In
these passages we are faced with a poet, still young, who doesn't yet

know just how seriously to take his own ideas. As a result, his poem is too often defensive, glib, or brash, and these qualities are reflected in lapsed diction and a mismatch of theme with form. It may be, as Edwin Muir believed, that Scottish poetry had simply not evolved forms capable of embodying modern dissociation. Viewed in this light, *A Drunk Man* leaves the reader stranded, at times, between the strenuous simplicity of its verse line and the complex uncertainties of its themes. In any case, this gap calls attention to the fundamental issue: voice.

Is the Drunk Man Hugh MacDiarmid? Yes and no. This is not just a formal problem, for much of our own response to what we hear depends on who is speaking. Unfortunately, in seeking to decide this, one finds contradictions constituting not a necessary expression of themes – such as those we have earlier praised – but a failed poetic strategy.

Some of the speaker's statements require that we believe he is a rural Scottish Everyman, yet others could only be made by a cosmopolitan artist. This lapsing in and out of *persona*, not caring about the reader's responses, makes the individual shifts less credible and the larger poem less coherent. To take an example, early on we hear:

> I ha'e nae doot some foreign philosopher
> Has wrocht a system oot to justify
> A' this: but I'm a Scot wha blin'ly follows
> Auld Scottish instincts, and I winna try.
> (149–53)

That MacDiarmid's own views on instinct derive from Shestov *et al.* would not matter if he had continued to express them in his persona's voice. Unfortunately, these same 'foreign philosophers' are flaunted, quoted, at one point even bragged about (436) in much of what follows. Similar gaps exist between the 'theiveless crony' / 'village drunk' image (183, 435) and 'we wha are poets and artists' (537). Passing over such combinations as 'T. S. Eliot, afore he wrote *The Waste Land* . . . by gum' (435), we might still wonder why a man whose ramblings draw upon 'vse-chelovek' (1654), 'shook foil' (1245) and Schoenberg (434) is married to a wife who differs in no respect from Tam O'Shanter's Kate.

Such flaws have been glossed over through the loose use of terms by which most critics have sought to characterize the poem. For instance, John Weston's otherwise fine 'Critical Note' to the 1971 edition says that the poem, spoken by a 'Tam O'Shanter type' is 'highbrow in the extreme' – yet Weston doesn't pursue this contradiction. Elsewhere the poem is variously called a monologue, an interior dramatic monologue, a stream of consciousness. None of these terms will do. The Drunk Man's words are neither freely associative (as are Molly Bloom's) nor an abstract verbalization of disembodied consciousness (as in 'Prufrock'). Composed in large part as speech to an imagined listener, the poem comes closer, in fact, to Browning's monologues; even when depicting confusion, the expository voice remains. Moreover, such professions at times entail intrusions on the persona which Browning himself would not have committed.

The uncertainty of exactly where MacDiarmid *is* in this work reflects his own uncertainty about the poem's ontological status. In *A Drunk Man*, the changes, the miscellaneousness, and the puzzle of how to take things the speaker says would seem better justified were the poet to claim only the authenticity of his personal vision. As is, however, the pastiche or quotations from other poetry work against such intensity, and bring the work as a whole closer to the looseness of the modern journal.[1]

It will have no doubt been noted that, in seeking to explicate *A Drunk Man*, much of one's task lies in selection, extraction and re-arrangement of what is already there. These procedures are really, in fact, just the final stages of composition. It seems a shame that the poet, believing so strongly in the 'mission' of verse (2584f.), could nevertheless not be bothered with its fine details. Insufficient revision suggests in part a lack of self-discipline and patience, in part an insecurity compensated for by repetition. As we have seen, *A Drunk Man* was originated, in large part, to demonstrate a theory, and where it reads most like a demonstration, it succeeds least well in verse.[2]

The result is an occasional air of performance; at times the persistent busy-ness of MacDiarmid's own voice makes him sound

---

[1] Unlike Prufrock, or Henry in Berryman's *Dream Songs*, the speaker is neither sufficiently distinguished from – nor integrated with – the poet's own voice. For a valuable discussion of this question of 'attribution' in modern verse, see Robert Pinsky, *The Situation of Poetry* (Princeton: Princeton University Press, 1976), especially chs. 2 and 5.
[2] Conversely, it is best where the poet stops saying 'This is what I am doing' and simply does it: 'Sic Transit Gloria Scotia', 'A Vision of Myself', 'Poets Pub', 'Ebb and Flow', 'Yank Oot Your Orra Boughs', and the closing thirty lines; and least successful in 'In The Keel of Heaven', 'Creation's Whirlygig', and 'The Emptiness At The End'.

like a character in Browning. This same quality is present in stretches of Ezra Pound's Cantos 2 through 12 as well – both poets come out of Browning – but in Pound the tone of busy extroversion gets carefully redressed immediately after. We find no equivalent to the mood of Canto 13 anywhere in *A Drunk Man*, and we miss it. There is too much Malatesta in the poem – and precious little Kung.

There are reasons for this. First, as curiously few critics mention, the poet was still a young man; Yeats, at the same age, was writing *The Wind Among The Reeds*. In *A Drunk Man*, MacDiarmid's ambition perhaps ran ahead of his poetic development. The poem's over-demonstrative aspect reflects a young poet's tackling themes in a manner he is not quite ready for. In addition, it must be remembered to his great credit that MacDiarmid was also a pioneer, attempting with no modern models and few allies to re-vitalize an entire literature. In such circumstances it is only natural to expect, along with the insecurity of the autodidact, the necessary false starts and backtrackings of the scout. These should not be carped at ungenerously. For in the last analysis, the form that is insufficiently worked out nevertheless accommodates great virtues which, taken together, produce an admirable, memorable work of art.

First, there is the extraordinary range of subject and mood, expressed with inexhaustible inventiveness and passion. Whether a reader agrees or disagrees with everything the poem contains, he is forced to confront his own 'thistleness' via the fundamental issues of twentieth-century life. Thanks to the poet's 'egalitarian imagination', all human needs, from spiritual to carnal, receive their due – and with a good deal more humour than one finds in, say, D. H. Lawrence.

Second, the poem contains much that is gothic in Ruskin's sense of the word – as a mark of freedom. Elsewhere MacDiarmid wrote that 'the essence of life lies in the movement by which it is trans-mitted'.[1] The energy with which *A Drunk Man* explores and changes makes each moment unpredictable; it underscores the role of chance. In doing so, it seeks to mitigate despair, suggesting hopeful future possibilities that cannot yet be foreseen.

Third, there is a quality (along with grotesquerie) of *mutation* in the way that images evaporate and pool. This aspect of the writing mimics processes of evolution in which its hopes reside. The

---

[1] 'The Never-Yet-Explored', in *Annals*, p.155.

knowledge that each organism can only change the gene pool infinitesimally, that Nature must kill, so to speak, to recycle its genetic raw material, reconciles the poet to his own limits, and mortality.

As a result, the poet's wild flights and self-inflicted injuries produce, at last, not a will to power or primitivism on the one hand, nor arch ironies on the other, but a ground of humane feeling on which rationality can stand.

Multiplicity, egalitarian concern, collective evolution – each would receive more focused treatment in poems to come, and shape MacDiarmid's interests for the next ten years. Great splash of talent though it is, *A Drunk Man Looks at the Thistle* must therefore be viewed not only as the culmination of the *Sangschaw* phase, but also as the fertile seedbed – still unweeded – of new growth to come.

CHAPTER FOUR

'Argue with these Stones'

Whatever may have been the case in years gone by, the true use for the imaginative faculty of modern times is to give ultimate vivification to facts, to science, and to common lives, endowing them with the glows and glories and final illustriousness which belong to every real thing, and to real things only.

WALT WHITMAN
'A Backward Glance O'er Travel'd Roads'

I was lonely amidst a world of *things* lit up by phosphorescent flashes of cruelty . . . I had to accustom myself gradually to the penalties which freedom involves.

HENRY MILLER
Henry Miller On Writing

A MacDiarmid short story published in 1923 concerned a character whose tendency

> was always to the whole, to the totality, to the general balance of things. Indeed it was his chiefest difficulty, (and an ever-increasing one that made him fear, at times, cancellation to non-entity) to exclude, to condemn, to say No. Here, probably, was the secret of the way in which he used to plunge into the full current of the most inconsistent movements, seeking, always in vain, until he was utterly exhausted . . . to find ground upon which he might stand foursquare.[1]

In *A Drunk Man Looks at the Thistle,* that ground was located, if not always occupied, and the poem's richness more than justifies its problematic aspects.

The same cannot be said of *To Circumjack Cencrastus.* Published in 1930, that poem resembles *A Drunk Man* in length and format. But now the structural disarray is imitative, not innovative; the sustaining fiction of drunkenness has disappeared, and with it the humour, vitality and personal warmth which pervade the earlier work. A sharp decline in the quality of writing suggests a poet who is merely going through the motions, who is 'utterly exhausted'.

Like *A Drunk Man, Cencrastus* is a lengthy sequence of fragments meant to coalesce around a central symbol. Once again that symbol links a specific memory of youth to a literary tradition, and its physical characteristics are seen to embody an underlying Idea. This time the symbol is Cencrastus, a serpent found in James Watson's *Choice Collection* (1709) which reminded MacDiarmid of a serpentine path called 'the Curly Snake' which he played on as a child.[2] The idea is that this beast, whose movements suggest the pattern and progress of consciousness, will be circumjacked, or lain around and about (Jamieson). In other words, that which emblematically envelops all will itself be grappled with, surrounded, encompassed by the poet's necessarily global mind.

Unfortunately – and with this particular poet the point cannot be

---

[1] In *Annals of the Five Senses* (Montrose: C. H. Grieve, 1923), pp. 194-5.
[2] Kenneth Buthlay, *Hugh MacDiarmid* (Edinburgh: Oliver & Boyd, 1964), p.56.

overstated – an *idea* for a poem does not a poem make. In fact the title's concept is rarely realized in the verse itself, and when it does appear it feels tacked-on. Moreover, unlike the thistle/octopus/leviathan of *A Drunk Man,* the serpent/sea monster in *Cencrastus* lacks a symbolic complement (such as moonlight/whisky/whiteness); no impulse toward wholeness transcends and withstands the stresses of complexity. The result is a lack of either counterpoint or continuity among the sections, and hundreds of lines like these:

> And mairtyrs to their ain stupidity
> You set Earth's generations a' alowe
> And the neist victim lauchs or grues to see
> His predecessor in the acid licht.
> The residue o' gowd is unco sma'
> And centuries gang to mak' a single grain
> While a' the dross o' pomp and circumstance
> Burns clear awa' as it had never been.
> The hopes and fears o' a' but twa-three men
> At best are foolish, syne null and void.

This is really rather bad. To see just how bad we need only compare these lines from the opening 'Address to Cencrastus' with a quatrain from the 'Address to Burns' in *A Drunk Man* with which they correspond:

> O gin they'd stegh their guts and haud their wheesht
> I'd thole it, for 'a man's a man', I ken,
> But though the feck ha'e plenty o' the 'a that',
> They're nocht but zoologically men.

The point of the two passages is identical, but what a difference in how it's made! On the one hand, the quatrain is cranky, idiomatic, humorous; from the reductive 'I ken' to the graceful use of Burns to the wonderfully dismissive 'feck' and 'zooLOGIcally', it had the pointed charm of deliberate loquacity. By contrast, the longer passage is devoid of personality. It seems written under hypnosis, or spoken by rote, and lacks the inflection of natural speech.

The failures of this writing are so evident that they need not be belaboured. A more useful question for what follows is not what went wrong (which is fairly obvious) but why. We may suggest three answers, having to do with poetic technique, a cultural dilemma, and the poet's personal affairs.

In technical terms, *Cencrastus* suffers from an inattention to language in general and the loss of Scots in particular. Without the resonant metaphoric language that distinguished preceding work, we lose the free associative mood which this method requires to succeed. As a result, pedantic plod supplants imagination. Instead of being asked to 'look at' we are told to 'circumjack'; instead of expressionist word play we get lectures on expressionism; instead of a personal 'letter' to Dostoyevsky, an announcement that 'Tyutchev was richt'.[1] Themes are not discovered in images, but forced upon them, thus:

> A' mankind/Writhes like the cut up pairts o' a snake

> What is Cencrastus but the wriggle
> O' Man's divided vertebrae . . .

> But you're no Truth in ony case, but Error.[2]

Such recourse to explanation indicates a failure of metaphor and/or loss of trust in the reader. Conversely, the use of connective phrases between sections (where none were supplied in *A Drunk Man*) suggests the poet has lost confidence in himself, and his method. That loss of confidence arises from a crisis of identity which he shares with earlier Scots poets.

Like Burns a century before, Hugh MacDiarmid was *in* a social class but never entirely *of* it. For both men, the dilemma which that status imposed was this: If one expresses, as voice of a class, the commonly accepted values and aspirations of that class, he will be limited creatively by its communal and conventional standards. But if he ventures too far beyond them, he will be seen as forsaking – *and will be forsaken by* – the very class he purports to represent.[3] MacDiarmid complains about this difficulty in *Cencrastus* when he writes

> For if it's no' by thocht that Poetry's wrocht
> It's no by want o' thocht
> The verse that flatters ignorance maun seem
> To ignorant folk supreme
> Sin' nane can read the verse that disna
> The damned thing bides as if it isna![4]

Given his radical, non-conformist goals (and his unrelenting

---

[1] In the *Complete Poems* (London: Martin Brian & O'Keefe, 1978), pp.189, 219.
[2] *Ibid.*, pp.188, 215.
[3] This thought is suggested and developed in relation to Burns by David Craig throughout *Scottish Literature and the Scottish People* (London: Chatto and Windus, 1961).
[4] *Complete Poems*, p.232.

pursuit of them) it was inevitable that he should find himself
increasingly cut off from the provincial life in which the roots of his
own feeling lay. Four years after having said, 'Like staundan water
. . . I pray I'll never be / Cut aff and self-sufficient' the poet now
writes, 'I am the mavis o' Pabal / A root cut aff frae the sea'. The
best portions of *Cencrastus* express this sense of personal isolation
within the context of cultural goals. One example is 'The Mavis of
Pabal' (just quoted); another is 'Lourd On My Hert':

> *Lourd on my hert as winter lies*
> *The state that Scotland's in the day.*
> *Spring to the north has aye come slow*
> *But noo dour winter's like to stay*
> > *For guid*
> > *And no' for guid!*
>
> *O wae's me on the weary days*
> *When it is scarce grey licht at noon;*
> *It maun be a' the stupid folk*
> *Diffusin' their dullness roon and roon*
> > *Like soot,*
> > *That keeps the sunlicht oot.*
>
> *Nae wonder if I think I see*
> *A lichter shadow than the neist*   next
> *I'm fain to cry: 'The dawn, the dawn!*
> *I see it brakin' in the East.'*
> > *But ah*
> > *– It's juist mair snaw!*

Here, despite the alienation it expresses, the verse itself has not lost
integrity; the grieving is a function of the love.

Unfortunately, in most of *Cencrastus* the mood is less direct and a
good deal more corrosive. As the poet increasingly defines himself
against others, he seeks arguments with countless stereotyped
adversaries. Sometimes these are addressed in specific terms:
'Aiberdeen doctors', 'university students', 'a fool (Plotinus he is
ca'd)', 'pigmies like Bruce or Hume'.[1] At other times this scorn is
generalized: 'The way that maist men think / And feel's beyond
contempt'.[2] The less certain the poet is that anyone will respond,
the more extreme his provocations grow. Poetry becomes palaver –
oral in form but not social in feeling. Like a drunk in the local the
poet stands too close and repeatedly asks 'Am I right?' because he's
not sure that anyone's listening.

[1] *Ibid.*, pp.216, 203, 217, 230.
[2] *Ibid.*, p.221.

In this respect the difficulties associated with cultural and class identity were exacerbated by adverse personal circumstances from 1926 to 1930. Since the publication of *A Drunk Man*, MacDiarmid had been beset by personal crises: faltering of the Renaissance movement; a failed start in London as editor of *Vox*; a fall from a moving bus that resulted in unconsciousness, hospitalization and (some say) lasting injury; a painful marital separation and denial of parental visitation rights; and an alcoholic period alone in Liverpool.[1] These individual setbacks coincided with the onset of the Great Depression, to which Scotland was particularly vulnerable, and from which it took especially long to recover. Thus, starting in the thirties, for twenty years MacDiarmid suffered isolation, critical neglect, and penury.

These factors shaped the background out of which succeeding books emerged. That background does not warrant pity, which MacDiarmid himself conspicuously never sought. It does command respect for the courage and endurance which continued to produce, in trying circumstances, poetry of lasting value. After *Cencrastus*, the legitimate intellectual and cultural issues upon which that particular poem had foundered were not avoided, but henceforth pursued in different ways. Given the ordeals this pursuit entailed, and the cost to himself, it is less remarkable that MacDiarmid produced some terribly flawed poems than that he wrote so many which are fine. Indeed, his best work of the thirties is chastened and strengthened, more innovative and accomplished, than anything he had previously achieved. His growth will be evident if we compare a passage from 1926 with another from 1935.

Halfway through *A Drunk Man*, the following lines appear:

I'm under nae delusions, fegs!	
The whuppin' sooker at wha's tip	*whipping sucker*
Oor little point o' view appears	
A midget coom o' continents	*comb*
Wi blebs o' oceans set, sends up	*drops*
The braith o' daith as weel as life	
And we maun braird anither tip	*grow*
Oot owre us ere we wither tae	

[1] Many of these details should become available in reliable form in a forthcoming authorized biography by Mr Dougald McMillan of the University of South Carolina at Chapel Hill. While such matters are of obvious importance, and I have necessarily taken account of information supplied by relatives, friends and colleagues of MacDiarmid, it would seem prudent (and only fair) to limit such discussion until full accounts, appropriately researched, appear in print.

> And join the sentrice skeleton   *scaffold*
> As coral insects big their reefs.   *build*

As verse these lines are not remarkable; statement cramps suggestion, the syntax is monotonous, the tetrameter plods. Yet they
contain a wealth of idea and image which MacDiarmid returned to
nine years later in 'On the Ocean Floor':

> Now more and more on my concern with the lifted
>   waves of genius gaining
> I am aware of the lightless depths that beneath them lie;
> And as one who hears their tiny shells incessantly raining
> On the ocean floor as the foraminifera die.

First, a gloss: foraminifera are protozoans which extend fine
pseudopods through patterned perforations in their chambered
shells. Their name refers to *foramina*, the openings that form
between adjacent chambers after a new chamber envelops the
preceding one. When they die, the protoplasm disappears, and
their chalky shells drift to the bottom. There they combine into
'foraminiferal ooze' that covers thirty per cent of the ocean floor,
turns into limestone and, when elevated by tectonic force, forms
new land. Thus, by virtue of both their individual structure and
collective function, they lend themselves, as image and analogy, to
MacDiarmid's central interests – evolution, multiplicity, the value
of individual existence viewed in light of processes that dwarf it.

The poem itself is built on paradox. First of all, a solid 'rains'
through a liquid. Second, though the movement of the verse is
downward – from 'lifted' to 'depths' to 'lie' to 'floor' to 'die' – and
focuses on what we do see, its real theme is the less visible, more
durable process of building up. This tension is further embodied in
the contrast between feminine endings, 'gaining' and 'raining',
with the masculine endings that still them, 'lie' and 'die'. Similarly,
the disproportionate number of monosyllabic words (which
suggest a myriad of tiny organisms) are propelled by a few suppler
phrases ('incessantly raining') as if in waves. The placement of
'gaining' in the first line expresses the action it describes, and the
movement from high-pitched to low-pitched vowels in line three
establishes downward drift. That, in turn, is heightened, most
subtly, by internal rhymes – 'More', 'more', 'floor', 'foraminifera'
– that fall from line to line, evoking the dying creatures' loveliness,
discovering music even in their scientific name.

While such art and delicacy were present in *Sangschaw*, here the
poet's hand is less visible. In place of vertiginous razzle-dazzle we

have quiet resonance evoked by simple language, and the result is both more poised and more charged. Along with the sort of time-transcending *aperçu* encountered previously, this poem constitutes a political statement. As Edwin Morgan explains:

> MacDiarmid is saying that he has been too self-centered; too concerned with individual genius, he had forgotten the great mass of ordinary mankind; but now, in the thirties, in the period of economic and political crisis, he suddenly becomes aware of what as a communist he should be aware of – the masses themselves, dying and falling anonymously like the foraminifera, but from whom something is going to rise up, a new society, like the chalk cliffs rising from the sea.[1]

Thus, these four brief lines subtly conflate natural imagery and topical polemic. In an almost Shakespearean manner, a view of political and social health is located within the larger processes of nature. The poem differs from earlier writing less in subject matter than in what the poet himself now brings to his subjects – a ballast of conviction. We are moving beyond mere perception towards comprehension. MacDiarmid now controls his images, not vice versa, and we sense that he has, as it were, grown into themes that were a size too large when first tried on.

With regard to politics *per se*, one might object that the passive filtering of frail corpses through flickering water is an unlikely metaphor for political action. The issue is central to an evaluation of all MacDiarmid's 1930s poems. For, as 'On the Ocean Floor' suggests, even where his views most resemble those of other writers of the thirties, the language and referents remain unique. In particular, there is an ongoing, idiosyncratic tension between (or fusion of) Scots rural elements and militant left wing positions. How do the nostalgic, luxuriant 'nature poems' which comprise half his thirties work relate to the more famous, urban, polemical ones? Is there a contradiction, and if so, which are more successful? Where does the 'real' MacDiarmid lie? Such difficult questions are best held in abeyance until we have examined each type of writing, and sorted out one from the other.

Many of the poems in *First Hymn to Lenin* (1931), *Scots Unbound* (1932), and *A Lap of Honour* (1967) celebrate 'sheer plenitude wi' its prevert face', the diversity and abundance of nature. Written in the early thirties, they draw on MacDiarmid's childhood more

---

[1] Edwin Morgan, *Hugh MacDiarmid* (Harlow, Essex: Longman, 1976), p.21.

directly than previous poems. As previously noted, Langholm at turn-of-the-century possessed

> . . . a bountifulness so inexhaustible that it has supplied all my subsequent poetry with a tremendous wealth of sensuous satisfaction, a teeming gratitude of reminiscence . . . of an almost tropical luxuri-ance of Nature – of great forests, of honey-scented heather hills, and moorlands . . . infinitely rich in little-appreciated beauties of flower-ing, of animal and insect life, of strange and subtle relationships of water and light . . . and a multitude of rivers. . . . [1]

Even today, the town retains its Edenic quality; along the Esk or by Wauchopeside in June, the sucking mud and steaming foliage filled with small animals and birds seem to take one back in time. MacDiarmid evokes and interprets this experience in 'Water of Life'. The poem begins

> Wha looks on water and's no' affected yet
> By memories o' the Flood, and, faurer back,   *farther*
> O' that first flux in which a' life began,
> And won sae slowly oot that ony lack
> O' poo'er's a shrewd reminder o' the time
>   We ploutered in the slime?   *floundered*
>
> It's seldom in my active senses tho'
> That water brings sic auld sensations as that
> (Gin it's no' mixed wi' something even yet
> A wee taet stronger); but in lookin' at   *somewhat*
> A woman at ony time I mind oor source
>   And possible return of course . . .

The double-entendre in the last two lines is taken up in a bit of bawdy later on:

> Ah, vivid recollection o' trudgin' that
> Crab-like again upon the ocean flair! –
> Juist as in lyin' wi' a woman still
> I feel a sudden cant and sweesh aince mair
> Frae Sodom or Gomorrah wi' yon Eastern whore
> T'oor watery grave o' yore.

In the next stanzas, a comic account of lovemaking moves back and forth in time, not only to a collective distant past, but also to a recent individual one:

---

[1] Hugh MacDiarmid, *Lucky Poet* (London: Methuen, 1943), p.219.

She clung to me mair tightly at the end
Than ane expects or wants in sic a case,
Whether frae love or no' I needna say,
A waste o' guid material – her face
Fastened on mine as on a flag a sooker   *iris | sucking insect*
    And naething shook her . . .

– The gowden pendants frae her lugs, her skin   *golden | ears*
Sae clear that in her cheeks the glints 'ud play *would*
As whiles wi' bits o' looking-glass as loons   *sometimes*
We'd gar the sun loup roon's.   *leap round us*

In much of MacDiarmid's earlier work, vulgarity and time disjunctions were intended to disorient and shock; here, the time changes are less stagey, and integrate diverse experiences with both grace and ease. The flow of water images becomes synonymous with the course of time, and a poem most immediately about the Wauchope is really about how memory reconciles us to change:

Nae doot the sudden predicament we shared
Has fixed her in my mind abune the lave,   *above the rest*
A kind of compensation for the way
She was sae tashed and lightlied by the wave   *soiled | tarnished*
Oot o' my recognition and slarried by   *muddied*
    The infernal sly.

These lines address the same question that Wordsworth pondered in 'Tintern Abbey', and the 'whore' who is swept out of the speaker's recognition by a wave (of both water and time) serves the same function as Dorothy in the earlier poem. Of course, the tone is quite different, as if Wordsworth were at ease with vulgarity, and had a sense of humour.

Like his great predecessor, MacDiarmid finds that he must resign himself to mortality, the passage of time, in order to make peace with it:

Nae man can jouk and let the jaw gang by.   *dodge | surge, swing*
To seem to's often to dodge a silly squirt
While bein' whummled in an unseen spate   *overturned*
Lodgin' us securely in faur deeper dirt
Or carryin' us to heichts we canna see
    For th'earth in oor e'e.   *eyes*

Nae gulfs that open 'neath oor feet'll find
Us hailly at a loss if we juist keep   *wholly*
The perspective the deluge should ha'gien's   *have given us*
And if we dinna, or if they're mair deep

Than even that is muckle guidance in,
    It's there altho' we're blin'.

Whatever is to be, what's been has been;
Even if it's hailly undune that deed'll bear
A sense o' sequence forever in itsel',
Implyin, and dependent on, what erst was there,   *once*
Tho' it's no' conscious o't – less conscious o't
    Than men o' their historic lot.

Still, MacDiarmid's poem is essentially *forward-looking*: it celebrates not only history and what endures, but also possibility in what is yet to come:

Hoo I got oot o' yon I dinna ken,
But I am ready noo at ony time
To be hurled back or forrit to ony stage   *forward*
O' ocht we've ever been twixt sun and slime
Or can become, trustin' what's brocht aboot   *brought*
    A' th'ither sequels to the water-shute.

If such lines suggest a greater openness to *future* possibility than one generally finds in Wordsworth, they also invite comparison with a modern poem by Robert Frost. In Frost's 'West Running Brook', a couple contemplate a brook that runs west 'when all the other country brooks flow east / To reach the ocean'. The man in the poem declares:

Speaking of contraries, see how the brook
In what white wave runs counter to itself.
It is from that in water we were from
Long, long before we were from any creature.
Here we, in our impatience of the steps,
Get back to the beginning of beginnings
The stream of everything that runs away.

The river, he explains, is unresisted 'save by some strange resistance in itself':

It is this backward motion toward the source,
Against the stream, that most we see ourselves in,
The tribute of the current to the source.
It is from this in nature we are from.
It is most us.

Though much more famous than 'Water of Life', 'West Running Brook' is surely in all respects the inferior poem. First of all, it is really a lecture – sententious, unself-chastising, philosophic in a way that belies personal involvement. The female speaker exists merely to establish how down-to-earth the male is, to ask which way is north (odd question for a countrywoman), or to say 'Go on, you thought of something'. Go on he does, and on:

> And it is time, strength, tone, light, life, and love –
> And even substance lapsing unsubstantial . . .

One hopes she is taking notes.

I am being harsh on Frost for a reason. He has been touted in our time as the pre-eminent voice of poetic plain-style wisdom. Yet this brand of self-conscious elevation, with its palliative folksiness as jam for the pill of Philosophy will not hold up when compared with the 'real thing' – a poet who, truly at home in the folk idiom, has something intellectually fresh to say. Compare Frost's lines

> The sun runs down in sending up the brook
> And there is something sending up the sun

with MacDiarmid's

> As whiles wi' bits o' looking-glass as loons
>   We'd gar the sun loup roon's.

MacDiarmid's image is a happy one, yet the phrase which describes it has darker overtones. For even as the 'loons' make the sun 'loup roon' them, playfully, in another sense the sun louping roon the earth denotes time passing, and with it the very innocence the image recalls. Moreover, since that image is used to describe a whore's face years later, it further embodies the passage of time. Compared with the Frost lines, which are inert declamation, Mac-Diarmid's link the happiness of childhood (localized by language) to the (generalized) pathos of adult recollection.

A similar contrast can be drawn between the two poets' conclusions. Frost alludes to 'contraries' and 'motion', but the poem itself feels curiously static, and the human relations in it are correspondingly fixed. MacDiarmid's conclusion is less riddled with Classic Poise, and more – well, more *fluid*. It too takes account of the classical view, indeed echoes Heraclitus in its penultimate stanzas. But having done so, 'Water of Life' moves on; it ends with an *opening* movement:

> Ah, weel I ken that ony ane o' them,
> Nae maitter hoo vividly I ca't to mind,
> Kennin' the world to men's as light to water,   *knowing*

Has endless beauties to which my een are blind,
My ears deaf – aye, and ilka drap a world   *every*
   Bigger than a' Mankind has yet unfurled.

In his autobiography, MacDiarmid quotes John Cowper Powys' statement, 'Deep within us is a secret fount, from whose channel, by a resolute habit of will, we can clear away the litter that obstructs the water of life'.[1] MacDiarmid's poem professes willingness to be borne along on that water to a destination yet unknown, and implies that to fear change is to dam(n) life. Few other twentieth-century poets could handle so large a topic with such good humour and conversational ease. When the water which runs through every stanza of this poem shivers into droplets, each of which reveals a world, all preceding images of sunlight, childhood, and future childhoods fuse. The resulting blend of vulgarity, amusement, nostalgia and metaphysics is warm, but not sentimental, and offers affirmation without bombast. It is a lovely poem.

'A perfect maze o' waters is aboot the Muckle Toon' wrote MacDiarmid in 'Water of Life'. The waters which symbolize process and change in that poem inspired experiments with language in others. One such, 'Water Music', begins with a nod to *Finnegan's Wake*:

> *Wheesht, wheesht, Joyce, and let me hear*   hush
>   *Nae Anna Livvy's lilt,*
> *But Wauchope, Esk, and Ewes again,*   see p.2
>   *Each wi' its ain rhythms till't.*   to it

MacDiarmid tries to capture the music of Langholm's rivers by combining thick border Scots with onomatopoeic inventions:

> Lively, louch, atweesh, atween,   *downcast | betwixt | between*
> Auchimuty or aspate,   *paltry*
> Threidin' through the averins   *heather stems*
>   Or bightsom in the aftergait . . .   *ample | outcome*
>
> Or barmybrained or barritchfu',   *wanton, giddy | troublesome*
>   Or rinnin' like an attercap,   *spider*
> Or shinin' like an Atchison,   *Scots coin*
>   Wi' a blare or wi' a blawp.   *yawn | belch*
>
> They ken a' that opens and steeks,   *shuts*
>   Frae Fiddleton Bar to Callister Ha',
> And roon aboot for twenty miles,
>   They bead and bell and swaw . . .   *gather | bubble up | ripple*

[1] *Ibid.*, p.3.

Brade-up or sclafferin', rouchled, sleek,	*neat / slovenly / ruffled*
Abstraklous or austerne,	*outrageous / austere*
In belths below the brae hags	*swirls / overhanging bank*
And bebbles in the fern. . . .	*droplets*

'Water Music' is one of a number of poems – others are 'Balefire Loch', 'In the Caledonian Forest', 'Tarras', 'By Wauchopeside', 'Once In A Cornish Garden', 'Whuchulls', and 'Scots Unbound' – which MacDiarmid described as *divertissements philologiques'* or 'primarily an exercise of delight in the Scots sense of colour'.[1] As one might expect, the quality of such experiments varies rather widely. Some do provide 'divertissement' ('Scots Unbound', for instance), whereas others ('In the Caledonian Forest', 'Vestigia Nulla Retrorsum') fall short of the mark. Because they attempt to capture nature's multiplicity with a correspondingly dense and specific language, they risk becoming catalogues, mere lists of names. 'Let me plunge where the undergraith's mair thick', MacDiarmid writes in 'Whuchulls',

> Pile up the facts and let me faurer ben.
> Multiply my vocabulary, ten times ten.
> Let me range owre a' prosody again,
> Mak' yon a lammergeir, no' juist a wren.   vulture

The difficulty, which these lines themselves reflect, is that interest in *vocabulary* is not the same as interest in *language,* such as one finds in Joyce. Without a corresponding playfulness regarding syntax, for instance, one loses the transfer of energy, hence relation, and hence meaning. Nouns piled together – even fascinating nouns – yield piles, and a verse comprised too much of them grows clubfooted where Joyce is nimble.

Still, one needn't make too much of this. For one thing, even in 1983 most lowland Scots understand many more of these words than they habitually employ, and to hear them put forth with such gusto 'unbinds' as MacDiarmid intended. Similarly, words which keep 'your tongue awak' in your mouth' inspire interest in the aural texture of verse, the melopoetic qualities of language. When MacDiarmid applied what he learned in these experiments to more

---

[1] The first phrase is the subtitle to 'Scots Unbound'; the second appears in a note to 'Balefire Loch'. It should be noted that though the 'sense of colour' is identified as Scots, the poems that express it are written in both Scots and English, and a mixture of the two. See 'Milk-Wort and Bog-Cotton' and 'Cattle Show', discussed in the following chapter.

serious ends, when the love of language and minute natural particulars was subsumed in a larger purpose, there emerged some
remarkable poems. Among them, 'On A Raised Beach' is pre-
eminent.

First things first: 'On A Raised Beach' is one of MacDiarmid's
most important poems, an extraordinary work which deserves a
place in modern poetry beside *The Waste Land*, Canto 47 and
'Sunday Morning'. Like each of these, MacDiarmid's poem con-
fronts the apparent fragmentation and indifference of a natural
world after loss of the inherited faith that formerly gave it coherence. In some respects, MacDiarmid's poem is as obscure and
idiosyncratic as those of Eliot, Pound and Stevens; in others, it is
less so. As in each of those works, the difficulties which make 'On A
Raised Beach' at first seem inaccessible are ultimately justified by
the intelligence and integrity of what it has to say.

'On A Raised Beach' begins with word play, the delight with and
fascination of language as sound:

> All is lithogenesis – or lochia,
> Carpolite fruit of the forbidden tree
> Stones blacker than any in the Caaba,
> Cream-coloured caen-stone, chatoyant pieces,
> Celadon and corbeau, bistre and beige,
> Glaucous, hoar, enfouldered, cyathiform,
> Making mere faculae of the sun and moon
> I study you glout and gloss, but have
> No cadrans to adjust you with, and turn again
> From optik to haptik and like a blind man run
> My fingers over you, arris by arris, burr by burr . . .

From the very start this language is so peculiar, so obviously *not* the
idiom of normal speech, that it signals a radical intention; unless
we are to throw up our hands and dismiss it at once, we must figure
out what this is. The first thing one notices about these words is
how diverse they are. MacDiarmid draws on vocabularies one
seldom encounters singly, let alone jammed together this way –
French, Norse, Scandinavian, Old Scots, Middle French, Greek,
American geological. All these terms, and the last in particular, are
extremely specific. Yet their exactness produces quite the opposite
effect from words like 'keethin' sicht' or 'watergaw' in earlier work.
Here, the more precisely each name suits what it signifies, the
fewer its connotations. A first-time reader is *right* to feel put off;
words like cyathiform (cup-shaped), arris (sharp edge where sur-

faces meet) and faculae (bright regions in the solar photosphere)
evoke no personal response. The reality of stones 'blacker than the
Caaba' precludes any religious, symbolic, or emotive value that
might accrue through more personal language that human beings
invent to describe them. Because their only meaning at this point is
apparently their resistance to meaning, they must be taken as 'fora-
minous' – an origin or zero-point of reference.

That is why, though these lines make perfect sense once one
takes the time to gloss them, they achieve their effect primarily as
incantation or tone poem. Words which are each so odd must be
read with deliberation, preferably aloud. A reader is forced to
detach one from the other, to 'handle' them like stones on a beach,
to 'tell' them, each by each, like beads on rosaries. As in MacDiarmid's other poems of plenitude, the aural texture approaches the
density and roughness of what it describes. The difficulty and
obliquity of that approach – of word to stone – becomes the subject
of the poem:

> Deep conviction or preference can seldom
> Find direct terms in which to express itself.
> Today on this shingle shelf
> I understand this passive reluctance so well . . .
>
> These stones with their resolve that Creation shall not be
> Injured by iconoclasts and quacks. Nothing has stirred
> Since I lay down this morning an eternity ago
> But one bird. The widest open door is the least liable to intrusion,
> Ubiquitous as the sunlight, unfrequented as the sun.
> The inward gates of a bird are always open.
> It does not know how to shut them.
> That is the secret of its song.
> But whether any man's are ajar is doubtful.
> I look at these stones and know little about them,
> But I know their gates are open too,
> Always open, far longer open, than any bird's can be,
> That every one of them has had its gates wide open far longer
> Than all birds put together, let alone humanity . . .

That last phrase, 'let alone humanity', exemplifies the 'reductive
idiom', a characteristic Scottish rhetorical figure which crops up
throughout MacDiarmid's work.[1] As used here it suggests a reverse
view of human capabilities *vis-à-vis* those of non-human nature.

[1] For instance, in *A Drunk Man*, 'Let there be licht, God said, and
there was / A little' (l.2101-2); 'My name is Norval. On the Grampian
Hills / It is forgotten, and deserves to be' (l.2192-3).

Language which aspires to capture the *quidditas* of reality necessarily creates exclusive, hence divisive categories and, to borrow
MacDiarmid's metaphor, closes the gates a little further. Hence
the poet's effort next becomes to get behind words, so to speak, to a
reality they cannot fragment.

All the rhetorical fumbles and apparent inadequacy of the ensuing lines serve to express the argument they advance:

I would scorn to cry to any easier audience
Or, having cried, to lack patience to await the response.
I am no more indifferent or ill-disposed to life than death is;
I would fain accept it all completely as the soil does;
Already I feel all that can perish perishing in me
As so much has perished and all will yet perish in these stones.
I must begin with these stones as the world began.

Like the inverted word order in 'On the Ocean Floor' (*supra*,
p.111), the rhetorical deliberation in these lines is strikingly Whitmanesque. This free verse is plodding and scrupulous, with a
touch of necessary awkwardness. There is little enjambment; each
line presents a false closure. It is not enough to imply the ellipses;
each is fully, ploddingly expressed, as if to suggest that elegance,
artful speech and other felicities of style are irrelevant to this
endeavour.

Recognizing the inadequacies of language is the first step toward
confronting the ultimate inadequacy of all our schemes and concepts. In philosophic terms, MacDiarmid still stands with Duns
Scotus against Aquinas, with an egalitarian interest in the quiddity
of things, rather than in hierarchies we construct to 'explain'
them.[1] Only now, in seeking the rock of underlying unity, he
begins to find *any* distinctions superficial. However carefully observed, or sensitively evoked, they remain merely incidents of the
surface:

. . . no general principle can be guessed
From these flashing fragments we are seeing,
These foam bells on the hidden currents of being. . .
Brilliant-hued animals hide away in the ocean deeps;
The mole has a rich sexual colouring in due season
Under the ground; nearly every beast keeps

[1] See *The MacDiarmids* (A Conversation – Hugh MacDiarmid and
Duncan Glen with Valda Grieve and Arthur Thompson) recorded at
Brownsbank, Candymill, 25 October 1968 (Preston, Lancashire:
Akros, 1970), pages not numbered.

Brighter colours inside it than outside.
What the sun shows is never anything to what it's designed to hide,
The red blood which makes the beauty of a maiden's cheek
Is as red under a gorilla's pigmented and hairy face.

These last two lines reflect the decision to reject romantic diction
('a maiden's cheek') in favour of some more precise though less
comforting terms ('pigmented and hairy face'). Similarly, in the
following stanzas various conventional metaphors are proposed
and then rejected. First is the notion that stars are exalted and
distinct from our reality:

We must be humble. We are so easily baffled by appearances
And do not understand that these stones are one with the stars.
It makes no difference to them whether they are high or low,
Mountain peak or ocean floor, palace, or pigsty.
There are plenty of ruined buildings in the world but no ruined stones.

Next comes the notion that ephemeral beauty is enough, that it is
adequate to 'live for today':

. . . It is easy to find a spontaneity here,
An adjustment to life, an ability
To ride it easily, akin to 'the buoyant
Prelapsarian naturalness of a country girl
Laughing in the sun' . . .

But no, MacDiarmid decides, it is *too* easy:

. . . It is wrong to indulge in these illustrations
Instead of just accepting the stones.
It is a paltry business to try to drag down
The arduus furor of the stones to the futile imaginings of men.

Among these 'futile imaginings' are any and all images, metaphors, insights or imaginative uses one attempts to make of the
stones. In what must be a response to Eliot, MacDiarmid states,
'This is no heap of broken images'. Nor does it allow the sustaining
fictions which other twentieth-century poets such as Stevens pro-
pose as a source of value. All it is is stone, and that is all. 'I must get
into this stone world now', the poet declares (1.149), and the
strongest passages in 'On A Raised Beach' are those in which he
does so:

We must reconcile ourselves to the stones,
Not the stones to us.
Here a man must shed the encumbrances that muffle
Contact with elemental things, the subtleties
That seem inseparable from a humane life, and go apart
Into a simpler and sterner, more beautiful and more oppressive world,
Austerely intoxicating; the first draught is overpowering;
Few survive it. It fills me with a sense of perfect form,
The end seen from the beginning, as in a song.
It is no song that conveys the feeling
That there is no reason why it should ever stop,
But the kindred form I am conscious of here
Is the beginning and the end of the world,
The unsearchable masterpiece, the music of the spheres,
Alpha and Omega, the Omnific Word.

Having rejected the specific words, images, songs which can only describe what is multiple and mutable, MacDiarmid is led from words to the Word.

But the Truth which these stones suggest to him is darker, less redemptive than the religious doctrine with which they invite comparison:

Listen to me – Truth is not crushed;
It crushes, gorgonises all else into itself.
The trouble is to know it when you see it?
You will have no trouble with it when you do.
Do not argue with me. Argue with these stones.
Truth has no trouble in knowing itself.
This is it. The hard fact. The inoppugnable reality,
Here is something for you to digest.
Eat this and we'll see what appetite you have left
For a world hereafter.
I pledge you in the first and last crusta,
The rocks rattling in the bead-proof seas.

It may seem perverse, having criticized such declamation in Frost, to now praise a similar sententiousness in MacDiarmid. The difference to be borne in mind is that 'On A Raised Beach' is spoken in solitude on a cold, desolate island. In effect, we overhear the poet talking to himself. Despite their finger-pointing quality and second-person pronouns, his statements comprise not an oration to others, but a meditation; coming to terms with the stones means reconciling oneself to death. Like more traditional poems in this genre, 'On A Raised Beach' also proceeds from thoughts of death to hopes for resurrection: 'These stones go through Man, straight to God, if there is one'.[1]

In pursuit of that 'if' MacDiarmid draws heavily on Christian reference: *Did* the stone move from the grave? Is there some transcendent meaning – love – which redeems us from death?

> 'Ah!' you say, 'if only one of these stones would move
> – Were it only an inch – of its own accord.
>   This is the resurrection we await,
> – The stone rolled away from the tomb of the Lord.'

Unhappily, however, MacDiarmid is led by his intellect to reject (as one more insufficient word-image-concept) the hope that exerts such a powerful hold on his imagination. The Word is just another word. The rock remains indifferent and unchanged. On that rock he builds his lack of faith, and speaks in sermonic cadences of 'stony limits':

> – I lift a stone; it is the meaning of life I clasp
> Which is death, for that is the meaning of death;
> How else does any man yet participate
>   In the life of a stone,
> How else can any man yet become
> Sufficiently at one with creation, sufficiently alone
> Till as the stone that covers him he lies dumb
> And the stone at the mouth of his grave is not overthrown?
> – Each of these stones on this raised beach
>   Every stone in the world,
> Covers infinite death, beyond the reach
> Of the dead it hides, and cannot be hurled
> Aside . . .

Ironically, in denying the consolations of Christianity, the speaker himself becomes Christlike. We have encountered this paradox before in *A Drunk Man* (see p.88ff.); here it is less explicitly evoked, less self-serving, and thus more affecting. Voice in the Wilderness – temptation in the desert[2] – however one construes these lines, they constitute the Passion of a man who scorns the comfort of all customary passions:

[1] The pattern is still more clear in lines which MacDiarmid deleted from an earlier draft: 'Behind the dullness, the silence, denial and despair / I impute to them, deep in the heart of each stone there / I see the unconquerable hope, the light of lights divine' (etc.). Hugh MacDiarmid papers, Edinburgh University Library, 'On A Raised Beach' original MS, Gen.887, ff.83-8.

[2] In *Life In the Shetland Islands* (1934), rpt. in *The Uncanny Scot* (London: MacGibbon & Kee, 1968), pp.80-92, MacDiarmid de-

> I am enamoured of the desert at last,
> The abode of supreme serenity is necessarily a desert.
> My disposition is towards spiritual issues
> Made inhumanly clear; I will have nothing interposed
> Between my sensitiveness and the barren but beautiful reality; . . .

Having considered and rejected all the various explanations that unify a senseless multiplicity, the speaker at last simply accepts his place within it. The personal cost is not less than everything. The payoff – such as it is – is a vision that, by surrendering consciousness to the brute beauty of things, is able to transcend time.

Having 'stepped out' of the process long enough to come to see it whole, the speaker re-enters, concluding in the style with which he began:

> Diallage of the world's debate, end of the long auxesis,
> Although no ébrillade of Pegasus can here avail,
> I prefer your enchorial characters – the futhorc of the future –
> To the hieroglyphics of all the other forms of Nature.
> Song, your apprentice encrinite, seems to sweep
> The Heavens with a last entrochal movement;
> And, with the same word that began it, closes
> Earth's vast epanadiplosis.

This language requires detailed glossing. *Diallage* (from the Latin for 'interchange') is a figure of speech by which arguments, after having been considered from various points of view, are all brought to bear on one point. *Auxesis* refers to a gradual increase in intensity of meaning; *ébrillade* means checking a horse by jerking one rein when he refuses to turn in the desired direction. *Enchorial* (from a word on the Rosetta stone) is used as the distinctive epithet of the popular (as distinguished from hieroglyphic and hieratic) form of the ancient Egyptian written character. *Futhorc* was the Runic alphabet. *Encrinites* are fossil crinoids anchored to the tropical sea-bottom, while *entrochal* refers to the wheel-like plates of which certain crinoids are composed. Biologically, *epanadiplosis* means 'reduplication'; in rhetorical terms, it means the beginning of a sentence, line, or clause with the concluding, or any prominent,

---

scribes three days spent alone and essentially without food on the rocky ledges and in caves of Linga, a tiny island near Whalsay. In a personal interview (Brownsbank, Biggar, 24 June 1980), Mrs Grieve has said that the raised beach could be any one of many on those islands; still, this particular account gives some idea of the sort of experience MacDiarmid was undergoing, indeed cultivating, at the time.

word of the one preceding (*OED*).

Can any set of meanings possibly justify such a peculiar and difficult – some might say affected – display of vocabulary? Granted adequate attention, a careful paraphrase suggests that it can. That paraphrase might run something like this:

> Although the wayward and semi-random movements of imagination cannot be reined in, and thus will not avail to distill various perspectives into one intense, clear, unifying Truth, the 'enchorial characters' with which we at best approximate such expression are preferable to the still more obscure 'hieroglyphics' of Nature, which have nothing to say to human beings. 'Song', by which we seek to create sufficient beauty and meaning, is the distinctively human contribution to the cosmic order. It establishes our place in a circular reduplicative pattern in which everything from the tiniest sea creature (crinoid) to the heavens themselves must turn (entrochally), and death, which is the final term in any individual existence, is also the next term in a larger equation of perpetual change.

Let us look more closely for just one moment more, for the very peculiarity of the expression constitutes its genius. This poem is set on a raised beach, that is, a beach that was once under water but is now out of reach of tidal change, and thus reminds us of a time when the contours of the earth were different.[1] This stony beach, now so cold and dead, once lay under a sea as tropical as that on whose floor the living crinoids grew. Song (poetry, intellect, belief) – our living attempt to describe and interpret Nature – will itself become extinct; hence life, and its modes of expression, are an apprenticeship to fossildom (apprentice encrinites). As the poem said earlier, this truth 'gorgonizes'. In the closing lines, a dense crush of language and concept expresses that process: the same terms which earlier described the turning of heavenly spheres (1.232) now recall the wheel-like, calciferous plates of tiny fossils.

The poem thus concludes that language, which at the outset attempted to capture and explain life, is but another component of the process which is inexplicable. Rather than encircling life, our words (and by extension, concepts and creeds) become caught in life's circular motion. Thus the poem moves from meaning, 'above' life, to pattern/form, and places life within it; from a quest for paradise to a vision of eternity; from a redemption that is moral and personal to transformation that is impersonal and biological.

That accounts for the tension between theological and scientific

[1] See Roderick Watson, *Hugh MacDiarmid* (Open University Press, Unit 25, 1976), p.48.

language in the poem. It may also explain what might otherwise be thought a glaring weakness – excessive alliteration. In the final stanza, for instance, a long series of esoteric 'e's' (ébrillade, enchorial, encrinite, entrochal, epanadiplosis) conjures images of the dictionary falling open to a given page. Supposing this to be the case – MacDiarmid himself would neither deny it nor apologize for it – it may be that rather than start with a context and then evoke its significance, MacDiarmid instead builds a context out of chance – in this case, whatever words inhabit one page of a dictionary. It's an astonishing idea, and supports two observations: first, that he succeeds in fashioning a coherent and serviceable statement; second, that the process in this stanza recapitulates the theme of the entire poem, down to its final recapitulative term – epanadiplosis.

This discussion began by asserting that 'On A Raised Beach' deserves a place in modern poetry beside *The Waste Land*, Canto 47, and 'Sunday Morning'. That view must now be qualified. For while MacDiarmid's poem is as affecting in its own way, it is not so consistently and fully realized in poetic terms. In pursuing what I take to be the poem's main 'line', I have been obliged to overlook several lapses, an unevenness. First, there are a number of unnecessary repetitions, as in lines 180ff. Second, the poem's principal image is used in conflicting ways.

In most of 'On A Raised Beach', stone signifies 'the barren but beautiful reality', 'the hard fact' that human social life cannot digest or embody:

> These stones have the silence of supreme creative power
> (234)

> Their sole concern is that what can be shaken
> Shall be shaken and disappear
> And only the unshakeable be left.
> (174–7)

Personified in this way, the stones may be thought to function as pantheist symbols of the inhuman, antisocial divinity and permanence of Nature.

But in other sections of the poem, stones are introduced as models for human behaviour:

> It will be ever increasingly necessary to find
> In the interests of all mankind
> Men capable of rejecting all that all other men
>   Think, as a stone remains

> Essential to the world, inseparable from it,
>   And rejects all other life yet.
> Great work cannot be combined with surrender to the crowd.
>   (256–62)

The first examples stress how different we are, intrinsically, from stones (i.e. from nature); the last example proposes that we become more like them. Whereas the former lines define what every human being shares – the common deprivations that unite us – the latter *emulates* the stones, and seems almost to envy their isolation. Whatever one thinks of this conceptual position, the manner in which it is introduced creates confusion.

In short, within a sustained and powerful long poem there are several regrettable lapses of judgment. Of course, that is true of many long poems, including *The Waste Land* prior to Ezra Pound's editing. With that valuable collaboration in mind, it is worth noting that throughout his life MacDiarmid never submitted his work to such editing, never trusted any fellow poet enough to nurture the sort of collegial respect (among differences) that existed between Eliot and Pound, Williams and Stevens, Yeats and Synge.[1] To my mind, this represents a weakness of character which had unfortunate consequences for MacDiarmid's art.

Nevertheless, despite its lapses, or perhaps because of the isolation that fostered them, 'On A Raised Beach' possesses a total impact, an integrity as great as that of the more polished works with which I have grouped it. MacDiarmid's poem is bleak. Moreover, this bleakness is not endearing, quotable or artful. Indeed, the poem's genuine desolation accounts for its strength; compared with Eliot's Sanskrit in *The Waste Land*, and Stevens' romantic resolution of 'Sunday Morning', the close of MacDiarmid's poem is more of a piece with what precedes. Whether or not it is 'lesser' art, it coheres at least as successfully as a vision.

Without indulging in misrepresentation that could make the poem more palatable, it is nevertheless possible to state what 'vision' is affirmed. First, there is the capacity to stare nothing in the face, and *not* make anything of it, to realize that desolation is not the opposite or absence of Nature, but an integral aspect of it. Out of this perception arises a greater capacity to look upon *internal* desolation as a part of one's *own* nature . . . to give it its due. The feeling is akin to that in Pound's 'Δώρια':

---

[1] An exception may prove to be the influence of Francis George Scott on the shaping of *A Drunk Man* . . .

> Be in me as the eternal moods
>   of the bleak wind, and not
> As transient things are –
>   gaiety of flowers.
> Have me in the strong loneliness
>   of sunless cliffs
> And of grey waters.

While this mood appeals most to those for whom desolate landscapes exert attraction and compulsion, any reader can appreciate the courage that refuses to palliate and obfuscate painful vision, but rather keeps it raw, close to the bone. Learning to do so results – so the poet contends – not in 'ataraxia' or 'fatalism' (201–2), but rather in a 'spartan impassivity':

> . . . An emotion chilled is an emotion controlled;
> This is the road leading to certainty . . .
>
> The deadly clarity of this 'seeing of a hungry man'
> Only traces of a fever passing over my vision
> Will vary, troubling it indeed, but troubling it only
> In such a way that it becomes for a moment
> Superhumanly, menacingly clear . . .
>   (321–7)
>
> It is essential to know the chill of all the objections
> That can come creeping into the mind, the battle between opposing ideas
> Which gives the victory to the strongest and most universal
> Over all others, and to wage it to the end
> With increasing freedom, precision, and detachment,
> A detachment that shocks our instincts and ridicules our desires.
>   (125–33)

Here, I believe, is the most truly radical MacDiarmid, the 'lone eagle', doing and saying what he'll be most remembered for. Even while rejecting Scots Calvinist doctrine, MacDiarmid retains something of its temperament. He regards a 'direct line' to God as his due. In this respect, 'On A Raised Beach' is a thoroughly Calvinist document, a sermon of disbelief – but a sermon nevertheless. To some extent, all modern poetry begins with desolation. Where the Anglican Eliot turned to the ecclesiastic structures of institutional religion, and the aesthetically-inclined Stevens extended the fictive strategies of French Symbolism, for MacDiarmid the temperamental Scots Calvinist new faith required validation by new works. The new faith was the stoicism formulated in 'On A Raised Beach'. The new works were his politics and political poems.

MacDiarmid's overtly political writings often employ the same terms and ideas as his poems of desolation and plenitude, and may be seen to grow out of them. For example, words which describe the stones in 'On A Raised Beach' are repeated eight years later to characterize a communist's commitment:

> Their sole concern is that what can be shaken
> Shall be shaken and disappear
> And only the unshakeable be left.
>   ('On A Raised Beach')

> His purpose is that what can be shaken . . .
>   (Introduction to *The Fury of the Living*)

The words are nearly the same, with a subtle change of emphasis from 'concern' (passive and neutral) to 'purpose' (active, directed).

Similar continuities are evident in recurrent references to 'growing up'. One stanza of 'On A Raised Beach' begins:

> O we of little faith,
> As romanticists viewed the philistinism of their days
> As final and were prone to set over against it
> Infinite longing rather than manly will . . .

An earlier manuscript version began with what is now the second line;[1] by inserting the first, MacDiarmid transformed accusations of others into a judgment of his own tendencies. The spirit of 'infinite longing' (in lyrics like 'Poet's Pub') is now considered an 'immature' response through which one must pass on to 'adult' exertion. 'First Hymn to Lenin' extends this metaphor:

> Christ said, 'Save ye become as bairns again.'
> Bairnly eneuch the feck o' us ha' been!   *majority*
> Your work needs men; and its worst foes are juist
> The traitors wha through a' history ha' gi'en
> The dope that gar'd the mass o' folk pay heed   *compelled*
>   And bide bairns indeed.

In 'On A Raised Beach', MacDiarmid declares 'Here a man must shed the encumbrances that muffle / Contact with elemental things' and 'Here where there is neither hope nor hesitation / Something at least of the necessary power has entered into me'. In 'First Hymn to Lenin', he celebrates someone who not only confronted that elemental power, but also assimilated it to himself, and directed it to social ends:

[1] Hugh MacDiarmid papers, Edinburgh University Library, TS, Gen.887, fol.86.

I glimpse again in you, that mightier poo'er
Than fashes wi' the laurels and the bays   *troubles*
But kens that it is shared by ilka man
    Since time began . . .

If first things had had their richtfu' sway
Life and Thocht's misused po'oer micht ha' been ane
For a' men's benefit – as still they may
Noo that through you this mair than elemental force
    Has f'und a clearer course.

'First Hymn' begins by comparing Lenin to the 'Churchills, Locker-Lampsons, Beaverbrooks' who will be less to him 'in history's perspective' than the 'Centurions to Christ' and adds:

Christ's cited no' by chance or juist because
You mark the greatest turnin'-point since him
But that your main redress has lain where he's
Least use – fulfillin' his sayin' lang kcpt dim
That whasae followed him things o' like natur'
    'Ud dae – and greater ! . . .   *would do*

Great things ha'e aye ta'en great men in the past
In some proportion to the work they did,
But you alane to what you've dune are nocht
Even as the poo'ers to greater ends are hid
In what's ca'd God, or in the common man,   *called*
Withoot your plan.

The notion that religion is the opiate of the people hangs over this whole poem, and the lines just quoted suggest a process of substitution that MacDiarmid shares with many thirties leftist writers – 'History' for deity, 'historical determinism' for a determining God. Nevertheless, the righteous man remains he who makes himself servant of the 'greater poo'er'. Still reflecting his traditional religious upbringing, MacDiarmid (more than others) seems inclined to make Lenin Christ's *heir*, and it is tempting to view this effort as a facile translation of Presbytery into Politburo, session into communist cell.

But that is at best a partial truth which fails to take seriously the actions such changes call for. In terms of altered imperatives, the individual's responsibility shifts from comprehension to organization; from imitation of Christ (as in *A Drunk Man* and 'On A Raised Beach') to imitation of Lenin, a mortal who restrains individual longings in order to bring about material change.

Radical change depends on planning backed by force, and the greatest problem for a writer who advocates the former is to justify the latter. In 'First Hymn', MacDiarmid argues that force exerted not for individual advancement but in the name of a greater common end is legitimate. Indeed, one's willingness to employ distasteful means, to dirty one's hands, is what marks the emergence from 'bairnhood':

> For now in the flower and iron of the truth
> To you we turn; and turn in vain nae mair,
> Ilka fool has folly eneuch for sadness
> But at last we are wise and wi' laughter tear
> The veil of being, and are face to face
>   Wi' the human race.
>
> Here lies your secret, O Lenin, – yours and oors,
> No' in the majority will that accepts the result
> But in the real will that bides its time and kens
> The benmaist resolve is the poo'er in which we exult
> Since naebody's willingly deprived o' the good;
>   And least o' a', the crood!

Unlike the poet and thinker, who as individuals are also ready for adulthood, the Lenin figure projects his mature vision over the whole field of human affairs. He pulls the entire society along with him, out of its primitive (or infantile) stage, leading them by his 'real' will into 'the good'.

Several responses to this view are possible. First of all, Plato's point (which the penultimate line misrepresents) was that though all men take what they themselves desire to be the good, it may not in fact be so; certitude (whether Calvinist or Bolshevik) does not prove rectitude. Second, with the benefit of hindsight, one must say that the 'real will' MacDiarmid admires brought precious little cause for 'laughter' where it was most efficiently exerted: in the USSR and Nazi Germany. And third, is there not something alarming in this sudden willingness to define an 'elect' after twenty years' opposition to such concepts?

On the other hand, it is crucial to consider MacDiarmid's view in 'First Hymn' in the context of its time. This poem was written in 1931. Like many intellectuals early in the decade, MacDiarmid had become enthralled with social *planning*. Compared with the deepening British economic collapse, and apparent inability of the National Government to arrest it, and based on information that was then available, Soviet social reorganization struck many as the one example of progressive change to have emerged from the Great War. For MacDiarmid personally, such 'reasoned planning' offered both a way to redress political injustice *and* an intellectual response to the issues of multiplicity and fragmentation. The two can be seen to come together in lines such as these:

> Today we are breaking up the chaste
> Ever-deceptive phenomena of Nature
> And re-assembling them according to our will.

Three years before the Reichstag fire and the first purge trials, six years before Guernica, some still found it possible to differentiate 'good' violence from 'bad', to believe that terror could be directed and contained. 'It is now or never, the hour of the knife / The break with the past, the major operation', said a Day-Lewis poem. And those of like mind said if there must be violence, let it be that of birth.

In modern times, the most pervasive example of controlled violence is the engine, the machine. On the one hand (as in Auden's *Poems 1930*), the machine stood for industrial wreck, the stagnation and paralysis of the 'old Society'. But on the other, it was also thought to provide the material basis for a new society. Moreover, as an example of a high degree of organization directed toward a common end, the machine could also be made to stand as a metaphor for rational social organization.[1] For many, the central issue was thus how to make the machine serve man, not *vice versa*. That is the subject of 'The Seamless Garment'.

Like many of MacDiarmid's political poems, 'The Seamless Garment' is spoken *to* someone, in this case not the leader of a revolution, but the ordinary worker whom that revolution claims to serve. The poem employs examples from mill work to expound a Marxist theory of labour in terms that the labourer will understand. This effort to state what one believes in simple yet accurate and appropriate terms deserves praise in itself; the resulting poem is beautifully achieved, thanks to its relaxed, colloquial Scots and the clarity of its central image:

[1] In this respect, it is interesting to wonder if, while turning away from nineteenth-century capitalism, twentieth-century Marxists were not also returning from nineteenth-century romanticism to mechanistic / rationalistic models more common in the eighteenth century. Certainly some of them thought so.

You are a cousin of mine
   Here in the mill.
It's queer that born in the Langholm
   It's no' until
Juist noo I see what it means
To work in the mill like my freen's.

I was tryin' to say something
   In a recent poem
Aboot Lenin. You've read a guid lot
   In the news – but ken the less o'm?   *of him*
Look, Wullie, here is his secret noo
In a way I can share it wi' you.

His secret and the secret o' a'
   That's worth ocht.
The shuttles fleein' owre quick for my een
   Prompt the thocht,
And the coordination atween
   Weaver and machine.

The haill shop's dumfoonderin'   *bewildering*
   To a stranger like me.
Second nature to you; you're perfectly able
   To think, speak and see
Apairt frae the looms, tho' to some
That doesna sae easily come.

A poem by John Singer, whom MacDiarmid admired, declares,
'Do not fear the machine, fear rather / The machine in yourself'. In
a similar vein, the 'coordination' MacDiarmid posits echoes two
tenets of Marxist theory: first, that only by mastering the means of
production will the masses no longer be limited by, or subservient
to, them; second, that just as 'primitive accumulation' provides the
necessary basis for social and cultural advance, so making necessary work habitual ('second nature') frees the individual for higher
things. When the worker is not alienated from his labour – so the
argument runs – the same care and quality he directs toward menial
tasks will extend to the 'higher thoughts' for which they free him:

Are you equal to life as to the loom?
   Turnin' oot shoddy, or what?
Claith better than man? D'ye live to the full   *cloth*
   Your poo'er's a' deliverly taught?   *continually*
Or scamp a' thing else? Border claith's famous
   Shall things o' mair consequence shame us?

As we might expect, 'The Seamless Garment' praises Lenin's ability to extend the organization and skill which runs mills onto a larger scale. More surprisingly – and this is where MacDiarmid is consistently more interesting than hack 'proletarian' writers – it equates Lenin's efforts with those of his equal in a very different realm:

> A poet like Rilke did the same
>> In a different sphere,
> Made a single reality – a' a'e 'oo –   *all one wool*
>> O' his love and pity and fear;
> A seamless garment o' music and thought . . .
>
> Lenin and Rilke baith gied still mair skill,
>> Coopers o' Stobo, to a greater concern   *[experts]*
> Than you devote to claith in the mill.
>> Wad it be ill to learn
> To keep a bit eye on their looms as weel
> And no' be hailly ta'en up wi' your 'tweel?[1]   *wholly*

The hope of the future is for people to cultivate in themselves the integrity which now exists in their products – not to reject modern life, but to make their social organization as advanced and as rational as their technology:

> The womenfolk ken what I mean.
>> Things maun fit like a glove,
> Come clean off the spoon – and syne
>> There's time for life and love.
> The mair we mak' natural as breathin' the mair
> Energy for ither things we'll can spare,
>> But as lang as we bide like this
> Neist to naething we ha'e, or miss.   *next*

The contrast between this poem and MacDiarmid's of the twenties is evident in the writing as well as the subject. 'The Seamless Garment' is so tightly, finely worked out as to seem disarming. And the poem is, to use MacDiarmid's own phrase, 'clean and clear'. But is it 'exact'? I think not. For, as Iain Crichton Smith suggests, the same factors that organize it limit it. What coheres so well as a structure succeeds as just that – a structure which never breaks out of its formulaic frame.[2] Having begun with Lenin, and moved on

---

[1] Cloth in which only threads at set *intervals* are interwoven; fig. texture or structure, pattern.
[2] 'The Golden Lyric', in Duncan Glen, ed., *Hugh MacDiarmid: A Critical Survey* (Edinburgh and London: Scottish Academic Press, 1972), p.127.

to challenge, 'Are you helpin? Machinery's improved, but folk?',
the poem concludes not with a call to revolution, or even (as in
Waiting For Lefty) to 'strike', but rather by merely affirming that
all good work has 'integrity':

> And as for me in my fricative work
>   I ken fu' weel
> Sic an integrity's what I maun ha'e,
>   Indivisible, real,
> Woven owre close for the point o' a pin
>   Onywhere to win in.

While the idea is fine, there is nothing in it as expressed that
requires a Marxist-Leninist view; indeed, the conclusion is hardly
distinguishable from Ruskin's argument (in *The Stones of Venice*)
that work should be judged by what it requires of the worker.

What accounts for this anti-climax? In part, the poem's setting.
For despite its mills, its power looms and class distinctions (which
MacDiarmid explored in a story, 'The Waterside Folk'), Langholm remains to this day a bucolic small town a world away from
the mass industrial and political conflict of Lenin's Petersburg,
Rosa Luxembourg's Berlin – or the Glasgow of John MacLean.
Not surprisingly, the least successful line in 'The Seamless Garment' is that which interjects the rhetoric of one milieu into the
other: 'Hundreds to the inch the threids lie in, Like men in a
communist cell'. Conversely, it is when the writing captures the
local flavour most closely (in the penultimate stanza), that the
anti-climax sets in. In short, we are faced with some sort of dis-
parity between author and audience. If radical revolution has
become MacDiarmid's faith, and political organizing its necessary
works, then 'The Seamless Garment' can be read as parable/ser-
mon for an unsophisticated rural congregation. Neither the fire
and brimstone of Clydeside rhetoric nor the doctrinal disputes of
Edinburgh are allowed to intrude. Here, for the first time, one
finds MacDiarmid limiting his own sense of complexity, simplify-
ing, toning down in deference to an audience, and a cause.

But not for long! Between 1930 and 1934, the pressure of events
would require a more detailed and articulated response. In those
years the economic situation deteriorated sharply, hitting hardest
where people were always poor – industrial Scotland, Southeast
Wales, Cumberland, the Tyneside, Birmingham. Though the job-
less rate in some districts (Jarrow, for instance) ran as high as 80

per cent, Britain was the only Western nation that did not adopt a policy of budget deficits to ease mass unemployment. Instead, the Government reduced expenditures on roads and education and relief. Hunger spread. When the Means Test was introduced, consumption of baked goods in Glasgow immediately fell by two-thirds. Meanwhile food was being dumped to shore up prices.[1]

Politically, the results of the October 1931 General Election could be read in the *Daily Express* headline, SOCIALISTS WIPED OUT. The same paper had been calling for an 'Empire Crusade' while the *Daily Mail* voiced enthusiastic support for German and Italian fascism. If for liberals the entrenchment of the National Government made effective parliamentary change seem hopeless, abroad the collapse of Weimar dissipated dreams of rational, tolerant solutions. As a response to Hitler, the 'Peace Pledge Movement' gave 'peace' a dirty name – and motivated its opponents toward militancy. In his widely-read *The Coming Struggle For Power* (1932), John Strachey wrote, 'We may leave such people to enjoy their tiny pleasures and comforts, for these will not remain long to them. They will find that in shrinking from the agony of birth they have chosen the agony of death'.[2]

In so increasingly polarized a climate, pressure upon writers to take sides increased. The movement toward 'socialist realism' was international, signalled in America by Granville Hicks' 'The Crisis in Criticism' (*New Masses*, 1933) and in Russia itself by the Soviet Writers Conference of 1934. Paradoxically, however, the call to make writing programmatic made the serious writer's response more problematic. For him, being a communist could no longer mean merely applying new tools of analysis (or prophecy); it now required re-evaluating, possibly renouncing, lifelong habits of feeling. Among the 'Auden group' one safety-valve for such internal pressures was ironical public school humour. By 1933, that movement had already become, according to one view, 'political in general intention' but 'religious in tone, and literary in its manifestations'.[3]

MacDiarmid's own class background and means of livelihood were more of a piece with his political sympathies, and in the

---

[1] Fenner Brockway, *Hungry England* (London: Gollancz, 1932), p.189. Food dumping is the subject of Auden's poem 'Hearing of Harvests'.
[2] Quoted by Julian Symons, *The Thirties (A Dream Revolved)*, 2nd ed. (London: Faber, 1975), p.51.
[3] Samuel Hynes, *The Auden Generation* (London: Bodley Head, 1976), p.112.

'Second Hymn to Lenin' (1934), he still sought to affirm that poetry and revolution are compatible. Nevertheless, because it addresses the role of the artist in particular, 'Second Hymn' is less public a poem than its predecessor, and unlike 'First Hymn', it airs ideological contradictions from the start:

> Ah, Lenin, you were richt. But I'm a poet . . .

The half-dozen 'buts' and 'yets' that follow suggest that the criteria for judging politics and art may be different after all; whereas the former must be ruthlessly singleminded, the latter cannot. As MacDiarmid wrote in 'Whuchulls':

> The poet hauds nae brief for ony kind,
> Age, place, or range o' sense, and no' confined
> To ony nature can share Creation's insteed. . . .
>
> Poetry isna some
> Society for Preservin' Threatened Types,
> But strokes a cat or fiddles on its tripes,
> And for inclusions or exclusions, fegs,
> Needna apologize while a'e bird's eggs
> Are plain, anither's speckled, beasts ha'e legs,
> Birds wings, . . .

In 'Second Hymn' this defence of art becomes one side of an internal debate:

> For a poet maun see in a' thing,
> Ev'n what looks trumpery or horrid,
> A subject equal to ony
> – A star for the forehead!
>
> A poet has nae choice left
> Betwixt Beaverbrook, say, and God,
> Jimmy Thomas or you,
> A cat, carnation, or clod.
>
> He daurna turn awa' frae ocht
> For a single act o' neglect
> And straucht he may fa' frae grace   *straight*
> And be void o' effect.

The other side of this debate responds that despite the necessary bread of poetry's subjects, its effects are insignificantly narrow:

> Great poets hardly anybody kens o'?
> Geniuses like a man talkin' t'm sel'? . . .

They're nocht but romantic rebels
Strikin' dilettante poses;
Trotsky – Christ, no' wi' a croon o' thorns
But a wreath o' paper roses.

A' that's great is free and expansive.
What ha' they expanded tae?
They've affected nocht but a fringe
O' mankind in ony way.

Barbarian saviour o' civilization
Hoo weel ye kent (we're owre dull witted)
Naething is dune save as we ha'e
Means to en's transparently fitted.

In these lines, MacDiarmid is trying to give both sides their due. It is this openness to 'the chill of all objections / That come creeping into the mind, the battle between opposing ideas' ('On A Raised Beach') that makes 'Second Hymn' a more vital poem than 'First Hymn' or 'The Seamless Garment'.[1]

Having defined the issues dialectically, 'Second Hymn' seeks to reconcile the opposing views by making that dialectic *temporal*, a matter of transition over time. In effect it posits a sequential change:

1) 'bairnly poetry': inadequate, rooted in fragmentary, 'bourgeois' sensibility;

2) 'politics': as first expression of integral thought (cf. 'The Seamless Garment'); social re-organization;

3) an outward expansion of such wholeness, integrity from the lesser (albeit necessary) realm of politics to the greater, subsuming realm of free thought, art. Thus:

Poetry like politics maun cut
The cackle and pursue real ends,
Unerringly as Lenin, and to that
Its nature better tends.

---

[1] Ironically, the dialectical tensions to which this poem owes its integrity are often ignored by those who seek in it confirmation of their own political stance. For instance, in their oversimple introduction to *The Socialist Poems of Hugh MacDiarmid* (London: Routledge, 1978) – which includes such 'socialist' poems as 'Crowdieknowe' and 'To Hell Wi' Happiness' – T. S. Law and Thurso Berwick quote the line I've cited as 'saviour of civilization' and by omitting the appellation 'barbarian' reduce a crucial poetic insight to cant. See p.xvii.

Wi' Lenin's vision equal poet's gift
And what unparalleled force was there!
Nocht in a' literature wi' that
Begins to compare.

Nae simple rhymes for silly folk
But the haill art, as Lenin gied
Nae Marx-without-tears to workin' men
But the fu' course insteed.

Despite the earlier jeer at Trotsky, the view that art and politics will converge at a future time has much in common with that of *Literature and Revolution*. Trotsky, it will be recalled, distinguished literature *of* the revolution (which he couldn't value) from literature that would be written *after* it. Instead of the coarse 'socialist realism' which Stalin later enforced, he foresaw a transitional revolutionary literature grounded in 'bourgeois' culture which would gradually give way not to 'proletarian' culture, but to 'socialist' (i.e. classless) culture:

> As the conditions for cultural creation will become more favourable, the proletariat will be more and more dissolved into a socialist community and will free itself from its class characteristics and thus cease to be a proletariat. . . . The cultural reconstruction, which will begin when the need of the iron clutch of a dictatorship unparalleled in history will have disappeared, will not have a class character. . . . The proletariat acquires power for the purpose of doing away forever with class culture and to make way for human culture.
>
> Engels spoke of the socialist revolution as a leap from the kingdom of necessity to the kingdom of freedom.[1]

This same desire to pass beyond necessity permeates MacDiarmid's 'Second Hymn':

> Oh it's nonsense, nonsense, nonsense,
> Nonsense at this time o' day
> That breid-and-butter problems
> S'ud be in ony man's way . . .
>
> We're grown-up folk that haena yet
> Put bairnly things aside
> – A' that's material and moral –
> And oor new state descried.

The sentiment is moving. Unfortunately, 'bairnly' as material

---

[1] Leon Trotsky, 'Literature and Revolution', in Paul N. Siegel, ed., *Leon Trotsky on Literature and Art* (New York: Pathfinder Press, 1970), pp.42, 60.

inequities and their deferred solutions are, they remain very much with us – and the dismissive ease with which this poem leaps beyond them to 'human culture' in the Marxist 'kingdom of freedom' is too facile. If the process MacDiarmid foresees were a chemical equation, it would read:

$$\begin{matrix} \text{bairnly poetry} \\ (\text{material, moral}) \end{matrix} + \begin{matrix} \text{politics} \\ (\text{adult}) \end{matrix} \xrightarrow{\text{revolution}} \text{'mature art'}$$

with present art and politics as reagents, revolution as catalyst, and spiritual growth (expressed in art) as product. The equation, alas, is not balanced. It ignores the respective valences of politics and art, omits by-products, and, by treating revolution as a catalyst, denies that the revolution itself may grow corrupt in process: 'Stalin is the Lenin of Today'.

Thus, when 'Second Hymn' addresses the succession from Leninist control to 'human culture' and 'mature art' (analogous to withering of the state), it does so in a highly romantic image revived from *A Drunk Man Looks at the Thistle*:

> You confined yoursel' to your work
> – A step at a time;
> But, as the loon is in the man,
> That'll be ta'en up i' the rhyme,
>
> Ta'en up like a pool in the sands
> Aince the tide rows in,
> When life opens its hert and sings
> Withoot scruple or sin.

The ability to abstract and romanticize historical struggle raises thorny questions indeed. Is MacDiarmid now so much the ideologue that he won't take account of the empirical facts, the totalitarian means and motives that belie the professed ideals? Or worse, is he so much the hardened party man that he *knows* the flesh and blood consequences yet believes that his theory of history makes them relatively insignificant? Politics is the art of the present, and the group, neither of which MacDiarmid ever seemed especially at ease with. Does the level of abstraction and rhetorical high-mindedness perhaps invalidate this writing as *political* statement altogether?

The last conclusion is supported by a number of pronouncements MacDiarmid made in various contexts. For instance,

> As a Socialist, of course, I am, it should be obvious, interested only in
> a very subordinate way in the politics of socialism as a political

theory; my real concern with socialism is as an artist's organized approach to the interdependencies of life.[1]

Mr. Singer, in other words, is a poet of 'Mental Fight' in William Blake's sense of the phrase, a Communist of that only authentic kind . . . of whom it has been rightly said that it would be better to call them 'Mentalists' instead of 'Materialists'.[2]

I do not believe in – or in the desirability of – any 'likemindedness', any 'common purpose', any 'ultimate objective' but simply in 'life and that more abundantly', in the lifting of all suppressions and thwarting agencies. *My communism in this sense is purely Platonic*. I am as all poets and dynamic spirits must be – purely 'irrational'. (The emphasis is on the 'purely'.)[3]

In short, we are back to Shestov (pp.78–9), only now the inconsistency which in 1926 was declared a prerogative of individual freedom is being extended into the public sphere, with inadequate regard for its different consequences. We might well ask what an 'artist's organized approach' to the purge trials would entail, or how a 'purely Platonic' Communist views Russian treatment of the POUM in Spain. Coming in 1936, 1939, and 1942, the statements just quoted have an air of never-never land about them. Doesn't MacDiarmid know that in the sort of dictatorship he advocates, 'mentalists' are – and were – the first to go?

The answer is yes, he does. What seems a maddening contradiction in his desires can perhaps be understood (if not justified) by returning to the notion of temporal sequence in 'Second Hymn'. We have seen that MacDiarmid, like Trotsky, distinguishes literature written during and for a revolution from that produced by people who have come through revolution – and places his hope in the latter. But whereas Trotsky envisages a future in which art will express widely accepted truths and limit itself to formal experiment, MacDiarmid believes that the essence of art is and must remain to challenge the accepted notions of *any* time: 'Nae Marx withoot tears to workin' men, But the fu' course instead'. MacDiarmid frequently quoted Thomas Hardy's 'Literature is the written expression of revolt against accepted things'.[4] The best case for MacDiarmid's position at this time can in fact be found in

---

[1] *Lucky Poet*, p.241.
[2] Introd., John Singer, *The Fury of the Living* (Glasgow: William McClellan, 1942), p.iii.
[3] C. M. Grieve in *New Scotland* (Alba Nuadh), No.27, Vol.1 (2 May 1936).
[4] *Lucky Poet*, pp.67, 232.

T. S. Eliot's review of V. F. Calverton's *The Liberation of American Art*:

> I should suppose it desirable that every country shall provide an environment in which its best minds flourish; it also seems desirable that these best minds should come to terms with their environment; but it is also possible that some amount of maladaptation is desirable... But the spectacle of the individual in conflict with the dominant tendencies and prejudices of his time, and consequently that of the individual in conflict with the dominant prejudices and tendencies of the coming time, does not influence critics like Mr. Calverton in favour of the individual....
>
> There are also people who, while recognizing the interest of the work of literature as a document upon the ideas and the sensibility of its epoch, and recognizing even that the permanent work of literature is one which does not lack this interest, yet cannot help valuing literary work, like philosophical work, in the end by its transcendence of the limits of its age, and by its speaking, in the language of its time and in the imagery of its own tradition, the word which belongs to no time. Art, we feel, aspires to the condition of the timeless; and Communist art, according to the sentence of those who foretell what it is to be, is bound to the temporal.[1]

Hugh MacDiarmid certainly aspired to the timeless. That is why the latter half of 'Second Hymn' insists that if or when it comes to a choice, the poet's first loyalty is to the latter:

> Unremittin', relentless,
> Organized to the last degree,
> Ah, Lenin, politics is bairns' play
> To what this maun be!

The same independent, insistently long-range thinking that led MacDiarmid to praise Lenin in 'First Hymn' and 'The Seamless Garment' requires, by 1934, that he demur even in the act of praise. From our vantage point, it may be hard to separate 'pure' Marxism from the regimes into which it has most often degenerated in practice. It may disturb us that MacDiarmid too easily overlooks the means and motives of totalitarianism; curiously, his quarrel is less with the *process* of securing power than with the nature of that control once it has been consolidated. For however much organization appeals to him in the abstract (at whatever abstract cost), his own deepest loyalties and instincts remain individual, libertarian, anarchic.

[1] T. S. Eliot, 'A Commentary', in *The Criterion* XII (1932-3), pp.247-8.

'Better a'e gowden lyric / Than a social problem solved', Mac-Diarmid wrote in a lyric of a few years before. By the mid-thirties, other leftist writers – even the most publicly strident – may have shared this inclination. But whereas in many it was concealed, repressed, or at best revealed obliquely – in cliquish reticence or schoolboy codes – MacDiarmid in 'Second Hymn to Lenin' kept his own priorities clear, and had the courage to declare them.

To insist on priorities is not, of course, to abandon sympathies. Quite apart from theoretical considerations, MacDiarmid's 'gut' sympathies were unshakeably radical-egalitarian, opposed to the British class system and its underlying economics. Throughout the thirties, dozens of his smaller – smaller *and lesser* – poems convey these sentiments, and MacDiarmid's reputation probably owes more to the tone of such poems than to the content of those we have just examined. This is regrettable, because they fall far short of the standard set by the best of his own poetic work and his critical pronouncements.

Along with the view of literature's purpose ascribed to Hardy, MacDiarmid was fond of quoting this statement by Ford Madox Ford: 'The only human activity that has always been of extreme importance to the world is imaginative literature . . . because it is the only means by which humanity can express at once emotions and ideas'.[1] Turning to the 'short range' poems with this in mind, one notes in fact a distinct *separation* of emotions and ideas; one wonders in what sense this writing is imaginative at all. Consider some representative titles: 'Why I Choose Red', 'The End of Usury', 'The Belly Grip', 'To Nearly Everybody in Europe To-day', 'Reflections in an Ironworks', '. . . *In* the Slaughterhouse', '*In* the Slums of Glasgow'. Such titles reflect an impulse less literary (as traditionally conceived) than 'documentary'.

For many artists of the thirties, intensifying political fervour was dogged by a sense of personal inadequacy arising from the purported irrelevance of intellectual work to the crises afflicting the masses. One way to bridge this gap was to redirect one's verbal talents toward analysis and exposition of social ills. This impulse led in the US to WPA anthologies (one entitled *Stuff*), strike literature, the photographic prose of *Let Us Now Praise Famous Men*, and (later) to the sentiment of William Carlos Williams' phrase,

[1] Quoted by Arthur Leslie [pseud.], 'The Politics and Poetry of Hugh MacDiarmid', 1925; rpt. in *Selected Essays of Hugh MacDiarmid* (London: Jonathan Cape, 1969), p.24.

'No ideas but in things'.[1] In Britain the same impulse is evident in the definite articles of Audenesque verse, the Left Book Club, the Unity Theatre, and the Mass Observation Movement. Out of such artistic reorientation arose a sense not equalled before or since that intellectuals as a *group* might gain access to power. In the US this can be dated precisely to the Sacco-Vanzetti Case and culminates in the great strikes of the CIO, while those who sought action in Britain found it, and lost it, in Spain.

The dual movement towards documentary detail and expressions of personal engagement is increasingly evident in MacDiarmid's short poems. What the infinite striations, tesserae, faculae are to 'On A Raised Beach', the ironworks, slaughterhouses, slums of the short range work are to the doctrine of 'The Seamless Garment': substantiating evidence – multiplicitous, objective, documentary:

> I am with the New Writers who waste no words
> On manifestoes but are getting down
> To the grim business of documentation.
> Not seeking a short cut to the universal
> But with all their energies concentrated
> On gaining access to the particular.

The intention, at least, was clear.

What resulted is another matter. How conspicuously words are wasted in this manifesto against waste and manifestoes! Here 'the particular' is a concept, as are 'the local', 'the vernacular', 'a changing conception of culture', 'a multiplication of regionalisms', and 'interesting and beautiful facts' in the lines that follow. Indeed, the entire thirty-three line poem does not contain a single concrete thing, a single image to indicate time or place.

Some of the shorter poems in *Scots Unbound* and *First Hymn*, and most in *Second Hymn*, share this deficiency. Over and over we are faced with this sort of thing:

> Only by the severest intellectual discipline
> Can one of the bourgeois intelligentsia win
> Up to the level of the proletariat
> On this side of the grave or that
> – The only goal worth aiming at . . .

[1] For a valuable extended treatment of this phenomenon, see William Stott, *Documentary Expression and Thirties America* (New York: Oxford University Press, 1973). See especially chapters 2, 3 and 4.

> There's no time to be arch
> On the revolutionary march . . .

> I am organically welded with the manual workers . . .

> For no religion, no form of government
>   Has ever had any sanction except
> Brute needs ruthlessly taken advantage of
>   And these science has now triumphantly o'erlept.

Many of these poems ('The Belly Grip', 'Etika Preobrazhennavo Erosa') are pedantic, brittle. Some are counterproductively strident – 'John MacLean', for instance. In some, such as 'Song Of the New Economics', an attempt at humour misses. In others, abstractness makes for ludicrous departures from common sense: prostitutes are 'greater' than wives and mothers because they serve 'nae man, but Man'; 'cancer, by crikey, kens nae compromise'. One senses MacDiarmid skimming his shallows rather than plumbing his depths; stance follows stance, each incomplete. The real excitement that derives in *A Drunk Man*, 'Whuchulls', or 'Second Hymn', from an engagement that risks the whole self, yields to the inverted complacency of anger. There is no exploration and hence no learning going on in these short political poems. They are proclamations, applause lines. That is why despite the charged rhetoric they lack process: they fail to *move* in either sense of the word.

We should be clear that our quarrel is not with the subject, content, or in most cases the sentiment of MacDiarmid's short range poems. There is truth in his remark (in 'Poetry and Propaganda') that 'any utterance that is not pure / Propaganda is impure propaganda for sure'. But a similar statement can be made about poetic style. In renouncing a 'literary' for a 'political' bias, MacDiarmid does not win free of mannerism; he merely trades one manner for another, becoming when least mannerly, most mannered. Where a poem fails, it is not because it is 'political', but because it is poorly written. And the failures that occur are largely failures of language.

As the examples of Milton, Donne, Pope, Wordsworth, and Pound suggest, a true revolution in thought entails a corresponding revolution of style. Similarly, as Auden's poems became more radical, he increasingly deleted connectives, added definite articles and injected syntactical oddities. But with MacDiarmid, as with Soviet 'socialist realists', the more self-consciously 'modern' his political ideas became, the more old-fashioned the forms in which they were cast.

The same can be said of his diction in the shorter political poems. These lack the accurate satiric detail of English leftist verse[1] and depend to a growing extent on automatic responses that certain code words might elicit at a meeting of the Left Book Club. Even invective – of which MacDiarmid is normally a master – grows uninventive: 'cheats', 'murderers', 'swindlers', 'ruthless', 'gross stupidity', and so forth. In a letter of 1934, Ezra Pound insisted to MacDiarmid that in poetry language cannot succumb to ideology. One wishes MacDiarmid had more consistently heeded his friend's advice.[2]

Flawed language allows flawed thought. In the group of poems presently under discussion, three tendencies suggest a parallel decline. First, there is the blithe rhetorical acceptance of mass terror. Second, there is a willingness to overlook undesired evidence, as when MacDiarmid compares – unfavourably – the fate of Scottish culture in Britain with that of minorities in the Soviet Union.[3] Nor can one plead ignorance; in 1951 he repeated the claim, which he added is confirmed by 'leading Soviet writers': Alexei Sutkov, Paolo Tychina, Konstantin Simonov. (Mandelstam, Pasternak, Solzshenitsyn *et al.* were apparently not available for interviews.[4]) And third, there is a willingness to idealize which suggests not a poetry of fact, but of ideology. Consider:

Personality crushed out? Slaves to machines?
What personality ever had they then? . . .

. . . Let poetlings moan
About primroses and skylarks and the Lord knows what;
Not the matters of crucial concern to most folk
Any poet worth a rap would be hammering at.

[1] For further discussion, see Watson, p.39ff.
[2] Letter from Ezra Pound to Hugh MacDiarmid, dated '7 Dec. Anno XII' [sic]. Hugh MacDiarmid papers, Edinburgh University Library (not yet numbered). In another respect, one might wish MacDiarmid were *further* from Pound's example. 'Etika Preobrazhennavo Erosa' includes such lines as: 'Bunches of hams and shysters / With all the fat thumb business / And a Yiddishkeit crunch . . .' While MacDiarmid's work is generally free of the anti-semitism and various racisms that infect the work of so many British writers of the time, and these lines are thus atypical, it is nevertheless important to note them – if for no other reason than as a warning that the type of coarse stance which sanctions inaccurate language and thought in poetry opens the door to far worse in other realms.
[3] *New Scotland* (Alba Nuadh), No.10, Vol.1 (14 December 1935).
[4] Arthur Leslie, p.29.

The only poet of value Glasgow ever had, Livingstone,
Knew better – he sang not of himself but of a cause,
Not of personal ambition, regret, disillusionment,
And held in contempt the weak yearnings of love,
Concerned with great historical forces . . .
    In Glasgow
Something infinitely more worth seeing can be found
In crank-heads flashing rhythmically between
Twin columns hiding flying crossroads and thrusting silver rods;
The starboard shaft oiled and shining in the blaze of the electric lights
Turning its eighty revolutions a minute. My sympathies
Are with the workers, not the country clods.
    ('Personalities and the Machine Age')

'Country clods'? From the man who wrote 'Crowdieknowe',
'Cattle Show', 'The Crying of the Fair', 'Milk-Wort and Bog-
Cotton'? How can this be accounted for? In part as a need to
idealize for ideological aims. Responding to this poem, a factory
worker wrote in to *New Scotland* in 1936. Noting first of all that
Lenin wanted women freed from the dull, oppressive, 'unproduct-
ive work of the home, in order to work in the factory', the correspondent questions which is really more dehumanizing. He adds,
'Whatever Lenin's experience of the home, he certainly had none
of the modern factory. And neither, as far as I know, had Hugh
MacDiarmid', and concludes that whoever owns the machines, the
tedious work of those who run them will not change. After sixteen
years in a factory, the correspondent says, he has yet to be inspired
by 'thrusting silver rods'.[1]

Moreover, even if MacDiarmid believes his own Stakhanovite
mythology of the Worker, that does not explain why he must
denigrate the countryman, why strength must be the opposite of
tenderness, why 'great historical' forces necessarily invalidate the
'yearnings of love'. To understand the source of such rigid dichotomies (from one whose lifelong habit had been to break them
down), we must acknowledge something deeper going on. To
borrow the psychological term, it is *compensation*, an effort to prove
that he is what he never was, and to write accordingly. The result,
in the worst of such poems, is a distortion of personality.

As so many of his poems make clear, the man possessed an

[1] 'G.H.', 'Personality and the Machine Age for Hugh MacDiarmid',
in *New Scotland* (Alba Nuadh), No.24, Vol.1 (21 March 1936). As one
who has spent a little time beneath the 'oiled starboard shaft' of a
modern ship, I too am impatient with MacDiarmid's strained raptures.

admirable sensitivity towards women and children. Those who knew him declare without exception that the man's gentleness, consideration, indeed shyness, contrasted markedly with the public and poetic stance of fire-eater. Add to this his slight physical stature, his reputation as a 'mama's boy' which he himself alludes to in *Lucky Poet*, and his hospitalization for nervous collapse in the early thirties, and one source of the intermittent attempt at machismo grows apparent. In poems where he regards his own sensitivity as an inadequacy (instead of the virtue that it is), thought gets divorced from the feeling, and what results rings hollow.

No poet was ever more drawn to the long view than Hugh MacDiarmid. But as Edmund Wilson remarked in 'Marxism and Literature', long-view writing is the sort least tolerated by totalitarian forms of government. Thus, where, possibly trying to prove himself, MacDiarmid embarks on short-view poems, one senses deliberate self-constriction. The resulting anger (not vision) confirms MacDiarmid's own point in 'Second Hymn to Lenin' that whatever the virtues of will in politics, it cannot displace imagination in art.

Finally, MacDiarmid himself was not an urban man; by temperament, upbringing, and lifestyle, he was a product and spokesman (albeit an eccentric one) of small town Scotland – Langholm, Montrose, Biggar. Beneath the political anger of many of the Glasgow poems and of 'Third Hymn to Lenin' lies an instinctive distaste for urban life – for its confinement, regimentation, and relative sensory deprivation. In spite of their theoretical stances, what these poems make clear is that MacDiarmid the man had little sympathy for, or sense of belonging to, an urban proletariat. His urban poems have little interest in the human landscape such as one finds in Fergusson, Baudelaire, or William Carlos Williams. And there is something curiously enervating about the lack of sensory detail, the abstraction from surroundings, which is quite at odds with the image of the busy comrade-poet. Conversely, his poems grounded in images of nature and rural Scotland are the most affecting; instead of a displaced (almost disembodied) poet, we hear a man speaking with a voice entirely his own.

It may seem odd, after having considered so many complex issues, to arrive at so simple a dichotomy. Yet this is the sort of judgment that most existing MacDiarmid criticism shrinks from, and precisely what is needed to assess properly so complex a figure. The distinction has led us to dismiss certain poems on which

MacDiarmid's popular reputation rests. It may also help us identify just what they lack, and extend our search for it in another direction.

What the work thus far addressed does not provide is the middle ground of day-to-day experience and personal relations. That cannot come from facing Death on solitary beaches, nor from 'Talking With Five Thousand People in Edinburgh' (the title of a poem). It must come from knowing not only what one believes, but also where one *belongs*. As has been seen, MacDiarmid faced internal conflict between two identities: freethinking individualist rebel and/or representative voice, still bearing the crown o' roses, with Scotland followin' on ahint as on Common Riding Day. On the one hand, the busy urban poetry could not resolve this inner conflict; rather, it evades or denies it, and the strain implicit in that denial may explain why some poems are so hyper-masculine and excessively controlled. On the other, poems such as 'On The Ocean Floor' do connect imagination and political conviction; in them the will to organize and the capacity to wonder coincide.

Even so, to achieve this synthesis the poet must 'chill' and 'control' emotion, and the end result can be too exclusively rational: 'spiritual issues / made inhumanly clear'. For all its clarity and style, the voice which contemplates communal fates can be markedly aloof. The resolution it provides is grand, but incomplete, externalized, abstract – the kind that may precede a fuller and more satisfying integration. We must seek for that fullness where the poet addresses his non-representative existence: not in the seamless garment but the seams, the rag-and-bone shop of *his* heart.

CHAPTER FIVE

'And Draw it to Me'

. . . To be able to see the portal of literature, that is to say: the portal of the imagination, as a scene of normal love and normal beauty is, of itself, a feat of great imagination . . . The chief problems of any artist, as of any man, are the problems of the normal . . . and he needs, in order to solve them, everything that the imagination has to give.

WALLACE STEVENS
The Necessary Angel

I was better with the sounds of the sea
    Than with the voices of men
And in desolate and desert places
    I found myself again.

HUGH MACDIARMID
Stony Limits

. . . .
  . . .
   . .
    .

JUST AS MACDIARMID'S poems of plenitude and politics show his renewed vigour after the hiatus of *Cencrastus*, so other verse he wrote in the early Thirties reveals a restored sense of humour, perspective, and (in the more intimate poems) a tenderness that had not been present for some time.

The humour can be seen in a flyting published in 1931. Entitled 'Prayer For A Second Flood', it begins:

> There'd ha'e to be nae warnin'. Times ha'e changed
> And Noahs are owre numerous nooadays,
> (And them the vera folk to benefit maist!)
> Knock the feet frae under them, O Lord, wha praise
> Your unsearchable ways sae muckle and yet hope
>   To keep within knowledgeable scope!

Here, from the first jaunty phrase, is the old MacDiarmid of 'Address to Burns' – relaxed, outrageous, assertive, entertaining – not declaring his own divinity (not directly at any rate!) but exhorting the Lord as one might cheer the centre-forward in a World Cup match.

In the following stanzas God becomes the coach, MacDiarmid the loyal fan, deriding the second string and demanding substitutions:

> Ding a' their trumpery show to blauds again.   *smash | bits*
> Their measure is the thimblefu' o' Esk in spate.
> Like whisky the tittlin' craturs mete oot your poo'ers *whispering*
> Aince a week for bawbees in the kirk-door plate,   *ha'pennies*
> And pit their umbrellas up when they come oot
>   If mair than a pulpitfu' o' You's aboot!

> O arselins wi them! Whummle them again!   *on their arse | overturn*
> Coup them heels-owre-gowdy in a storm sae gundy   *upend | head-over-heels | fier*
> That many a lang fog-theekit face I ken   *moss-thatched*
> 'll be sooked richt doon under through a cundy   *drain*
> In the High Street, afore you get weel sterted
>   And are still hauf-herted!

Now the poet is in his element, literally and figuratively, back where he belongs. The result is the sharp, incisive satire that only intimate knowledge of a place provides: details such as the long fog-theekit face, the joyful use of Scots, and the diabolical inventions, as in 'pulpitfu' of God'. Even here, MacDiarmid is, to use his own words, still 'hauf-herted'. But he's warming to the subject. Having got 'weel started', he proceeds in earnest:

> Scour't to the bones, and mak' its marrow holes
> Toom as a whistle as they used to be   *empty*
> In days I mind o' ere men fidged wi' souls,   *itched*
> But naething had forgotten you as yet,
>   Nor you forgotten it.[1]

> Up then and at them, ye Gairds o' Heaven.
> The divine Retreat is owre. Like a tidal bore
> Boil in among them; let the lang lugs nourished   *ears*
> On the milk o' the word at least hear the roar
> O' human shingle; and replenish the salt o' the earth
>   In the place o' their birth.

Some prayer! This bit of cheerleading for the apocalypse presents a familiar theme, MacDiarmid's relation to 'the feck o' folk', yet addresses it in a new way. What makes it satisfying, and so different from *Cencrastus* on the one hand and his verse pronunciamentos on the other, is that this time the anger is *ventilated*, not turned in on itself to issue forth as flat abstraction. Here the poet gives back as good as he gets. 'Let yourself gang' he advises God, and in so advising he lets himself go; the familiarity which can thus 'whummle' adversaries delights – and finds value in – itself.

As a result, when MacDiarmid approaches the same theme more directly, he is less defensive, and has greater poise. In fact many poems of this period can be read as paired responses to a single subject, in which one poem is autobiographical, while the other employs more detached and philosophic terms.[2] In the present case for instance, 'Prayer' is followed almost at once (in

[1] The protracted 'plagiarism' controversy over MacDiarmid's poem 'Perfect' which filled the pages of *The Times* in 1965 will not be exhumed in this study. However, those for whom it still holds interest might note the similarity of conception, imagination, imagery and feeling between 'Perfect' and this poem, written four years before MacDiarmid first read the source of the other. Even if MacDiarmid didn't 'find' 'Perfect', he might well have written something very similar.

[2] A 'table' which divides some of the more important poems into two such groups may be found in David Craig's *The Real Foundations: Literature and Social Change* (London: Chatto and Windus, 1973), p.253.

First Hymn . . .) by a highly personal poem unlike any we have seen thus far:

> *Charisma and My Relatives*
> No' here the beloved group; I've gane sae faur
> (Like Christ) yont faither, mither, brither, kin
> I micht as well try dogs or cats as seek
> In sic relationships again to fin'
> The epopteia I maun ha'e – and feel
> (Frae elsewhere) owre me steal.

Having brooded about this topic in *Cencrastus* and laughed about it in 'Prayer . . .', MacDiarmid is able to move on from the obvious problem – how he differs from his relatives – to the more difficult question of what he and they might share:

> A fiercer struggle than joukin' it's involved.   *dodging*
> Oorsels oor greatest foes. Yet, even yet,
> I haud to 'I' and 'Scot' and 'Borderer'
> And fence the wondrous fire that in me's lit
> Wi' sicna' barriers roond as hide frae'ts licht
>   Near a'body's sicht.
>
> And cry 'as weel try dogs or cats as seek
> In sic relationships again to fin'
> The epopteia' that, yet f'und, like rain
> 'Ud quickly to the roots o' a' thing rin
> Even as the circles frae a stane that's hurled
>   In water ring the world.
>
> Sae to my bosom yet a' beasts maun come,
> Or I to theirs, – baudrons, wi' sides like harps,   *cats*
> Lookin' like the feel o' olives in the mooth,
> Yon scabby cur at whom the gutter carps,   *sings*
> Nose-double o' the taste o' beer-and-gin,
>   And a' my kin.
>
> And yet – there's some folk lice'll no' live on,
> I'm ane o' them I doot. But what a thocht!
> What speculations maun a man sae shunned
> No' ha'e until at last the reason's brocht
> To view acceptable, as the fact may be
>   On different grun's to them and me.   *grounds*

The openness of this writing speaks for itself; just as the natural voice was apparent in the Scots diction of 'Prayer . . .', here it is present in the true Scots syntax, which differs from that of English, and cannot be faked. Together these give the poem a slightly prodigal tone, a sense of accepting (or at least desiring anew) what was previously denied. In this respect two moments in the final stanza are telling. The first comes in that stanza's second line. Immediately preceding, the verse has been rising from the vivid sensory details, through lice, toward the kind of expressionist 'scunner' that recalls *A Drunk Man*. In this case, however, the speaker 'catches' himself, exclaims with wry amusement, 'But what a thocht!' In other words, he can now recognize the excess for what it is – the masked self-deprecation of a man who feels 'sae shunned'. And as a result of this recognition, he does not pursue the tangent, but gets back to the main point at hand.

That leads to the second key phrase: 'the reason's brocht / To view acceptable'. Though understated and hence easily missed, this marks significant growth as well. Even in MacDiarmid's greatest early poems, the resolution or coming to terms was most always posited within the poet's self. By contrast, in this case he is concerned with not only what he can give *them* (as artist, thinker, political teacher) but also what they, despite their limitations, can give him: what is 'acceptable' in both directions.

In a well-known letter, Rainer Maria Rilke wrote:

> When what is near you is far, then your distance is already among the stars and very large; rejoice in your growth, in which you naturally can take no one with you, and be kind to those who remain behind, and be sure and calm before them and do not torment them with your doubts and do not frighten them with your confidence or joy, which they could not understand. Seek yourself some sort of simple and loyal community with them, which need not necessarily change as you yourself become different and again different; love in them life in an unfamiliar form . . .[1]

In 'Charisma and My Relatives' MacDiarmid seems ready to consider at least the latter half of what Rilke advised his correspondent. True, the poem's ending is ambiguous. The reconciliation it ponders is limited, and not that happy, if possible at all. Nevertheless, it does move past the occlusive bitterness of *Cencrastus* and the sometimes evasive hyperbole of 'proletarian' verse. The expression of personal pain is simplified. Indignation yields to more tractable, responsive recognition, coming home.

Other poems written at this time express that recognition in more limited ways. They are generally undramatic in conception and expression. Often, renewed attention to particularities of land-

---

[1] Rainer Maria Rilke, *Letters to A Young Poet* (New York: Norton, 1934; rev. ed., 1954), p.39.

scape signals allegiance to those who inhabit it. One such poem starts off, 'Country folk, bein' wice, are content . . .'; another begins, 'This is the kirk o' my faithers / And I ken the meanin' at last . . .' 'Kinsfolk' presents an atypically intimate account of MacDiarmid's relationship with his father on the one hand, and his own children on the other.[1] And though less specific, a poem addressed *to* his father is still more direct:

> At My Father's Grave
> The sunlicht still on me, you row'd in clood,   *wrapped*
> We look upon each ither noo like hills
> Across a valley. I'm nae mair your son.
> It is my mind, nae son o' yours, that looks,
> And the great darkness o' your death comes up
> And equals it across the way.
> A livin' man upon a deid man thinks
> And ony sma'er thocht's impossible.

Throughout his career MacDiarmid composed a number of poems in which a living speaker addresses a departed loved one, still half expecting to receive what the dead have taken with them.[2] In this sense, 'At My Father's Grave' may be usefuly considered as a later version of 'The Watergaw'. As in the earlier poem, the speaker looks up from the immediate human sorrow to surrounding nature, and there finds terms to evoke, but not explain, his loss. This poem does not possess the early lyric's exquisiteness; indeed, it explicitly denies the situation's drama. Of course that only makes it more compelling. For the dignity of the disclaimer lends an emotional weight and completeness that the less mature poem did not achieve.

Whereas conventional elegies use intimate detail to personalize the sorrow, 'At My Father's Grave' employs an opposite strategy. Nothing about this father or this son is individuated. The details are archetypal, the situation stark, the tone bereft and uniformly calm. 'I'm nae mair your son' the speaker says, and then repeats the thought at once, as if forcing himself to believe it. His specific choice of words emphasizes that the loss is not only of a relation, but also of *relationship*, which the speaker so badly needs in order to define himself. In its sudden absence, all he can say is what he is not: 'It is my mind, nae son o' yours, that looks . . .'

Though harsh, this acceptance bears an implicit affirmation. It

[1] This poem first appears as 'Work in Progress' in *The Modern Scot*, July 1931.
[2] For instance: 'Wheesht, Wheesht', 'Country Life', 'Ode To All Rebels', 'Kinsfolk', and 'Crystals Like Blood'.

implies that what makes us more than 'minds' is also that which makes us 'sons' – the connection to our 'father(s)'. By expressing that connection (or what of it endures) in elemental terms, the speaker locates it not in 'smaller thoughts' over which a father and son, or a poet and his people, inevitably disagree, but in the 'hills' that have shaped and encompass the shared aspect of their lives, and the 'valley' where he, like his father, will some day lie. Read in this way, the poem is at once highly personal and universal, deeply felt *and* totally objective. When most displaced by grief, the poet seeks, and finds, a way to place himself once more.

What places the poet in 'Cattle Show' is simply his own pleasure:

> *Cattle Show*
> I shall go among red faces and virile voices,
> See stylish sheep, with fine heads and well-wooled,
> And great bulls mellow to the touch,
> Brood mares of marvellous approach, and geldings
> With sharp and flinty bones and silken hair.
>
> And through th'enclosure draped in red and gold
> I shall pass on to spheres more vivid yet
> Where countesses' coque feathers gleam and glow
> And, swathed in silks, the painted ladies are
> Whose laughter plays like summer lightning there.

To get the full effect of these lines, one must hear the words as MacDiarmid spoke them, with the Border accent rolling over 'mellow', 'marvellous', and 'flinty bones', and practically gargling 'gleam' and 'glow'.

On the printed page more subtle pleasures emerge: the relaxed line endings and daring adjectives; the relationship of countesses 'swathed in silk' to the 'silken hair' of geldings, of bulls and mares in their enclosure to painted ladies awaiting red-faced men in theirs. In this context, the term 'spheres' is perfectly poised between gentle humour and wonder; MacDiarmid can now imply in one word the connections which 'The Bonnie Broukit Bairn' took eight lines to proclaim. Indeed, this whole poem exudes connectedness, both among its parts and (through affection) between the speaker and that which he observes. There is an old Scottish genre of poems about agricultural fairs which extends from 'Christ's Kirk On the Green' through Fergusson and Burns. In 'Cattle Show' MacDiarmid extends that genre, not by commenting on it, but by participating in it. He can remain detached, yet celebrate communal life in his own distinctive voice.

The primary impulse in most of MacDiarmid's early work was to de-stabilize and challenge. As his talent ripened and settled in the early Thirties, he wrote a number of small poems which may be thought to smooth the earlier work's sharp edges, to express thematically and technically the balance he now required.

Once again, we may find that balance expressed in both personal and more philosophic poems. The personal statement is 'The Little White Rose', a signature poem which requires no gloss:

> The rose of all the world is not for me.
> I want for my part
> Only the little white rose of Scotland
> That smells sharp and sweet – and breaks the heart.

The complementary metaphysical poem also uses imagery of local flora to balance pride against heartbreak. Entitled 'Milk-Wort and Bog-Cotton', it is arguably (as the poet himself believed) his best short lyric poem.[1]

> #### Milk-Wort and Bog-Cotton
>
> Cwa' een like milk-wort and bog-cotton hair!   *come away / eyes*
> I love you, earth, in this mood best o' a'
> When the shy spirit like a laich wind moves   *low*
> And frae the lift nae shadow can fa'
> Since there's nocht left to thraw a shadow there
> Owre een like milk-wort and milk-white cotton hair.
>
> Wad that nae leaf upon anither wheeled
> A shadow either and nae root need dern   *hide*
> In sacrifice to let sic beauty be!
> But deep surroondin' darkness I discern
> Is aye the price o' licht. Wad licht revealed
> Naething but you, and nicht nocht else concealed.

Removed from its origins, the metaphor of 'roots' has become something of a commonplace, in the US at any rate, in our time. For MacDiarmid, however, the metaphor lies much closer to its literal basis; wherever it appears in his work, one feels the individual imagination reaching back to its organic source, the childhood days in nature, close to Langholm. Because the metaphor is more specific, it is more vital than more recent popular counterparts. It is also less sentimental, for it stresses the costs as well as gains of

[1] According to Valda Grieve, personal interview, Brownsbank, by Biggar, 24 June 1980.

rootedness. From 'The Sauchs in the Reuch Heuch Hauch' to the Drunk Man's thistle ('tyauvin' wi' this root-hewn Scottish soil') to *Cencrastus* ('Bigger and blacker the roots strike back'), there is always a persistent fear of being caught. When 'Milk-Wort and Bog-Cotton' addresses that same fear, the pivotal feeling is itself *derned* – hidden, buried – in an old Scots word. When the speaker cries 'Wad that nae root need dern' his 'wad that' implies that indeed it must. To accept that here, as to renounce the rose of all the world, is to yield one's grandest aspirations in exchange for available pleasure.[1]

The poet wrote 'Milk-Wort and Bog-Cotton' in one sitting, in England, on bog paper – a series of coincidences best left to the reader's own interpretation. The year was 1931; the place, the village of Thakeham, Surrey, to which MacDiarmid had recently moved with Valda Trevlyn. By her account, they had been drinking with friends at the White Lion pub. As the night wore on, MacDiarmid grew characteristically drunk but uncharacteristically quiet. All at once he demanded paper. None could be found. The muse was insistent. So Valda rushed into the ladies', and returned with what was required. There and then, MacDiarmid scrawled and recited 'Milk-Wort and Bog-Cotton'.[2]

The story and the poem seem to typify that short period in the poet's life. After the disasters of London and Liverpool, MacDiarmid's return to a village milieu proved a godsend. When a divorce from Peggy Skinner finally came through in 1932, he and Valda married; in July of that year, their son Michael was born. Perhaps Thakeham evoked, in some fashion, Langholm, or perhaps domestic stability inspired clarity and tolerance. In any case, poems written during this period, including 'Water Music', 'Tarras', and 'Second Hymn to Lenin', do seem to blend with unusual evenness an open-minded curiosity and sensory detail.

Unfortunately, this respite proved brief. Flat broke, MacDiarmid soon moved the family to Edinburgh, where he edited a political journal called *The Free Man*. Shortly thereafter (in 1933) he quarrelled with the National Party of Scotland and was expelled; the following year he joined the Communist Party of Great Britain. By then MacDiarmid was less able than ever to earn a living, and

---

[1] For another example of how MacDiarmid's writing had matured, compare 'Milk-Wort and Bog-Cotton' to 'Shadows That Feed On the Licht' in *To Circumjack Cencrastus* (*Complete Poems*, p. 190-1).
[2] According to Valda Grieve, personal interview, Brownsbank, by Biggar, 24 June 1980.

drinking heavily. Friends secured him a cottage on the Shetland island of Whalsay. The Grieves took up island living for the next eight years.

The move to Whalsay affected MacDiarmid's writing in two significant ways.

First, and more obviously, it meant great physical isolation from other artists, from day-to-day political events in Scotland, and most of all from the lowland milieu in which his creative sources lay.[1] The move induced a toning down of diction and palette; a shift in prevailing metaphors from water to stone; a turn from derivative metres and diction to more expansive, idiosyncratic verse whose long lines pile up like waves. Moreover, with no-one close at hand whom he could claim to represent, the masks which MacDiarmid had intermittently donned were also less available. Henceforth he abandoned the lapsing in and out of 'representative' roles for an unabashedly individual – and very lonely – voice.

Though such tendencies were dominant (and would grow stronger in time), the years on Whalsay also brought an opposite effect. For the first time in his life, MacDiarmid found himself among others – ordinary people – who seemed equally in touch with 'elemental things', and no less lonely. In MacDiarmid's sympathetic view, they possessed the dignity whose absence he had lamented in provincial mainland culture, and a spirituality much like his own. While the islanders were self-reliant, they were also interdependent. Their isolation from the rest of the world made life on the islands paradoxically more truly social, and their finest individual qualities were expressed in the austerity of their social forms. What these meant to MacDiarmid may be seen most clearly in his long poem 'Island Funeral', which begins as follows:

> *Island Funeral*
> The procession winds like a little snake
> Between the walls of irregular grey stones
> Piled carelessly on one another.
> Sometimes, on this winding track,
> The leaders are doubled back
> Quite near to us.

[1] Many of the more strident political poems were written *after* Mac-Diarmid went to Whalsay, and was distanced from the events they address. In addition, the move helped restrict his available reading to what was available in cheap and/or pamphlet editions; this may account in part for the growing eccentricity of his allusions.

It is a grey world, sea and sky
Are colourless as the grey stones
And the small fields are hidden by the walls
That fence them on every side.

Seen in perspective, the walls
Overlap each other
As far as the skyline on the hill,
Hiding every blade of grass between them,
So that all the island appears
One jumble of grey boulders.
The last grey wall outlined on the sky
Has the traceried effect
Of a hedge of thorns in winter.

We have obviously arrived at a different world, far away from
the Scots 'delight in colour', and that world dictates a new poetic
style. Thus the highly distinctive language and sprightly rhythms
give way to an apparently artless free verse. In fact, this writing's
apparent artlessness reflects just how skilled it is. Unlike most
supposedly 'free' verse, which is often a somewhat random movement in and out of concealed metres, this prosody successively
resists the discernible metric patterns toward which verse always
pulls the poet. The result is a compelling limpidity much like the
best of Ezra Pound. As in Pound's 'Song of the Bowmen of Shu',
for example, each line bears roughly the same durational value,
regardless of its length;[1] each thus falls in an unemphatic sequence
like one footstep in a funeral march. And within that sequence, the
constant subtle off-rhymes and repetitions – of 'grey', 'stone' and
'wall' – make the image double back upon itself like the particular
procession it describes.

Significantly, we are first given the landscape, and then the
people who emerge out of it, through mist on the machair, like
Elizabeth Bishop's moose on a foggy road:

The men in the stiff material
Of their homespun clothes
Look like figures cut from cardboard,
But shod in their rawhide rivelins
They walk with the springing step of mountaineers.

MacDiarmid's best poems often have a highly cinematic quality, as
has been seen in the 'jump cuts' and 'zooms' in the early lyrics, and

[1] See Donald Davie, *Ezra Pound: Poet As Sculptor* (New York:
Oxford University Press, 1964), p.45.

some of the thistle sections in *A Drunk Man*. 'Island Funeral' is also cinematic, but more like the opening frames of an epic film shot at a slower pace, on a larger scale. Thus, having set the scene, and cut briefly to the people, the poet's 'camera' now looks up and out again to the surrounding country:

> A line of tawny seaweed fringes the bay
> Between high-water mark and low.
> It is luminous between the grey of rocky shore
> And the grey of sullen water.
>
> We can now and then look over a wall
> Into some tiny field. Many of these
> Are nothing but grey slabs of limestone,
> Smooth as any pavement,
> With a few blades of grass
> Struggling up through the fissures,
> And the grey surface of that rock
> Catches and holds the light
> As if it was water lying there.
>
> At last the long line halts and breaks up,
> And, like a stream flowing into a loch,
> The crowd pours from the narrow lane
> Into the cemetery where on an unfenced sandhill
> The grey memorial stones of the island
> Have no distinction from the country.
> The coffin lies tilted sideways
> On the dark grey sand flung up from the grave.

This is poetry which takes its time. Despite the resulting amplitude, it is minimalist verse. It is verse not because the rhetoric is heightened, but because it is deliberately lowered; it eschews the variety of prose. In the lines just quoted, MacDiarmid continues to sustain the unstressed free verse, the internal and off-rhyme (bay/grey of; rock/loch; lies/tilted sideways) and the repetition, as if in free-verse villanelle, of the key words 'little', 'rock' and 'stone'. As for 'grey', that unassuming adjective has now been used eleven times to describe the world, sea, sky, stones, fields, sand, tombs – and the people whose lives and deaths they mark. Even so, it is scattered so skilfully throughout the text that it does not obtrude.

In the stanzas that follow, the procession reaches the grave. 'A little priest arrives' wearing bicycle clips on his trousers. The service begins. The poet's thoughts move on. In all of the faces gathered round, he notices

> a strange remoteness.
> They are weather-beaten people with eyes grown clear
> Like the eyes of travellers and seamen,
> From always watching far horizons . . .
>
> Among these mourners are believers and unbelievers,
> And many of them steer a middle course,
> Being now priest-ridden by convention
> And pagan by conviction,
> But not one of them betrays a sign
> Of facile and self-lulling piety,
> Nor can one see on any face
> 'A sure and certain hope
> Of the Resurrection to eternal life'.

'Priest-ridden by convention and pagan by conviction.' The words might just as well describe an exiled lowland poet who had changed his name from Christopher to Hugh. By describing these islanders in terms that might describe himself, MacDiarmid posits a relationship of individual to the group that is new for him. He goes beyond accommodation (as in 'Charisma and My Relatives') to respect. Nor is this respect an abstract proposition (as in 'Second Hymn to Lenin') of what might be. Rather, here we have common people who, more than their country counterparts or the 'feck o' folk' in Glasgow, *already* seem to share the poet's natural doubts, and preternatural yearnings. Like MacDiarmid himself, they possess no certain creed; they do not expect their faith, such as it is, to shelter them from elemental things.

As a result, 'This burial is just an act of nature . . .' writes MacDiarmid.

> It is unlike the appointed funerals of the mainland
> With their bitter pageantry
> And the ramp of undertakers and insurance companies
> That make death seem incredible and cruel.
> There are no loafing onlookers.
> Everyone is immediately concerned
> In what is taking place.

'Concern' is a simple yet powerful word, derived from the late Latin *concernere*, 'to mix or mingle together'. As a central term in American Quaker practice, it denotes a strong conviction based upon a spiritual insight, at once highly private and capable of being shared during largely silent Quaker 'meeting'. MacDiarmid's use of the word in 'Island Funeral' may be thought to signal a similar

sharing, wherein difference is accepted, and respect can be assumed. The poet is clearly different from the others present, yet
given their mutual concern he does not feel compelled to defend or
pronounce or exclude. Because he need not strain so hard to
justify, he can more modestly affirm.

Of course, the form this affirmation takes *is* funeral elegy, not
only for one islander but also for traditional island culture. Anyone
who has witnessed such a funeral, or walked among abandoned
homes, or attended the Gaelic evening service in an island church,
has experienced the broader, almost unspeakable sadness which
MacDiarmid next addresses in his poem. Citing one of the island's
proverbs – 'Every force evolves a form' – he then remarks:

> While this thing lasted
> It was pure and very strong.
> In an old island room the sense is still strong
> Of being above and beyond the familiar,
> The world as we know it,
> In an atmosphere purified,
> As it were, from the non-essentials of living . . .

Then, moving from the rooms to those who inhabited them, the
poem adds:

> They lived as much like one another as possible,
> And they kept as free as they could of the world at large.
> It is not their creed as such, however,
> That explains them and the beauty of their work.
> It is rather the happiness with which they held it,
> The light-heartedness with which they enslaved themselves
> To the various rituals it demanded,
> And also the circumstance that they were all
> Poor people – whose notions of form
> Were both ancient and basic.
> They began with the barest patterns, the purest beginnings
> Of design in their minds, and then
> Something converted them into artists
> With an exalted lyric gift . . .

Though the sentiment of these lines is moving, the poet has, alas,
begun to lecture, and in the remaining passages of 'Island Funeral'
the quality of writing declines. Nevertheless, lines such as these
hold substantial interest for reasons beyond the immediate text at
hand. One reason has to do with ritual; the other, with time.

In most of MacDiarmid's poetry up to this point, social reality is either strenuous or comic. Conversely, spiritual/intellectual work is solitary; it entails self-willed, and hence heroic, tragedy. In this respect a world 'purified . . . from the non-essentials of living' suits a man whose 'disposition is toward spiritual issues / made inhumanly clear', who 'will have nothing interposed / Between my sensitiveness and the barren but beautiful reality' ('On A Raised Beach'). But in 'Island Funeral', a later poem, we find new readiness to *have* something 'interposed' – or rather, to concede that the sum of others' experience, embodied in ritual and tradition, might indeed express, without belittling, the poet's own. Thus, here we are presented with a social ritual that is not festive, satiric, strenuous or comic, but dignified and tragic. As such, the funeral procession on Whalsay complements and at long last completes the procession through Langholm on Common Riding Day. The poet finds a social form for grief as well as for strife and triumph. To be able to mourn with others is to be less alone.

Similarly, there is a suggestion that the speaker, in remaining distanced but *not* inhumanly detached, may learn from these people what Wordsworth learns from the old leech-gatherer, and what Yeats sent Synge to the Aran Islands to acquire: a depth of constancy, and a more forgiving attitude toward time. To put it more simply, he acquires patience. He slows down.

This changing, more expansive sense of time is expressed more happily in a sequence of nine 'Shetland Lyrics', and especially in its opening poem:

> With The Herring Fishers
>
> 'I see herrin'.' – I hear the glad cry
> And 'gainst the moon see ilka blue jowl
> In turn as the fishermen haul on the nets
> And sing: 'Come, shove in your heids and growl.'
>
> 'Soom on, bonnie herrin', soom on,' they shout,   *swim*
> Or 'Come in, O come in, and see me,'
> 'Come gie the auld man something to dae.
> It'll be a braw change frae the sea.'
>
> O it's ane o' the bonniest sichts in the warld
> To watch the herrin' come walkin' on board
> In the wee sma' 'oors o' a simmer's mornin'
> As if o' their ain accord.
>
> For this is the way that God sees life,
> The haill jing-bang o's appearin'   *whole lot*
> Up owre frae the edge o' naethingness
> – It's his happy cries I'm hearin'.

'Left, right – O come in and see me,'
Reid and yellow and black and white
Toddlin' up into Heaven thegither
At peep o' day frae the endless night.

'I see herrin',' I hear his glad cry,
And 'gainst the moon see his muckle blue jowl,
As he handles buoy-tow and bush-raip
Singin': 'Come, shove in your heids and growl!'

In this and the following Shetland Lyrics, MacDiarmid's use of the fishermen's speech and songs, and his feeling for the fish-eating birds that surround them, express more appreciation of manual labour – and, intermittently, a more affecting regret for his own distance from it – than any dozen self-consciously 'proletarian' poems. *This* co-operative labour scheme includes not only men and women, but also animals, and God! As usual in MacDiarmid's most relaxed verse, local idiom and natural detail weave one bright continuum; mysteries which gestate in the depths are celebrated on the surface. Diverse members of Creation share similar characteristics; each acts 'o' its ain accord', and by being most itself best expresses what they all share.

Just as 'On A Raised Beach' conveys the devastating impact of isolation and precedes a short stay in hospital for nervous collapse, the 'Shetland Lyrics' may be seen to reflect the salubrious effect of going sailing with the fishermen once MacDiarmid had come home.[1] In a similar recuperative time, another poet wrote 'It is gorgeous to live and forget. / And to feel quite new'.[2] Some of MacDiarmid's most pleasing poems of the mid- and late-thirties are those in which he allows himself, for a while, to 'live and forget'. One such poem is called 'Happy on Heimaey'. It reads as follows:

Happy On Heimaey

Meanwhile, the last of the human faculties
To be touched by the finger of science,
Still unanalysed, still immeasurable,
The sense of smell is the one little refuge
In the human mind still inviolate and unshareable
Because communicable in no known language,
But some day this the most delicate of perceptions
Will be laid bare too – there will be

---

[1] MacDiarmid was hospitalized in Perth (at the expense of F. G. Scott) in September 1935; he returned home seven weeks later.
[2] D. H. Lawrence, in 'Spring Morning'.

Chairs of osmology in our universities,
Ardent investigators searching out, recording, measuring,
Preserving in card indexes
The departing smells of the countryside.
Hayfields will be explained in terms of Coumarin,
Beanfields in Ionone, hedge-roses in Phenyl-Ethyl-Propionate,
Hawthorn as Di-Methyl-Hydroquinone.
(But will they ever capture the scent of violets
Among the smoke of the shoeing-forge, or explain
The clean smell of a road wet with summer rain?)
Until that day, on Heimaey, 400 miles due North-West
Of Rona in the Hebrides, I am content to walk out
Into an unreal country of yellow fields
Lying at the foot of black volcanic cliffs
In the shadow of dead Helgafell,
And watch a few farmers scything
(Careful of the little birds' nests,
Iceland wheatear, snow bunting, white wagtail, meadow pipit,
And leaving clumps of grass to protect them)
A sweet but slender hay-crop
And tell its various constituents to myself
– White clover, chickenweed, dandelion,
A very large buttercup, silverweed, horsetail,
Thrift, sorrel, yellow bedstraw,
Poa, carex, and rushes –
Or look out of my bedroom window
In the farmhouse near Kaupstadur
On a garden planted with angelica,
Red currant, rhubarb, and the flower of Venus,
Or at midnight watch the sun
Roll slowly along the northern horizon
To dip behind the great ice-caps
And jokulls of distant Iceland.
'Mellach lem bhith ind ucht ailiuin
        for beind cairrge,
Conacind and ar a mheinci
        feth na fairrci.'[1]
Ah me! It is a far better thing to be sitting
Alive on Heimaey, bare as an egg though it were,
Than rolled round willy-nilly with yonder sun.

MacDiarmid is one of only a handful of poets (another is Rim-
baud) with a special interest in smell, the one sense which is least

[1] From an ancient poem ascribed to Colum Cille, meaning: 'Pleasant,
methinks, to be on an isle's breast, on a pinnacle of rock, that I might
see there in its frequency the ocean's aspect' (MacDiarmid's note).

subject to the censorship of conscious (cerebral) control. What is so nice about this poem is the way MacDiarmid pokes fun at MacDiarmid-style pedantries, and then contrasts the list of chemicals with the lovely birds and flowers, each affectionately called by name. Look at these names again: 'a very large buttercup', 'chickenweed', 'horsetail', 'flower of Venus', 'scent of violets among the smoke of the shoeing-forge'. One can feel the poet's pure pleasure here, and his solicitude for other life in the metaphor of careful scything, i.e. leaving something untouched and unknown. Such things should remind us that this poet, known for his ferocity, also possessed an extraordinary, true capacity for gentleness, and care.

This quality of care is also evident in 'Bracken Hills in Autumn'. Considering bracken, yet another wild, perennial and densely rooted plant, MacDiarmid writes, 'These beds of bracken, climax of the summer's growth / Are elemental as the sky or sea'. Realizing that 'this flinty verdure's vast effusion is the more / Remarkable for the shortness of its stay', he is once again inspired to

> Look closely. Even now bog asphodel spikes, still alight at the tips,
> Sundew lifting white buds like those of the whitlow grass
> On walls in spring over its little round leaves
> Sparkling with gummy red hairs, and many a soft mass
>> Of the curious moss that can clean
>> A wound or poison a river, are seen.

> Ah! well I know my tumultuous days now at their prime
> Will be brief as the bracken too in their stay
> Yet in them as the flowers of the hills 'mid the bracken
> All that I treasure is needs hidden away
>> And will also be dead
>> When its rude cover is shed.

Ten years before, MacDiarmid could have drawn on one or the other quality of the moss in order to evoke either miracles or 'scunner'. Here, he can just observe, and acknowledge, both qualities. And in the subsequent thoughts which the object of his gaze inspires, he can address his own mortality with equal clarity, and no less balance.

Such poise, a product of the poet's middle years, is united with the charm of his early work in the following small poem:

> O Ease My Spirit
> O ease my spirit increasingly of the load
> Of my personal limitations and the riddling differences

> Between man and man with a more constant insight
> Into the fundamental similarity of all activities.
>
> And quicken me to the gloriously and terribly illuminating
> Integration of the physical and spiritual till I feel how easily
> I could put my hand gently on the whole round world
> As on my sweetheart's head and draw it to me.

These lines express two kinds of impulse in two different kinds of language. One is the highly abstract, intellectual idiom of 'Scotch metaphysics'; the other, the normal diction of 'low' Scots culture. They may thus be taken to express the divisions in Scottish sensibility discussed in Chapter One, and the corresponding conflict in the poet himself – between, as it were, Hugh MacDiarmid and Christopher Grieve. To some readers, the poem might seem to offer the worst of both, to combine the bombast of one with the bathos of the other in a decidedly offhand way. This verse *is* unselfconscious. However, like art critics seeking proof of a master's own hand in details which a copier wouldn't think to forge, we may perhaps use this minor poem to discern its author's truest voice. In discussing the early lyrics, it was remarked that they characteristically begin with opposing categories, which are then broken down or inverted in surprising ways. With that pattern in mind, let us look at the present poem again.

'O Ease My Spirit' opens on a note of internal intellectual struggle, conveyed by highly rhetorical and belaboured diction, and grandiose, hortatory phrasing. By contrast, the poem closes with a radical simplification, a gesture of almost apologetic sweetness. The entire poem has only eight lines, yet the speaker inhabits one mood as completely in the end as he was possessed by its opposite at the outset. How is this transition made? Through language.

The speaker's first words are a supplication: 'O ease'. Ease what? The thorny complications next expressed in the glottal stops of the first two lines, the 'inc', 'gl', 'dl', and 'ng' sounds, and the polysyllabic, somewhat pompous words which distance us from ourselves even as we speak them:

> O ease my spirit increasingly of the load
> Of my personal limitations and the riddling differences
> Between man and man with a more constant insight . . .

Though these lines look even paced, they in fact progress in rhythmic fits and starts. After rolling past the first two lines, we are

suspended momentarily, stuck (appropriately) on the phrase
'between man and man'. Then the verse resumes its forward
progress, as if by force of will, in the words 'with a more constant
insight'. Moving again, it picks up speed, grows fluid: 'into the
fundamental similarity of all activities'. Notice the echo of 'al – ity'
(singular) and 'all – ities' (plural); sound reveals sense. This is not
stiff declamation after all; in fact, it is highly expressive writing.

Stanza two begins with the desired activity, leaning forward on
the iamb 'and quicken'. In the lines that follow, 'physical' and
'spiritual' are both consonant with 'fundamental', as with each
other. The 'l' sounds that before expressed congestion become
unstressed; opening out from 'gloriously' to 'terribly' to 'easily'
and 'gently', they develop a music of their own, whose sound *is* the
integration which their sense demands. In the process, thought
imperceptibly 'quickens' into feeling. Runover lines produce a
stretched grammatic period that accelerates through thirty-seven
words from 'and' to 'and'. And . . . what?

'Draw it to me.' That's all. Four simple monosyllables and the
poem's first active verb now counterbalance all that came before.
Metrically, this closing line is incomplete. The rhythm, like the
thought, breaks off; the long syntactic structure so elaborately
built up dissolves. What remains is a pause, an empty space. And
having found that space, a tenderness expressed with due simplicity encompasses the 'whole round world'.

So perhaps 'O Ease My Spirit' is not so tossed off or negligible as
it may have first appeared. Nevertheless, it is a remarkably unselfconscious and unprotected statement, and in this respect a note of
caution is in order. It would be wrong to read the poem's closure as
a dismissal of the opening struggle. For MacDiarmid, abstraction
has its own imperatives and pleasures, not to be denied. Unlike
poets with a more psychological bent, he does not view impersonal
thought as camouflage for what we 'really' feel. In the work this
chapter has considered, his goal is never to *overcome* intellection,
but to re-integrate it with emotion. Thus one must willingly incur
the struggle of the first stanza to achieve the ease of the second; and
that ease, once found, does not turn inward, but once again reaches
out to the 'whole round world'. What is unique about this poet is
his insistence that both activities are fundamentally similar. What
is courageous is the tenacity and utter lack of embarrassment with
which he persists in giving voice to each.

'O Ease My Spirit', 'Bracken Hills in Autumn', and 'Happy on
Heimaey' may not be 'important' poems; they have neither the

originality of the Lenin hymns nor the sparkle of *A Drunk Man*. Yet they are solid, well-made poems, important by virtue of what the poet achieved for himself in writing them: the middle ground of experience, and an increased emotional breadth. Just as the Thakeham poems helped resolve dilemmas of personal alienation, so these ease his obsession with the pressures of time. In 'Balefire Loch' MacDiarmid writes, 'Bide whaur ye are / There's time eneuch / To plumb and scale the infinite.' That realization presages the true detachment that need not proclaim itself. It fosters a maturation from prophet of doom, wishing himself above and outside time, to a more humane contemplative, content to imagine beyond time while accepting his own place within its natural processes.

These developments bear fruit in the final poem we shall consider, perhaps MacDiarmid's greatest. It is called 'Harry Semen'.[1] First, the text:

Harry Semen

I ken these islands each inhabited
Forever by a single man
Livin' in his separate world as only
In dreams yet maist folk can.
Mine's like the moonwhite belly o' a hoo   *dogfish*
Seen in the water as a fisher draws in his line.
I canna land it nor can it ever brak awa'.
It never moves, yet seems a' movement in the brine;
A movin' picture o' the spasm frae which I was born,
It writhes again, and back to it I'm willy-nilly torn.
A' men are similarly fixt; and the difference 'twixt
    The sae-ca'd sane and insane
Is that the latter whiles ha'e glimpses o't
    And the former nane.

Particle frae particle'll brak asunder,
Ilk ane o' them mair livid than the neist.   *each one*
A separate life? – incredible war o' equal lichts,
Nane o' them wi' ocht in common in the least.
Nae threid o' a' the fabric o' my thocht
Is left alangside anither; a pack
O' leprous scuts o' weasels riddlin' a plaid
    Sic thrums could never mak'.   *ravelled thread*

[1] Typically, despite its quality the poem was not available in accurate form for many years. It was excised from the first edition of *Stony Limits* by the publisher, Victor Gollancz, and replaced with 'The Progress of Poetry'. And it is printed incorrectly in the *Collected Poems*.

Hoo mony shades o' white gaed curvin' owre
To yon blae centre o' her belly's flower?
Milk-white, and dove-grey, wi' harebell veins.   *Scottish bluebell*
Ae scar in fair hair like the sun in sunlicht lay,
And pelvic experience in a thin shadow line;
Thocht canna mairry thocht as sic saft shadows dae.

Grey ghastly commentaries on my puir life,
A' the sperm that's gane for naething rises up to damn
In sick-white onanism the single seed
Frae which in sheer irrelevance I cam.
What were the odds against me? Let me coont.
What worth am I to a' that micht ha'e been?
To a' the wasted slime I'm capable o'
Appeals this lurid emission, whirlin' lint-white and green.
Am I alane richt, solidified to life,
Disjoined frae a' this searin' like a white-het knife,
And vauntin' my alien accretions here,
Boastin' sanctions, purpose, sense the endless tide
I cam frae lacks – the tide I still sae often feed?
O bitter glitter; wet sheet and flowin' sea – and what beside?

Sae the bealin' continents lie upon the seas,   *festering*
     Sprawlin' in shapeless shapes a' airts,   *in all directions*
Like ony splash that ony man can mak'
     Frae his nose or throat or ither pairts,
Fantastic as ink through blottin'-paper rins.
But this is white, white like a flooerin' gean,   *wild cherry*
Passin' frae white to purer shades o' white,
Ivory, crystal, diamond, till nae difference is seen
Between its fairest blossoms and the stars
Or the clear sun they melt into,
And the wind mixes them amang each ither
Forever, hue upon still mair dazzlin' hue.

Sae Joseph may ha'e pondered; sae a snawstorm
Comes whirlin' in grey sheets frae the shadowy sky
And only in a sma' circle are the separate flakes seen.
White, whiter, they cross and recross as capricious they fly,
Mak' patterns on the grund and weave into wreaths,
Load the bare boughs, and find lodgments in corners frae
The scourin' wind that sends a snawstorm up frae the earth
To meet that frae the sky, till which is which nae man can say.
They melt in the waters. They fill the valleys. They scale the peaks.
There's a tinkle o' icicles. The topmaist summit shines oot.
Sae Joseph may ha'e pondered on the coiled fire in his seed,
The transformation in Mary, and seen Jesus tak' root.

This poem embodies the perfection of techniques and culmination of thematic concerns whose development we have followed through the previous four chapters. To see how these elements merge here, how one facilitates the other, we may begin with technical matters.

'Harry Semen' is written in rhymed free verse stanzas, each consisting of three *abcb* quatrains, with a couplet inserted between the second and third.[1] Some stanzas (the second for instance) employ the truncated cut-lines of Habbie Simpson metres and much of Burns, whereas others are elliptical and Whitmanesque: 'White, whiter, they cross and recross as capricious they fly'. While the individual line lengths thus vary greatly – from four to eleven words – the rhyme scheme is regular. The resulting blend of loosely structured discourse and tightly woven form serves MacDiarmid well. From the start, the tone is uniquely MacDiarmid's own, yet the rhymes, analogies (such as 'belly o' a hoo') and metre of the first stanza's final quatrain help keep that individual tone in contact with a representative voice; they place his complicated statement in an approachable, inviting context.

In the second stanza, the first four lines are again unmistakeably MacDiarmid. Their hint of apocalypse and fear of fragmentation (reflected in a broken question and reversal) recall the middle section of *A Drunk Man*:

> Particle frae particle'll brak asunder,
> Ilk ane o' them mair livid than the neist.
> A separate life? Incredible war o' equal lichts
> Nane o' them wi' ocht in common in the least.

Then the quatrain that follows again lowers the rhetoric, domesticates and humanizes the declamation:

> Nae threid o' a' the fabric o' my thocht
> Is left alangside anither; a pack
> O' leprous scuts o' weascls riddlin' a plaid
>   Sic thrums could never mak'.

Among the fine Scots words, 'thrums' warrants special attention. Literally, 'thrum' means 'thread' and by extension a pervasive thread or streak in one's character (Jamieson). 'Thrum' is also a technical term for the warp thread in the end of a loom, a shred or

---

[1] In stanzas four and five the couplet is missing. If available, the manuscript may reveal whether these were dropped by accident, or simply never written.

scrap of no value. Kin to weavers, the poet certainly would have known this usage, as well as its slang derivatives: 'thrum cutter' – a derogatory name for weaver – and 'thrum descent' – of lowly origin (*SND*). His use of the word here recalls the language of weaving in 'Seamless Garment' but goes beyond it. For in the earlier poem, when he translates his notions into their terms to teach them what he thinks they need to know, there is a slight hint of quaintness, of the exercise, or gambit. Here, by contrast, MacDiarmid describes himself in language which they might employ to assess *his* situation. To convey his marginality he reaches into the common language; the words which concede how he doesn't 'fit' paradoxically reaffirm how he does.

In its next lines the poem asks:

> Hoo many shades o' white gaed curvin' owre
> To yon blae centre o' her belly's flower?
> Milk-white, and dove-grey, wi' harebell veins.
> Ae scar in fair hair like the sun in sunlicht lay,
> And pelvic experience in a thin shadow line;
> Thocht canna mairry thocht as sic saft shadows dae.

The mystery here is not what is happening – the speaker is beginning to excite himself – but why, now, and how this relates to what just preceded. True, there is the vaguest association of 'her' belly with 'the belly of a hoo' in line five, and with his own, now presumably exposed. But by and large, the jump is inexplicable. What's going on? The connection may be deliberately obscure; perhaps the poet is having a small joke on those whose critical seriousness leads them to ask. He knows that the baffled reader will want to marry thought to thought, to 'make sense' of this, yet mischievously leaves us baffled. Thus unaccounted for, the memory inaugurates a feeling of frustration and irrelevance, which expands in the following stanza:

> Grey ghastly commentaries on my puir life,
> A' the sperm that's gane for naething rises up to damn
> In sick-white onanism the single seed
> Frae which in sheer irrelevance I cam.
> What were the odds against me? Let me coont.
> What worth am I to a' that micht ha'e been?
> To a' the wasted slime I'm capable o'
> Appeals this lurid emission, whirlin' lint-white and green.
> Am I alane richt, solidified to life,
> Disjoined frae a' this searin' like a white-het knife,

> And vauntin' my alien accretions here,
> Boastin' sanctions, purpose, sense the endless tide
> I cam frae lacks – the tide I still sae often feed?
> O bitter glitter; wet sheet and flowin' sea – and what beside?

Two points should be made about this writing. First of all, let us not, in 1983, pretend to more shock, amusement or disdain than we feel. Of course the speaker is masturbating as he thinks. The movement of the stanza as a whole expresses the act described, and those who admire the Nausicaa section of *Ulysses* need not quail at MacDiarmid's similar intention.[1]

Secondly, we need not project, as one critic does, 'revulsion from the flux of living', and 'desperate disgust at sexual experience, not resolved by the rationalizing and fleering humour that he brings in to handle the revulsion'.[2]

One may more usefully approach the poem as one expression in a long line of others of MacDiarmid's fascination with necessity and probability, how spirit 'solidifies' to flesh – the relationship of what is to 'what micht hae been' and to what might be. That question figures largely in *A Drunk Man,* and in 'Kinsfolk', his most nearly confessional poem, where MacDiarmid says of his father,

> Gin he had lived my life and work micht weel
> Ha' been entirely different, better or waur,
> Or neither, comparison impossible.
> It wadna ha' been the same. That's hoo things are.

Viewed in this light, the 'irrelevance' from which Harry Semen 'cam' does not connote self-hatred, just an admission that nothing in human experience – not even our own identity – has the logical inevitability we might wish to ascribe to it. The 'odds against me' (my becoming *me,* as I've turned out) are of course incalculable, as are the odds that any particular sperm will achieve conception. By offering rhetorically to 'coont' those odds, the speaker brings home the incapacity of such reckoning – 'sanctions, purpose, sense' – to provide the answers which we so desire.

In this regard we must bear in mind that the stanza just quoted constitutes only one step in a dramatic monologue which is moving *through* bafflement and solipsism toward some other resolution. Far from being merely 'fleering humour', the multiple meanings of 'marry', 'rises up', and 'coming' foreshadow that resolution, as

[1] The stanza's last line is a well-known schoolboys' 'send-up' of a Victorian poem.
[2] Craig, p.238.

shall be seen. By forcing himself, and the reader, to acknowledge the extent to which our personal realities are randomly determined, the poet prepares us to recognize and acknowledge still larger mysteries. The speaker next declares:

> Sae the bealin' continents lie upon the seas,
> Sprawlin' in shapeless shapes a' airts,
> Like ony splash that ony man can mak'
> Frae his nose or throat or ither pairts,
> Fantastic as ink through blottin'-paper rins.

By this point 'Harry Semen' as a whole seems almost a compendium of favourite MacDiarmid devices: fish seen under water, 'moon-white' bellies, imagery of weaving, sunlit erotic memories, slime, off-colour humour, the self as tide. While familiar, these are nevertheless interwoven with refreshing subtlety. For example, wasted sperm is described as 'lint-white', the colour of flax and of sloughed-off waste fabric. Black ink in blotting-paper (waste words that won't be printed) is analogized with white sperm (blotted in a wet sheet) that won't achieve conception. And a continent's 'shapeless shape' can only be described in terms of what it came to be, what 'tides' have made it. In short, the poet's imagination is at full force.

On the other hand, one salient characteristic of his earlier poetry is conspicuously absent – the insistent 'Am I right?' of *Cencrastus*. Indeed, despite its paraphrasable content, we would be hard pressed, after forty-two lines, to say what this poem is 'about'. Its development appears to be essentially associative and random, its only logic the 'logic' of imagination, leading where it will. But if this development is not ordered in the usual sense, neither is it uncontrolled. Images are not flung about with cacaphonous abandon, but gently introduced and folded into one another, like ingredients in self-rising batter. Despite the poem's constantly expanding scope, the speaker's tone remains, if not at ease, good natured; his avuncular cosmology rubs off on us. The result is compelling, yet not threatening; within a 'shapeless shape' the poem's evocative details are handled beautifully – paced, and yet primed to explode.

The 'explosion' of meaning is prepared in the penultimate stanza's final lines, as all the preceding images begin to cohere:

But this is white, white like a flooerin' gean,
Passin' frae white to purer shades o' white,
Ivory, crystal, diamond, till nae difference is seen
Between its fairest blossoms and the stars
Or the clear sun they melt into,
And the wind mixes them amang each ither
Forever, hue upon still mair dazzlin' hue.

A word about 'crystal': at various stages of his career, MacDiarmid's poems show an uncanny identification with particular 'elements' in the classical sense. In *First Hymn to Lenin and Other Poems* and in *Scots Unbound*, nearly half the poems use water to embody memory, movement, connection, change. In *Stony Limits* ('I must get into this stone world now'), a half dozen stone poems express isolation and finitude, and equate explicit definitions with lost possibility. In 'Harry Semen' we find both the watery hope and stony fear in one representative substance, clear as water, hard as stone – in crystal.[1]

Let us look at these last five lines again. Notice how, with the introduction of this new imagery, the imaginative flow itself now crystallizes. Each word, each stressed metrical unit – ivory, crystal, diamond – lifts the vision and makes it more definite. Line endings that sound like closures one instant ('sun', 'stars', 'into') are immediately run-over, taken up in the line that follows. The movement of this verse replicates that of windblown crystals at the start of a snowfall. In the final stanza, this becomes a veritable storm:

Sae Joseph may ha'e pondered; sae a snawstorm
Comes whirlin' in grey sheets frae the shadowy sky
And only in a sma' circle are the separate flakes seen.
White, whiter, they cross and recross as capricious they fly,
Mak' patterns on the grund and weave into wreaths,
Load the bare boughs, and find lodgments in corners frae
The scourin' wind that sends a snawstorm up frae the earth
To meet that frae the sky, till which is which nae man can say.
They melt in the waters. They fill the valleys. They scale the peaks.
There's a tinkle o' icicles. The topmaist summit shines oot.
Sae Joseph may ha'e pondered on the coiled fire in his seed,
The transformation in Mary, and seen Jesus tak' root.

[1] Crystal appears increasingly in MacDiarmid's later visionary poems, such as 'Crystals Like Blood', 'At Lenin's Tomb', 'The Monument', 'The Terrible Crystal', and 'Diamond Body'. Along with passing references to the 'poetry of knowledge', the last title suggests a possible interest and reading in tantric buddhist sources – something worth looking into.

The power of this vision, the marvellous verse movement, the graceful introduction and repetition of 'sae Joseph' and the shining conclusion are all self-evident. Less apparent are two little words which unobtrusively determine that conclusion, and may reveal its full significance.

The first is 'frae'. Throughout most of 'Harry Semen''s first four stanzas, the word 'frae' denotes a backward glance lamenting waste or separation, as in 'the sperm *frae* which I was born'; 'particle *frae* particle'll brak asunder'; 'the seed *frae* which in sheer irrelevance I cam'; 'disjoined *frae* a' this searin''; 'the endless tide I cam *frae*'; 'the splash that ony man can mak' *frae* his nose' (etc.). However, with the onset of snow and whiteness in the fourth stanza, 'frae' suddenly acquires the forward sense of progression – of 'passin' *frae* white *to* purer shades o' white'. And in the final stanza, where the word appears four times in eight lines, it begins to confound directions altogether; snow falls 'frae' the sky, 'frae' the wind, 'frae' the earth, thereby blurring distinctions between hill and valley, ground and sky . . . just as the Incarnation blurred distinctions between earth and heaven, man and God.

With the other little word, 'sae', we seem at last on the verge of an explanation, or causal connection. But it does not materialize. What we get instead are two sets of implied correspondences for which we have not been consciously prepared.

The first set of correspondences is visual – between the 'grey commentaries' of 'whirlin'' seed and the snowstorm 'whirlin' in grey sheets', between the alien accretions of sperm and the 'capricious' accumulations of 'separate flakes'.[1] The second correspondence is linguistic – between the descent of snow and of Christ, whose advent also temporarily transfigured the visible world. Here the visual echo of a snowy Christmas morning is reinforced by connotative language. Flakes 'cross and recross'; though akin to thrums, they are nevertheless woven into 'wreaths'; they find 'lodgement' on earth much as, in folklore, the Holy Family seeks lodging at the inn.[2] That godhead should emerge in one humble

[1] Laurie Anderson, whose multi-media 'performance art' is currently the rage of New York's Soho, in fact projects overlapping images of snow and sperm in one segment of her current touring show called 'U.S.A'. Watching the snow turn into sperm, and hearing the audience respond as she intones 'Which one will make it?', one is tempted to cry out: 'It's been done already . . . fifty years before!'

[2] Reminiscent of the 'roofless ingles' which the snow seeks out in 'Hymn to Dostoyevsky' in *A Drunk Man*. In addition, the flooerin' gean (cherry tree) may recall the well-known ballad of that name, in

child, crystallize, as it were, in one flake among all the countless and apparently meaningless millions, cannot be explained by the conventional union of Mary and Joseph, any more than thought can *marry* thought (stanza two) to explain the 'coming' of Harry Semen. This inadequacy of literal, causal explanation brings with it a third correspondence. *Any* human child could have been made the Christ. If Christ came 'randomly' as any snowflake in a storm, and snowflakes are analogous to blizzards of wasted sperm, then 'sae Joseph', forced to contemplate the coming of the one, may have 'pondered' just like Harry, searching for the meaning of the other.

In the biblical account of Christ's birth, all that is specified about Joseph's feeling is his concern for Mary: 'When she was found to be with child, her husband, being a just man and unwilling to put her to shame, resolved to divorce her quietly' (Matthew 1, 19). Similarly, in their consuming interest for the virgin birth *per se*, most authors who have made use of it were (and are) concerned only with its divine protagonist(s). Hugh MacDiarmid is the only poet who comes to mind who addresses the Incarnation from Joseph's point of view, first in 'O Wha's the Bride' and here, in 'Harry Semen'.[1] Harry is the modern Joseph. Baffled, surrounded by improbable, indeed miraculous, events which he himself cannot determine or explain, he finds his own role limited, at best, to testimony. And yet, to look on in the proper spirit, to appreciate and strive to understand, *is* to participate in a fully human way. Such witness is . . . sufficient. He accepts it. He does not find peace. He affirms by having seen.

This shift from imitation of Christ (as in 'On A Raised Beach') to identification with Joseph reflects that recognition of the common life, and kinship, whose growth has been traced throughout this chapter. Significant for MacDiarmid personally, it has broader implications for modern poetry.

Hugh MacDiarmid was a declared atheist. He was also a deeply spiritual man. Like many of his contemporaries who had rejected the specific content of their parents' faith, he yet employed the Christology, its mythic and fictive power, to nourish the preternatural self, and sustain his hopes for the race's spiritual evolution.

---

which the cherry trees bow down their heads so that Joseph may gather fruit for Mary.
[1] One does get Joseph's point of view in the medieval mystery cycles, and though not about Joseph, Hardy's 'The Oxen', and Yeats' 'The Magi' voice similar concerns.

Re-imagining the Christ story from Joseph's point of view at once renounces doctrinal certitudes and restores the primitive sense of wonder. Compared to this, the 'fire and rose' of Eliot, the *Anathemeta* of David Jones, seem (to this writer's mind) cold compilations of ecclesiastic symbols; they predicate belief upon received, elaborate definitions. By comparison, MacDiarmid's secular wonder is a manger faith. It asserts no explanation, expects no arbitration, discounts no possibility; keeps itself open, utterly, to all that it can't define.

At this point in our discussion, some readers might concede the poet's emotional growth and yet still find the poems that reflect it uninteresting. They might contend, for instance, that MacDiarmid's renewed appreciation of his 'roots' restricted him to the narrow ground in which they lay, on which he wrote well; that the work which achieves personal integration is also the most conventional and old-fashioned. The real issue here is of course not where or when a work of art is set, but whether it transcends its temporal and geographic setting. We may judge MacDiarmid's poetry in this regard by briefly comparing 'Harry Semen' to a work set in a very similar milieu: 'The Great Hunger', by the Irish poet Patrick Kavanagh.

Written eight years after 'Harry Semen', 'The Great Hunger' tells the story of bachelor ploughman Patrick Maguire, 'the man who made his field a bride', and whose happiest dream was

> To smoke a pipe
> In a sheltered gripe
> In the middle of July –
> His face in a mist,
> And two stones in his fist
> And an impotent worm on his thigh.

Before proceeding with this bitter tale, the poet asks

> If we watch them an hour is there anything we can prove
> Of life as it is broken backed on the Book
> Of Death? Here crows gabble over worms and frogs
> And the gulls like old newspapers are blown clear of the hedges, luckily.
> Is there some light of imagination in these wet clods?

This question is posed in the poem's opening section. As we 'watch from the doorway the years turn back', the thirteen sections that follow present, without mitigation, the Irish farmer's life of stultifying drudgery and sexual repression. Sometimes lyrical, sometimes ironic, Kavanagh mingles graphic details and colloquial speech with his own bitter commentaries, such as 'For the strangled impulse there is no redemption.' The poem's vulgarity and relentless anti-clericism, which scandalized some, made it for others an act of personal courage and cultural service.

Despite these evident similarities, 'The Great Hunger' differs from 'Harry Semen' in two significant ways. First of all, whereas 'Harry Semen' really does seek 'some light of imagination' among wet clods, in 'The Great Hunger' Kavanagh's question is a bit sardonic and rhetorical. The work begins with 'Clay is the word' and ends with an 'apocalypse of clay in every corner of this land', and one can't help feeling that despite his poem's integrity, the poet's own imagination has been blighted by the circumstances it describes. Second, the conclusions are tied so specifically to the situation of *this* land that they do not resonate sufficiently beyond it. For non-Irish readers this apocalypse is too particular; we may appreciate Maguire's plight, but are not made to feel it as our own.[1]

'Harry Semen', by comparison, is not a poem about impotence, celibacy, sex fear, or thwarted sexuality *per se,* nor about repression, nor the particular mores that enforce it. It is a poem about fatherhood and creation, about conception in the broadest sense, which uses sexual *frustration* to dramatize intellectual and spiritual waste. Moreover, though set in a distinctive milieu which is the poet's own, the poem is not a lament for Scotland, nor a quarrel with the Scottish clay – but a Scottish person's universal vision of 'coiled fire'.

That vision is the crowning achievement of this poet's career. It goes beyond realism. It is neither impersonal nor confessional. Each of these terms, and the verse it describes, entails bringing to one's subject an attitude that precedes it, and selecting and defining what one sees accordingly. In verse, as in everyday life, this is habitual to us – second nature. But MacDiarmid seeks to restore us to our elemental, *primary* nature. Rather than use the characteristics of the external world to express internal states of mind (the so-called objective correlative), he regards himself as one phenomenon among countless others, and studies the correspondences among them, looking 'sae that nae difference is seen'. He avows no present meanings, and accepts no future limits. Deferring a need for structure in order to more clearly discern pattern, and discover-

---

[1] Kavanagh himself eventually dismissed the poem as 'documentary', and some of his subsequent poetry is a good deal more imaginative and open. See, for instance, 'Canal Bank Walk' and 'Innocence'.

ing patterns in nature, he does not define our lot outside them, but secures us, forever, within. In 'Harry Semen' MacDiarmid comes as close as a writer can to purging himself of preconceptions. The result is *objective* poetry: the cosmological vision still retained, but tempered by social experience – cleansed of crankiness, and pride, and fear.

The loneliness remains – what vision could escape it? Yet in 'Harry Semen' and associated poems, the poet has accomplished what he first set out to do. His own intensity of concern for a large objective purpose is expressed in a common language, with geniality and patience and feeling. Read one by one, these poems delight and inspire. As a group, they are all that poetry can be: powerfully imagined, richly articulated, fully developed; humanely achieved.

CHAPTER SIX

Tribute to Chance

The more I read and teach, the more convinced I am that obscurity and idiosyncracy of style in young poets is inevitably symptomatic of fear: the fear of saying something apprehensible which others might then criticize for its content. If one says something arty . . . only partially, or in code, or fashionably, one is less vulnerable. Sometimes I think that the growth of a poet to some extent depends on his or her becoming less and less embarrassed about more and more.

MARVIN BELL
Old Snow Just Melting

Surrendering and dispersing his identity
He yet made the world feel him at last
As something tough, something singular,
    something leathery with life.

HUGH MACDIARMID
A Kist of Whistles

. . . .
. .
.

IN 1938 MacDIARMID wrote 'I turn from the poetry of beauty
to the poetry of wisdom – of "wisdom", that is to say, the poetry of
moral and intellectual problems, and the emotions they generate'.[1]
Most critics have accepted this distinction as MacDiarmid first
defined it, and refer to his subsequent writing – most notably *In
Memoriam James Joyce* (1955) and 'The Kind of Poetry I Want'
(1961) – as his 'later work'.

This terminology can be misleading. In the first place, dates of
publication should not be confused with dates of composition,
which are frequently much earlier.[2] According to Valda Grieve,
her husband wrote an enormous amount of verse when they lived
on Whalsay but little thereafter.[3] And attempts to date his work are
complicated further by his habits of describing projected projects
as *faits accomplis*, and re–using lines and passages from early poems
repeatedly in later writing.[4] In short, much of the so-called 'later
work' was written not by an old man (such as the 'later' Yeats), but
some time before, by a poet in early middle age. Rather than break
absolutely with the communist verse, poems of plenitude and island
poems, the 'later work' merely accentuates certain tendencies –
encyclopaedic, anarchic, orotund – that were present all along.

The quote with which this discussion began first appeared in a
preface to 'Direadh I'. That title, Scots Gaelic for 'act of surmount-
ing, or ascending', reflected MacDiarmid's deepening interest in
the didactic and improvisational aspects of Gaelic verse. His on-

---

[1] *Voice of Scotland* (Dec. 1938-Feb. 1939), p.13.
[2] To take a few examples: 'Ode to All Rebels', which appeared in
1947, was written in 1934, but deleted from *Stony Limits*, along with
'Harry Semen', by the publisher. The opening sections of 'Cornish
Heroic Song for Valda Trevlyn', published in 1939, 43 and 47, were
composed in 1936. The *Complete Poems* (London: Martin Brian &
O'Keefe, 1978) does much to sort out the chaos of the *Collected Poems*
(New York: Macmillan, 1962), and is thus essential for studying dates
and sources.
[3] Personal interview, Biggar, Lanarkshire, 24 June 1980.
[4] Thus many of the short poems in *Second Hymn to Lenin* (1935) are
merely 'Englishings' of the Scots passages in the earlier 'Ode to All
Rebels'. One such passage, re–titled 'One Of the Principal Causes of
War' in *Second Hymn*, was published in Scots yet again, as 'Jeannie
MacQueen' in 1970.

going fascination with individual words, especially the 'misfits' and 'funny ones', comprised a second source of inspiration.[1] Language viewed as a tool of evolutionary synthesis became the subject and in effect the hero of his massive *In Memoriam James Joyce*, itself part of *A Vision of World Language*. No longer content to work in one tongue, whether Lallans or English–geological (as in 'On A Raised Beach'), MacDiarmid now sought to employ simultaneously a host of disparate vocabularies. This effort led him to a third linguistic source – contemporary science.

In broadest terms, the 'later poetry' represents an effort to 'ascend' to a level of consciousness where conventional linguistic and intellectual categories may be 'surmounted'. This poetry's main subject is that effort itself; its form, a rambling discourse which incorporates a wide array of sources enlisted as evidence in a running argument:

I dream of poems like the bread-knife
Which cuts three slices at once,
Of poems concerned with technical matters
(Poems braced by Carducci's cold bath of erudition . . .

A poetry that goes all the way
From Brahma to a stock,
A poetry like pronouncing the Shemhameporesh . . .

. . . a poetry such that if someone asks
As of the forest by the river Kundalini
'Of what nature is the monk
Who adds glory to the forest?' [etc.]

[A poetry not] ignorant like those who prate of empty air
Unaware of its ceilings and vaults, the Heaviside Layer and the Appleton Layer
Along which the sound waves run . . .
    ('The Kind of Poetry I Want')

A language, a poetry in keeping with the new quantum mechanics
(The non-intuitive handling of data, introduced by Heisenberg
The translation of the matrix calculus
Into operational and 'Poisson brackets' methods,
And finally . . .
    ('In Memoriam James Joyce')[2]

The scope and diversity of reference in such lines are indeed astounding. Yet even a cursory glance at grammar and syntax suggests that this verse does *not* 'cut three slices at a time'; rather, it

[1] 'In Memoriam James Joyce' in *Complete Poems*, p.741.
[2] *Ibid.*, p.782.

tears through an unleavened sequence of analogies, expressed or implied. This writing either lacks technique – or is attempting something technically quite different from preceding work.

In 1935, MacDiarmid praised the Celtic bardic system which in his view had 'reduced the personal element to a minimum and subjected the young poets to a vigorous technical training . . . during which they graduated from the use of certain simple technical forms to the more complex ones'.[1] In addition to literary forms, MacDiarmid had in mind the *Ceol Mor*, the classical Highland pipe music renowned for its blend of intricate form and complex improvisation. It was the latter aspect which MacDiarmid most admired, and which he conceived of his own 'later work' as embodying. That the pipers' improvisation existed within – indeed was made possible by – a rigid formal pattern, is a fact MacDiarmid overlooked. In this sense, his own poem, 'Lament For the Great Music', notably lacks the formal control it praises; 'organized in the last degree' is precisely what it is *not*.[2]

Turning to the more immediate inspiration, Joyce, one finds a similar gap between MacDiarmid's own techniques and that of the man he regarded as his modern master. In order for language to embody and transmit energy, syntax must be either obliterated – as in some of Hopkins, Ted Hughes, Berryman, and Roethke – or perfected – as in Herrick, Pope, or Yeats. The prose of *Ulysses* spans both strategies, yet locates each within a larger, counter-balanced structure. By contrast, *In Memoriam James Joyce* lacks both that structure on the one hand, and transmogrifying language on the other. And unlike the obscurity of *Finnegan's Wake*, which is intrinsic and continuous, the obscure passages in MacDiarmid's poem stick out from the rest, and can be skipped over.[3] Without that 'happy madness of the word' which *In Memoriam James Joyce* praises, but evinces at best sporadically, the cumulative effect of its lists, alternative word choices, transparently false claims and ostentatious footnotes is, when not oppressive, comic:

---

[1] *New Scotland (Alba Nuadh)*, 7 Dec. 1935, p.3.
[2] Not knowing Gaelic himself, MacDiarmid can hardly claim to have incorporated its *technical* achievements into his own work. A notable contrast presents itself in the Irish poet Austen Clarke, who steeped himself in the Irish Gaelic, and employed its poetic techniques, such as assonantal rhyme, in his own verse in English.
[3] For a fuller discussion see Edwin Morgan, 'Ju-Jitsu For the Educated', in *Twentieth Century* (September 1956), p.228.

'Elsewhere I have quoted in this connection
MacCruitin, O'Heffernan, O'Hosey, and other Gaelic bards . . .
    ('Direadh I')

Germane to this poem, and most amazing instance perhaps
Of the lengths to which malicious misrepresentation goes
And the *suppressio veri* that accompanies it everywhere
Is the great question of Sinus Tone Production . . .

That this degenerated into the characteristic French nasality
Is neither here nor there . . .
    ('In Memoriam James Joyce')

Why, then, one might ask, is it in the poem? And what possible
personal reaction are such lines meant to elicit?

Clearly, any favourable response on the reader's part entails
expectations that differ from those we normally bring to verse.
What MacDiarmid seems to be demanding in these lines (and
thousands of others equally unfocused and prosaic in standard
terms) is no less than a revision of critical values by which we define
poetry, and judge it.

The critic who has responded most sympathetically is Edwin
Morgan. In 'Poetry and Knowledge in MacDiarmid's Later Work',
Professor Morgan argued that this verse seeks a balance between
'sense impressions' and 'information', and likened it not so much
to an organism as to a colony,

> highly organized in parts, but not prescriptively with regard to the
> whole. . . . Shape and architectonics are not so important as the quick
> movements of the thought – the feelers in the water, moved partly by
> the surrounding currents and partly by their own volition and partly
> in response to the movement of neighbour tentacles, while a suc-
> cession of images, illustrations and analogies is presented to it. As
> zoologists may argue whether a colony is an organism, critics may
> hesitate to say that the kind of *poetry* MacDiarmid wants is a kind of
> *poem*. [1]

In a later essay, Morgan describes MacDiarmid's method as
'aleatory' and 'undoubtedly wasteful', yet argues that this waste is
necessary to surprises that could not be sprung by other means:
'What MacDiarmid is doing, what he has done all through his life,
is to insist on the importance of the multiplex, as against simplistic

[1] 'Poetry and Knowledge in MacDiarmid's Later Work' (1962); rpt.
in Edmund Morgan, *Selected Essays* (Manchester: Carcanet, 1974),
p.208.

solutions, and this involves paying tribute to chance'.[1]

Whether this is special pleading, and whether or not an 'improvisational' art will always be a lesser art, Morgan's spirited defence makes it clear that any satisfactory consideration of MacDiarmid's 'poetry of wisdom' will depend on critical approaches and assumptions significantly different from those that have governed this study. Having suggested a likely direction such future work may follow, we will therefore leave the most problematic writing of a problematic career to other hands.

Having traced the growth of MacDiarmid's verse through each of its varied phases, we may now attempt to sum up his contribution to Scottish literature, and suggest his place in twentieth-century letters.

The Scottish literary renaissance that Hugh MacDiarmid initiated in the early 1920s had several goals: to revive lowland Scots as the national literary language; to promote the study of Scottish Literature independently, rather than as a subordinate category of English Literature; and to bring contemporary Scottish writing into closer touch with other literatures, while insisting that it be judged by the same criteria.

Though the Scots Revival produced individual works of beauty and lasting value, the movement did not endure. Looking back in 1976, two years before his death, MacDiarmid wrote:

> I had hoped that . . . it would be in Scotland as it had been in Ireland with its Irish Literary Revival and that the reawakened national genius would throw up in the course of a single generation an unparalleled host of exceptional personalities. Varied as were the men and women who in fact contributed to that development, the number of any real significance remained disconcertingly small.[2]

If this statement includes work in English – and the Irish comparison suggests that it must – then the generation MacDiarmid alludes to produced only three writers of major stature: MacDiarmid, Edwin Muir, and Lewis Grassic Gibbon. If consideration is limited to work *in Scots*, MacDiarmid stands alone.

In his own synthetic Scots, words borrowed from the literary past were effective and accessible because the colloquial words with which they were blended were still spoken freely at that time.

[1] 'MacDiarmid at 75', *ibid.*, p.216.
[2] Introd., *Contemporary Scottish Studies*, 1925-27; rpt. 1976 (Edinburgh: *The Scottish Educational Journal*), p.iii.

However, as the spoken component of that synthesis lost currency, the 'on-dings' and 'yow-trummles' came to sound less like the language one spoke as a child, and more like expressions found only in books. As Maurice Lindsay notes, 'In an age where the word "lift" is now used only in daily life as Glaswegian for "hoist", it is perhaps questionable if even the lyric genius of a MacDiarmid could achieve again such linguistic revivifications as were still miraculously possible in the 1920s'.[1] MacDiarmid's use of Scots remains widely admired – but is rarely imitated any more.[2]

By contrast, nearly all his hopes for Scottish studies have been realized. Most Scottish universities now have autonomous departments of Scottish Literature, and the School of Scottish Studies at Edinburgh University is world renowned. The Makars are no longer called 'Scottish Chaucerians', and the authors and issues MacDiarmid addressed in shotgun fashion (fifty articles in three years in one magazine alone!)[3] are now the subjects of numerous books, biographies, symposia, *festschrifts* and films. Of course, the post-war burgeoning of Scottish scholarship and art has many varied causes. Nevertheless, the institutional support for such work emerged in large part as a response to the ferment initiated and sustained over decades by one man above all.

The style of MacDiarmid's advocacy, sometimes hyperbolic or inconsistent (but as often sensitive and shrewd), made it difficult to agree with him much of the time – but also impossible to ignore the issues he continually raised. He was not a consolidator so much as an initiator. Not a subtle political thinker himself, he instilled political awareness in countless others; not a fastidious scholar, he

[1] Maurice Lindsay, *History of Scottish Literature* (London: Hale, 1977), p.395. Of course, MacDiarmid himself had stopped using Scots, to all intents and purposes, by the start of World War II.
[2] Inspired by MacDiarmid's example, poets of the next generation did write in Scots; including Sidney Goodsir Smith (1915-75), Robert Garioch (1909-80), and Alexander Scott (b.1920). Nevertheless, most younger Scottish writers today regard the Scots of MacDiarmid and Garioch as part of the irretrievable past. Whereas for the young MacDiarmid, the language of everyday meant Lallans, for current writers such as Scott it may mean the idiosyncratic, nearly unintelligible slang of Glaswegian street gangs. Efforts to capture this argot with orthographic and phonetic experiments represent exactly the sort of 'proletarianization of our actual language' that MacDiarmid opposed in *Left Review*, 1 (February 1935), p.182.
[3] 'Contemporary Scottish Studies', in *The Scottish Educational Journal*, were devoted to Scottish thinkers and issues in a variety of fields. Subjects included 'J. M. Barrie', 'A. S. Neill', 'Scottish Education', 'Rhythm and Culture', etc.

inspired generations of scholarship. This study began with a proposition: that the real task of any modern Scottish writer – and that
by which he or she must ultimately be judged – is to restore some
parity among discontinuous traditions, and to re-integrate the
capacities which they had come, in isolation, to embody.

Did MacDiarmid succeed in the first task? Brilliantly.

Did he accomplish the latter? Sporadically. For despite the
greatness of individual poems, the career is dogged throughout by
insecurity and bluster. As the last forty years in particular make
clear, this poet could not sustain the integration of head and heart
which his finest poems achieve. He could not resolve, in much of
his own life, the contradictions in his culture.

And yet, by internalizing those contradictions, by expressing
them with beauty, loyalty, intelligence and passion, he made other
Scots desire that integration; he helped future Scots achieve it.
What Pound said of Whitman may well be said of Hugh MacDiarmid, born Chris Grieve: he split the wood.

What is MacDiarmid's place beyond Scottish letters? Like other
poets who were born around 1890 and came to prominence after
the Great War, he regarded his own work as both the restoration of
a literary tradition and a revolution within that tradition. Like
others, most notably Eliot and Pound, MacDiarmid sought new
inspiration in non-mainstream or neglected literatures and cultures. And like them, he viewed literary goals as part of a broader
cultural restoration, and insisted that art earn and claim a social
role. All of these poets were also active polemicists, who felt a deep
commitment to the teaching of literature and re-definition of artistic values. Like Eliot (with whom he corresponded) and Pound (a
lifelong friend), MacDiarmid became the central figure of a literary
movement which influenced several generations; and in old age he,
too, acquired nearly mythic status. A writer for the *Sunday Times
Magazine* may have had such similarities in mind when he entitled
a 1978 article, 'MacDiarmid the Brave – Last of the Giants'.[1]

While his interests and intentions coincided in many respects
with those of his more famous contemporaries, MacDiarmid's
verse itself differs from most modernist poetry in two important
ways: it is a verse of advocacy, and of oral discourse.[2]

[1] Neil Ascherson, *Sunday Times Magazine* (14 May 1978), pp. 58-65.
[2] With the notable exception of the early lyrics. Given its variety of
styles and subjects, MacDiarmid's career as a whole does not lend
itself easily to generalization. In the comments that follow, an attempt

Given this poet's allegiances to a culture and a class, he had a tendency, like Burns, to represent the interests of that class to the outside world. While the resulting advocacy is most explicit in the political poems, the need to provoke and convince carries over into other writing too. Indeed, despite marvellous forays into symbolism, expressionism, and surrealism, the bulk of MacDiarmid's output may be thought to have an 'argument' much as one finds in Milton, or in Blake. This frequently allows discussion of a poem's paraphrasable meaning as distinct from its means of expression.[1] It admits – at times demands – a response of 'right' or 'wrong'. Whether or not this response is desirable, it is certainly different in kind from that which most modern verse seeks to elicit. Try to decide whether Hart Crane's *The Bridge* or Williams' *Paterson* or Ted Hughes' *Crow* is 'right' and the difference will be clear. As readers we are not much attuned these days to a verse of exhortation and overt opinion; where MacDiarmid's writing offers this it is closer in feeling to Victorian than to modern poetry.

This leads to our second distinction. None of the three works just mentioned presents an identifiable, and hence accountable, speaker. By contrast, most of MacDiarmid's verse is based primarily in oral discourse; much of the time there is a clear first-person voice which, specified or not, approximates the poet's own. Except in *A Drunk Man Looks at the Thistle*, we are a long way from the modernist revolution in narrative technique, and its central experiments with voice and point-of-view. In these areas, MacDiarmid lacked interest or sophistication. For him, verse remained by and large a heightened form of exposition, meditation, speech.

Of course, the same might be said of most major poets in the language up until his time, and in following suit he echoed not only Burns (and the native tradition of direct speech) but also Wordsworth, and Walt Whitman. Like them, MacDiarmid is essentially a meditative lyric poet.[2] His vast eclectic reading and avant-garde pronouncements notwithstanding, in his own poetic practice he cleaves unselfconsciously to Wordsworth's notion that the poet

---

has been made to identify qualities which cut across genres and periods (discounting the 'later' poems), and with the *caveat* that such selection may well, at nearly every point, be qualified.

[1] This obviously does not apply to the early lyrics, nor to many sections of *A Drunk Man*, and the impact of 'Harry Semen' owes much to non-discursive qualities within a discursive frame. Indeed, this sort of combination might be thought a hallmark of MacDiarmid's most successful poems.

[2] Discounting, again, the 'Poetry of Knowledge'.

must be centrally and simply a man speaking to men.

Is MacDiarmid thus a 'modern poet'? Intellectually he was ferociously modern. The ideas in his poetry are more fundamentally radical and progressive than anything in Eliot or Auden, Graves or Lowell, and hold broader implications than anything in Roethke, Berryman or Plath. On the other hand, the most instructive comparisons for MacDiarmid as *artist* may be with more rooted figures such as Hardy the adapter of hymnal forms, and Yeats, mining oratorical traditions that survived in Ireland but had long since disappeared from other lands.[1] Crossing genres for a moment, we may certainly place MacDiarmid closer to D. H. Lawrence's concerns than those of Ford Madox Ford. Do the views it contains make *Women In Love* a modern novel? Is 'On The Ocean Floor' a modern poem? It depends on what we're looking at – and for.

MacDiarmid's frequently old-fashioned style accounts in part for his critical neglect outside of Scotland. The limited size of his non-Scottish readership may also be explained by practical matters. Most obviously, there is the language. That Scots should comprise an obstacle says more about the provinciality and lethargy of readers than about the writer, but the problem is nevertheless there. Moreover, much of MacDiarmid's loveliest poetry is not immediately accessible out of context. Even with glosses, a reader who stumbled on 'The Eemis Stone' without some background knowledge might make little of it. Much of the finest verse also consists of short poems and fragments whose full meaning emerges only in relation to others – and are hence not suited for anthologies. Conversely, because MacDiarmid wrote so much bad poetry, a new reader who opens the *Complete Poems* at random may be quickly discouraged from browsing on. These obstacles will most likely be overcome by the more helpful and accurate editions of recent years, and by forthcoming critical studies.[2]

---

[1] Among poets of our own time, useful comparisons might be drawn with Odysseus Elytis and Czeslow Milosz. Like MacDiarmid's work, Elytis' often seeks to redeem the neglected, non-classical, non-rational aspect of his nation's culture. All three poets are strongly national figures with supra-national cosmopolitan concerns.

[2] The best selection of MacDiarmid's work to date is the *Selected Poems* of 1970, edited by David Craig and John Manson (Harmondsworth: Penguin). The most attractive and helpful edition of *A Drunk Man Looks at the Thistle* is John C. Weston's (Amherst, MA: University of Massachusetts Press, 1971). Readers are advised to avoid the *Collected Poems* in either the 1962 or 1967 editions – they are quite inaccurate – and use instead the *Complete Poems* (London: Martin Brian & O'Keefe, 1978).

Other difficulties which the poet brought on himself are less easily surmounted. In *Cencrastus*, for example, he declares himself 'Wrang heidet – but heidet – that's the thing', a line which several critics cite approvingly. Is this not special pleading? To be 'heidet' (i.e. intellectual, thoughtful) may distinguish one Scot's work from kailyard writing, but surely we assume as much about any poet of major stature, and what makes us take him seriously is not the strength of his opinions, but their intrinsic merit. In MacDiarmid's case, his vehemence too often overrode his judgment. We find, from time to time, an alarming susceptibility to Great Ideas: the liberalization of Presbyterian culture by Irish Catholic emigres; the Social Credit scheme of C. H. Douglas; a federation of pan-Celtic soviets; a 'parallelogram of forces' stretched between Cornwall and Moscow, not to mention a score of still more abstruse and unexamined notions. Some of these are so implausible as to be comic. Others – that Stalin's purges were a 'mere bagatelle', that 'what we need in Scotland is another Ulster' – cannot be excused on grounds of eccentricity, or non-literal intent.[1] We may infer from what's best in the poetry that MacDiarmid's own loose talk misrepresents his better self. Nevertheless, such statements *were* made; they *do* exist, and contribute to the poet's reputation as a crank.

There is also the disturbing question of unacknowledged sources. Here again, MacDiarmid's anxious, sometimes ill-considered 'heidet-ness' led him to claim knowledge he did not possess, to publish 'translations' of languages he did not know, to incorporate others' words and ideas into the later poems without appropriate citation. In this case the explanation may well be initial naivete and eccentricity, rather than ill intent; the manner of his borrowings suited MacDiarmid's notion of encyclopaedic art, of verse as compilation and amalgamation of the world's best thought. Thus, in the 1965 controversy over 'Perfect' (a fine little poem he made by breaking another man's prose into lines) the shameful thing was not what MacDiarmid had done, so much as his perverse

---

[1] The full statement from which my first quote comes reads: 'Even if the figures of the enemies of Communism were accurate, the killings, starvings, frame-ups, unjust judgment and all the rest of it are a mere bagatelle to the ... damnable consequences of the profit motive, what must be laid to the account of the so-called "free nations of the West"'. This was written not in 1939, or 1948 – but in the *Daily Worker* of 28 March 1957, after the Soviet invasion of Hungary. The comment on Ulster came in a radio broadcast in the seventies, and was quoted to me in Scotland by several different sources.

refusal to acknowledge it, even when caught.

The larger point, as in the flirtation with Stalinism, is that there are certain standards a responsible person does not play fast and loose with, and that to do so weakens our trust in him or her both as a person and as a writer. Even if MacDiarmid really was a Stalinist or plagiarist, or both, he was certainly much more than that. The pity is that his shoddiness on these issues made it harder to credit him as a thinker on others, and easier to overlook him as a poet. Consistency may be the hobgoblin of small minds, but accountability is still the hallmark of complete ones. Whatever the foibles of an artist's life, in his work he must, as nowhere else, be scrupulous. A writer owes this to the reader. And the reader has a right, indeed a duty, to demand it.

Having said as much, we must ourselves be fair. MacDiarmid was certainly no more of a crackpot than some of his great contemporaries; he wasn't the only poet to espouse the Social Credit, nor the only one to publish a great deal of bad verse. And despite other authors' erratic private lives, their overt fascism and covert anti-Semitism, racism and class prejudice, their poems are widely known and rightly praised. Therefore, in seeking to explain the gap in reputation between MacDiarmid and these other figures, we must move on from extrinsic factors to the verse itself. Having assessed his Scottishness, his modernity and credibility, we must finally ask the hardest, simplest, most important question: *Is MacDiarmid a poet of the first rank? Just how good, and how important, are his poems?*

As has been seen, this poet wrote too much, too fast. He revised too little and reversed himself too often. In contrast to the magic of his Scots (alone, or combined with English), his English can lack flexibility and nuance, bordering at its worst on cliché. His critical judgments were erratic – especially in regard to his own verse – and the period in which his great work was written is distressingly brief.

That work cannot compare with Eliot's for subtlety, precision and control. After the early books, it lacks Pound's understated genius – his fine ear – and rarely approaches the brilliance of diction and metaphor that one relishes in Wallace Stevens. We might wish that the poetry as a whole were a bit less strenuous, a bit more inward.

On the other hand, MacDiarmid has a liberality of invention, a broader range of feeling than either Eliot or Stevens, and his subject matter is intrinsically more interesting. He is often more tolerant, and less enamelled and obscure, than Pound; and unlike Stevens, makes a place for flesh-and-blood human beings in his verse. He has a sense of humour. He writes *hospitable* poems.

The intellectual preoccupations which all these modern figures share are balanced in MacDiarmid by a greater comfort with, indeed affection for, the flesh, the challenges and opportunities of day-to-day. Put simply, MacDiarmid, more than any of the others, seeks to ballast intellectual *modernism* with abiding *humanism*.

This sensibility may be attributed, in part, to personal circumstances. In addition to the Auld Makars (who served the same function for MacDiarmid as did the Metaphysical poets for Eliot, or Provençal poets for Pound), MacDiarmid drew more immediately on resources of a culture whose vestiges he had known personally as a child. Thus, 'Water of Life', 'Whuchulls', 'Cattle Show', and 'The Crying of The Fair' offer not an elegiac lament for an ancient loss, but bittersweet celebration of a tradition in which the poet himself took part. Many of MacDiarmid's poems possess a groundedness not present in the work of American exiles, particularly those who renounced their nationality. That groundedness in some degree offsets epistemological doubt, fragmentation and loss, and provides the kind of commitment and loyalty which cannot be obtained from literary precedent alone.

Beyond such biographical facts, MacDiarmid's strengths reflect the Scottish intellectual and educational heritage. In contrast to English practice, which stressed specialization and erudition, precedent and rule of thumb, the Scottish system traditionally emphasized general education, metaphysics and moral philosophy, experiment, discussion of first principles, and debate of specialized topics in the language of every day. MacDiarmid's use of science in 'Dytiscus', 'Thalamus', 'Crystals Like Blood' and 'On The Ocean Floor' echoes the determination of nineteenth-century Scottish professors to teach mathematics as 'a culture course, concerned with the relations of the subject to social life and the plain man'. And when in *In Memoriam James Joyce*, MacDiarmid protests 'the exclusion of value / from the essence of matter of fact', he re-affirms a predecessor's definition of 'the Northern ideal' as 'learning with a large human soul'.[1]

[1] George Elder Davie, *The Democratic Intellect* (Edinburgh: The University Press, 1961), pp.13, 168. The characterizations in the preceding paragraph are illustrated and discussed at length in Davie's study.

These emphases differ markedly from prevailing critical trends throughout and since MacDiarmid's own career. For all it had to teach about close reading, the New Criticism also implicitly removed poetry from its historic, political and social contexts, and taught us to value most the most precisely wrought, and most hermetic, poems. Later approaches, conceived in part as a corrective, emphasized phenomenology, structure or, most recently, poetic influence. Again, these have been helpful. Yet they too are largely unreceptive to direct verse; they too can obfuscate and belittle the place of the actual poet in the poem, and of the poem in non-literary culture. As a result, these critics and the poets whom they champion seem as abstracted and self-distanced from the communal life of our time as the Edinburgh Augustans were from theirs.[1]

Such writing pursues its relatively narrow subjects from a broad, cosmopolitan base. By contrast, MacDiarmid reaches out to a wide range of concerns from a concentrated base of place and class and history – of responsibilities which no interpretation, however *recherché* or subtle, can evade. Early on, an urgent desire for the betterment and fulfilment of those in low circumstances formed the core of his writing. As MacDiarmid's stature grew, the hope for betterment became more universal. Ranging elementally from beach to ghetto, from water to stone, it inspired three small bodies of great verse: the early lyrics, *A Drunk Man Looks at the Thistle*, and especially two dozen or so later poems. Sensual, personal, political, visionary, these share one theme: the struggle, grounded in nature, to fulfil the promise in our own nature; to search for what makes possible our individual and social evolution into fuller human beings.

Compared to much verse now in vogue, these poems provide 'a more strenuous moral experience . . . a more exigent conception of the self and of what being true to it consists in, a wider reference to the universe and to man's place in it, and a less acceptant and genial view of the social circumstances of life'.[2] The authenticity of MacDiarmid's poetry subsumes the fragmentary nature of his

[1] A contrasting – and more rewarding – impulse in contemporary poetry exists in the work of Seamus Heaney, Derek Walcott (especially in his brilliant long poem 'The Schooner *Flight*'), and for the more diffuse American culture in verse such as Robert Pinsky's book-length poem, *An Explanation of America*.

[2] Lionel Trilling's definition of authenticity, as distinct from mere sincerity, in *Sincerity and Authenticity* (Cambridge: Harvard University Press, 1972), p.11.

poems. Like the snowflakes in 'Harry Semen' and the foraminifera incessantly raining, these poems *stick*, accrete, accumulate transforming power. Written in a period of impending holocaust, they offer something we, in no less difficult times, could use: a sense of hope in what we can't yet know; an impulse to redeem.

Poetry assessed in such terms might strike some as dated, middle-brow, naive. It is certainly rare. It may be indispensable. It deserves, and rewards, attention.

BIBLIOGRAPHY

I. HUGH MACDIARMID (C. M. GRIEVE)

1. Verse

Early Lyrics of Hugh MacDiarmid. Introd. J. K. Annand. Preston, Lancashire: Akros Press, 1968.

Sangschaw. Edinburgh: Blackwood, 1925.

'Water Music.' Holograph MS, Gen. 767/1(e). Hugh MacDiarmid Papers, Univ. of Edinburgh.

'On A Raised Beach.' MS, Gen. 887, ff.83-8. Hugh MacDiarmid Papers, Univ. of Edinburgh.

In Memoriam James Joyce. Glasgow: MacClellan, 1955.

Collected Poems of Hugh MacDiarmid. New York: Macmillan, 1962.

A Lap of Honour. London: MacGibbon & Kee, 1967.

More Collected Poems. London: MacGibbon & Kee, 1970.

The Hugh MacDiarmid Anthology: Poems In Scots and English. Ed. Michael Grieve and Alexander Scott. London: Routledge, 1972.

The Socialist Poems of Hugh MacDiarmid. Eds T. S. Law and Thurso Berwick. London: Routledge, 1978.

The Complete Poems of Hugh MacDiarmid. 2 vols. Ed. Michael Grieve and W. R. Aitken. London: Martin Brian & O'Keefe, 1978.

2. Prose

Ed. *Northern Numbers, being representative selections from certain living Scottish poets.* Edinburgh: T. N. Foulis, 1920, 21; Montrose: C. M. Grieve, 1923.

'Scottish Books and Bookmen.' Dunfermline Press, 5 August 1922.

'Following Rebecca West in Edinburgh.' *Scottish Chapbook* 1, 3 (October 1922).

'Causerie.' *Scottish Chapbook* 1, 3 (October 1922).

'Causerie.' *Scottish Chapbook* 1, 7 (February 1923).

'Causerie.' *Scottish Chapbook* 1, 8 (March 1923).

Annals of the Five Senses [poetry and prose]. Montrose: C. M. Grieve, 1923.

'Abracadabra Plus X' [serial column]. *The New Age* 34 (3 April, 17 April, 1 May, 15 May, 29 May 1924).

'Mannigfaltig' [serial column]. *The New Age* 34 (10 April, 24 April, 8 May, 22 May 1924).

'Books and Bookmen.' *The Glasgow Herald*, 17 December 1925.

Contemporary Scottish Studies. 1925; Rpt. 1976. Edinburgh: The Scottish Educational Journal.

'Paul Valéry.' *The New Age*, Vol.XLII, No.5 (1 December 1927).

Albyn, or Scotland and the Future. London: Kegan Paul, 1927.

Letters about *To Circumjack Cencrastus*. Gen.886, ff.6, 7, 11, 14, 81-9. Hugh MacDiarmid Papers, Univ. of Edinburgh.

'Scotland and the Arts.' *The Bookman* 86 (September 1934), 285-6.

At The Sign Of the Thistle. London: S. Nott, 1934.

With Lewis Grassic Gibbon. *Scottish Scene*. London: Jarrolds, 1934.

And Valda Grieve. Letters (78) to Helen B. Cruikshank, 1922-64. Gen.886, ff.4, 5, 35, 79. Hugh MacDiarmid Papers, Univ. of Edinburgh.

'Scotland, France, and Working Class Interests.' *New Scotland (Alba Nuadh)*, Vol.1, No.3 (26 October 1935).

'Communism and Literature.' *New Scotland (Alba Nuadh)*, Vol.1, No.9 (7 December 1935); cont. Vol.1, No.10 (14 December 1935).

'Notes of the Quarter.' *Voice of Scotland* 1, 1 (June-August 1938).

The Islands of Scotland. New York: Scribner's, 1939.

'Editorial [against the English literary left]. *The Voice of Scotland* 2, 1 (June-August 1939).

Introd. *The Fury of the Living*. By John Singer. Glasgow: MacClellan, 1942.

Lucky Poet: A Self Study in Literature and Political Ideas. London: Methuen, 1943.

Ed. *The Voice of Scotland*, a quarterly magazine of Scottish arts and affairs (March 1948-April 1958).

Introd. *Selected Poems of William Dunbar*. Edinburgh: Oliver & Boyd, 1952.

'Why I Rejoined.' *The Daily Worker*, 28 March 1957.

Introd. *Selected Poems of Robert Henryson*. Harmondsworth: Penguin, 1973.

'Burns Today and Tomorrow.' Edinburgh: Castle Wynd Printers, 1959.

'David Hume: Scotland's Greatest Son.' Lecture, Edinburgh University, 1961; Rpt. Edinburgh: Paperback Bookshop, 1961.

The Company I've Kept. London: Hutchinson, 1966.

The Uncanny Scot: A Selection of Prose. Ed. and introd. Kenneth Buthlay. London: MacGibbon & Kee, 1968.

Selected Essays of Hugh MacDiarmid. London: Jonathan Cape, 1969.

Letter to Geoffrey Ellborn, 7 July 1968 [assessment of Yeats and Eliot]. AAF. Hugh MacDiarmid Papers, Univ. of Edinburgh.

'Growing Up In Langholm.' *Listener* LXXVIII (17 August 1968), 204-6.

And Duncan Glen. *The MacDiarmids: A Conversation*. (*See* Glen, Duncan.)

II. OTHERS

Abrams, M. H. 'The Correspondent Breeze: A Romantic Metaphor.'
The Kenyon Review 19 (1957).

Ackerman, Diane. 'Hugh MacDiarmid's Wide-Angle Poetry.' *Parnassus*
9, 1 (Spring/Summer 1981).

Aney, Edith Trelease. *British Poetry of Social Protest in the 1930's: The
Problem of Belief in the Poetry of W. H. Auden, C. Day-Lewis, 'Hugh
MacDiarmid' and Stephen Spender.* Diss. U. of Pennsylvania, 1954.

Angus, Robert. 'The Barren Thistle: A Poetic Tour-de-Force.'
Scots Observer 1, 14 (1 January 1927), p.15.

Annand, J. K., Introd. *Early Lyrics By Hugh MacDiarmid.* Preston,
Lancashire: Akros Press, 1968.

Ascherson, Neil. 'MacDiarmid the Brave: The Last of the Giants.'
London Times Sunday Magazine, 14 May 1978.

Bateson, Gregory. *Mind and Nature: A Necessary Unity.* New York:
Dutton, 1979.

Bell, Adrian. 'English Tradition and Idiom.' *Scrutiny* 2, 1 (1933), p.47.

Bergonzi, Bernard. *Reading The Thirties: Texts and Contexts.* London:
Macmillan, 1978.

Bogan, Louise. 'Two Poets' [Rev. of Collected Poems of MacDiarmid
and Neruda]. *The New Yorker*, 17 November 1962, 238-40.

Boutelle, Ann E. 'The Thistle and the Rose: A Study of the Poetry of
Hugh MacDiarmid.' Diss. New York University, 1972.

Brockway, Fenner. *Hungry England.* London: Gollancz, 1932.

Buchan, David (ed.). *A Scottish Ballad Book.* London: Routledge, 1973.

Buthlay, Kenneth. *Hugh MacDiarmid.* Edinburgh: Oliver & Boyd, 1964.

—— 'The Appreciation of the Golden Lyric: Early Scots Poems of Hugh
MacDiarmid.' *Scottish Literary Journal* 2, 1 (July 1975), 43-9.

Cookson, William (ed.). With Tom Scott. *Hugh MacDiarmid and Scottish
Poetry.* [Special double issue of] *Agenda* 5, 4-6, 1 (Autumn-Winter,
1967-8).

Corkery, Daniel. *The Hidden Ireland; a study of Gaelic Munster in the
eighteenth century.* 1925; Rpt. Dublin: Gill, 1941.

Craig, David. *Scottish Literature and The Scottish People 1680-1830.*
London: Chatto and Windus, 1961.

—— *The Real Foundations: Literature and Social Change.* London:
Chatto and Windus, 1973.

Craigie, Sir William A., and others. *The Scottish Tongue.* London:
Cassell, 1924.

—— (ed.). *A Dictionary of the Older Scottish Tongue.* 5 vols. London:
Oxford University Press, 1931-67.

Daiches, David. 'Hugh MacDiarmid and the Scottish Renaissance.'
Poetry (Chicago) 72, 3 (June 1948).

—— 'MacDiarmid and Scottish Poetry.' *Poetry* (Chicago) 72, 4
(July 1948).

Daiches, David. *Robert Burns*. New York: Rinehart, 1950.

—— Rev., *Collected Poems of Hugh MacDiarmid*. *New York Times Book Review*, 25 February 1962.

Davidson, John. *Ballads and Songs*. London and New York: The Bodley Head, 1898.

Davie, Donald. 'The Poetic Diction of John M. Synge.' *Dublin Magazine* n.s., 27, 1 (January-March 1952).

—— ' "A'e Gowdn Lyric".' *New Statesman* (10 August 1962).

—— *Ezra Pound: Poet As Sculptor*. New York: Oxford University Press, 1964.

Davie, George Elder. *The Democratic Intellect: Scotland And Her Universities In The Nineteenth Century*. Edinburgh: The University Press, 1961.

Day-Lewis, C. *The Lyric Impulse*. Cambridge: The Harvard University Press, 1965.

—— *A Hope for Poetry*. 1939; Rpt. 1976 Westport, Connecticut: Greenwood Press.

Deutsch, Babette and Avrahm Yarmolinsky. *Russian Poetry: An Anthology*. Rev. ed. New York: International Publishers, 1927.

Dickinson, William Croft and George S. Pryde. *A New History of Scotland*. London: Nelson, 1959.

Rev. of *A Drunk Man Looks At the Thistle*. *Times Literary Supplement*, 22 September 1927, pp.6501-2.

Duval, K. D. and Sidney Goodsir Smiths (eds). *Hugh MacDiarmid: A Festschrift*. Edinburgh: Duval, 1962.

Edwards, David Herschell (ed.). *Modern Scottish Poets*. 18 vols. Scotland: Brechin, 1880-97.

Eliot, T. S. 'A Commentary.' In *The Criterion* XII (1932-3), pp.247-8.

—— 'The Music of Poetry.' In *On Poetry and Poets*. New York: Farrar Strauss, 1957.

Fergusson, Robert. *Works*. Ed. A. B. G. London, Edinburgh, Dublin: Fullarton, 1851.

Forrester, W. F. Postcard, 13 April 1934 ['C.M.G. is past praying for']. Gen.1929/59/48. Hugh MacDiarmid Papers, Univ. of Edinburgh.

Frost, A. C. 'M'Diarmid: Scotland's Vortex Maker.' *Bookman* (London) 86 (1934).

Gillam, Barbara. 'Geometrical Illusions.' *Scientific American* 242, 1 (January 1980).

Glen, Duncan. *Hugh MacDiarmid and the Scottish Renaissance*. Edinburgh and London: Chambers, 1964.

—— (ed.). *The MacDiarmids* [A Conversation – Hugh MacDiarmid and Duncan Glen with Valda Grieve and Arthur Thompson]. Recorded at Brownsbank, Candymill, 25 October 1968. Preston, Lancashire: Akros, 1970.

—— Hugh MacDiarmid interview. *Akros* 5, 13 (April-May 1970).

Glen, Duncan (ed.) *Hugh MacDiarmid: A Critical Survey.*
Edinburgh and London: Scottish Academic Press, 1972.

'Gog' [pseud. Oliver St John Gogarty]. 'Literature and Life: *A Drunk Man Looks At the Thistle.*' *The Irish Statesman* 7, 18 (8 January 1927), p.432.

Gordon, Ian. 'Modern Scots Poetry.' In *Edinburgh Essays on Scots Literature.* Edinburgh: Oliver & Boyd, 1933.

Grant, William and David Murison (eds). *The Scottish National Dictionary,* 10 vols. Edinburgh: The Scottish National Dictionary Association Ltd, 1931-76.

Gray, Alexander. 'Lallans: A Plea for the Kailyard.' *Burns Chronicle* 1950, p.11.

—— Pref., *Four-And-Forty: A Selection of Danish Ballads Presented In Scots.* Edinburgh: The University Press, 1954.

Grieg, John Young Thompson. *Breaking Priscian's Head, Or English As She Will Be Spoke and Wrote.* London: Kegan Paul, 1928.

Grieve, Valda. Personal interview. 24 June 1980.

'G.H.' 'Personality and the Machine Age – for Hugh MacDiarmid.' In *New Scotland (Alba Nuadh),* Vol. 1, No.24 (21 March 1936).

Heaney, Seamus. 'Tradition and an Individual Talent.' *Hibernia,* 3 November 1972, p.11.

Henderson, T. F. *Scottish Vernacular Literature.* London: Nutt, 1938.

Hughes, John. 'Humanism and the Orphic Voice.' *Saturday Review,* 22 May 1971, 31-3.

Hynes, Samuel. *The Auden Generation.* London: Bodley Head, 1976.

Jamieson, John. *An Etymological Dictionary of the Scottish Language,* 1808. New Edition, John Longmuir and David Donaldson (eds). 4 vols. Paisley: Alexander Gardner, 1879-82.

Jay, Peter. Introd. *Triquarterly* 21 (Spring 1971), xi-xx.

Jung, C. G. *Two Essays In Analytical Psychiatry.* New York: Dodd Mead, 1929.

Kinsley, James (ed.). *The Poems and Songs of Robert Burns.* 3 vols. Oxford: Oxford Univ. Press, 1968.

Lindsay, Maurice. *The Scottish Renaissance.* London: Serif Books, 1948.

—— *History of Scottish Literature.* London: Robert Hale, 1977.

MacDiarmid, Hugh. Edinburgh: National Library of Scotland, 1967. Catalogue No.7.

'MacDiarmid – the Man.' *Jabberwock* [Edinburgh University Review], Vol.v (1958), 14-16.

McDiarmid, Matthew. 'Hugh MacDiarmid and the Colloquial Category.' *Agenda* 5 4/6, 1 (Autumn 1967-Winter 1968).

MacLaine, A. H. 'New Light on the Genesis of the Burns Stanza.' *Notes and Queries,* Vol.198, No.8 (August 1953).

Miller, Karl. 'Scotch On the Rocks.' *New York Review of Books,* 2 December 1971, 13-16.

Morgan, Edwin. 'Dunbar and the Language of Criticism.' *Essays In Criticism* ii (1952), 138-58.
—— 'Ju-Jitsu For the Educated.' *Twentieth Century* (September 1956).
—— 'Hugh MacDiarmid: The Poet at 70.' *Glasgow Herald*, 11 August 1970.
—— *Selected Essays*. Manchester: Carcanet, 1974.
—— *Hugh MacDiarmid*. Harlow, Essex: Longman, 1976.
Muir, Edwin. 'Scottish Letters in 1931.' *Scots Observer* 6, 273 (17 December 1931), 15.
—— *Scot and Scotland: The Predicament of the Scottish Writer*. London: Routledge, 1936.
—— *Latitudes*. 1924; rpt. New York: Viking, 1972.
Nicholson, Frederick J. 'Thomas Carlyle and Hugh MacDiarmid.' Edinburgh: The Carlyle Society, 1974.
Orage, A. R. Rev. of 'First Hymn to Lenin.' *The Modern Scot*, January 1932.
Ouspensky, P. D. *Tertium Organum (The Third Organ of Thought)*. Trans. Nicholas Bessaraboff and Claude Bragdon. Rochester, NY: Manas Press, 1920.
Rev. of *Penny Wheep*. *Times Literary Supplement*, 24 March 1927, p.214.
Pinsky, Robert. *The Situation of Poetry*. Princeton: Princeton Univ. Press, 1976.
Pound, Ezra. Letter to Hugh MacDiarmid, dated '7 Dec. Anno XII' [sic]. Hugh MacDiarmid Papers, Univ. of Edinburgh. [Not yet catalogued.]
—— *ABC of Reading*. 1934; Rpt. New York: New Directions, 1960.
Pritchard, William H. *Seeing Through Everything: English Writers 1918-1940*. London: Faber, 1977.
Ramsay, Allan. *The Tea-Table Miscellany or A Collection of Choice Songs, Scots and English*, 1724; 12th ed. 2 vols. London and Edinburgh: Alexander Donaldson, 1775.
Rilke, Rainer Maria. *Letters To A Young Poet*, 1934; rev. ed. New York: Norton, 1954.
Ross, Iain (ed.). *The Gude and Godlie Ballatis*. Edinburgh: The Saltire Society, 1939.
'Revival of the Scottish Language.' *Times Literary Supplement*, 8 January 1954, p.29.
'A Scottish Literary Renaissance.' [Review of *Sangschaw*] *Times Literary Supplement*, 7 January 1926.
Seurat, Denis. 'Le Groupe de la Renaissance Ecossaise.' *Revue Anglo-Americaine*, April 1924.
Shestov, Leon. *All Things Are Possible*. New York: McBride, 1920.
Simpson, J. Y. *Man and the Attainment of Immortality*. 2nd ed. London: Hodder & Stoughton, 1923.
Smith, G. Gregory. *Scottish Literature*. London: Macmillan, 1919.

Smith, Iain Crichton. *The Golden Lyric: An Essay On The Poetry Of Hugh MacDiarmid*. Preston, Lancashire: Akros Publications, 1967.

Smith, Sydney Goodsir. *A Short Introduction to Scottish Literature*. Edinburgh: Serif Books, 1951.

'Solovyev, Vladimir.' *Encyclopaedia Brittanica*, 1978 ed.

Speirs, John. *The Scots Literary Tradition: An Essay In Criticism*. 2nd ed. London: Faber, 1962.

Spence, Lewis. 'Scots Poetry Today.' *The 19th Century and After* 106, 630 (August 1929).

Stevens, Wallace. *The Necessary Angel: Essays on Reality and the Imagination*. New York: Knopf, 1952.

Stott, William. *Documentary Expression and Thirties America*. New York: Oxford Univ. Press, 1973.

Symons, Julian. *The Thirties (A Dream Revolved)*. 2nd ed. London: Faber, 1975.

Tapscott, Stephen. Rev. of *The Hugh MacDiarmid Anthology*. *Georgia Review* 32, 2 (Summer 1978).

Thomas, R. S. 'A Welsh View of the Modern Scottish Renaissance.' *Wales*, vol. VIII, No. 30 (November 1948), 600-4.

Trilling, Lionel. *Sincerity and Authenticity*. Cambridge: Harvard University Press, 1972.

Trotsky, Leon. 'Literature and Revolution.' In *Leon Trotsky on Literature and Art*. New York: Pathfinder Press, 1970.

Watson, Roderick. *Hugh MacDiarmid*. Open University Press, Unit 25, 1976.

Weston, John C. *Hugh MacDiarmid's A Drunk Man Looks At the Thistle*. Preston, Lancashire: Akros Publications, 1970.

—— Preface. *A Drunk Man Looks At the Thistle*. Amherst, MA: Univ. of Massachusetts Press, 1971.

Wilson, Edmund. *Axel's Castle*. 1931; Rpt. New York: Scribner, 1936.

—— 'Marxism and Literature.' In *The Triple Thinkers*. London: John Lehmann, 1952.

Wilson, Sir James. *Lowland Scotch As Spoken In the Lower Strathearn District of Perthshire*. London: Oxford Univ. Press, 1915.

Wittig, Kurt. *Scottish Tradition In Literature*. Edinburgh: Oliver & Boyd, 1958.

SELECT GLOSSARY

abordage, boarding
abstraklous, outrageous
abune(heid), above (overhead)
afore, before
aftergait, outcome
aiblins, perhaps
airels, musical tones
airt, direction
alunt, on fire
antrin, rare
arselins, sternforemost
Atchison, James VI coin
atour, over
atweesh, between
attercap, spider
auchimuty, paltry
aucht-fit, eight-foot
austerne, austere
awa', *ava'*, away
ayont, on the far side of

back-lill, thumb hole in the back of the lowland chanter
bairn, child
barmy-brained, foolish
barritchfu', harsh
baudrons, affectionate name for a cat
bauld, audacious
bawbee, half-penny
beal(ing), festering
bebble, to tipple
beddiness, sexually covetous
benmaist, furthest in
bide, dwell, await
big, build
bightsome, active
bish, to revolve
blare, to bleat
blate, bashful
blawp, belch
bleb, a bubble
blinter(ing), to glimmer

bouk, retch
braird, to sprout, grow
braw, splendid, brave
breenge, to plunge, to drive
breist, breast
broukit, dirt-smeared, neglected
buirdly, stalwart
bumclock, flying beetle
byous, wonderful

ca' canny, go carefully
cairney, a stony hill
callant, stripling
carle, man
carline, woman (disparaging)
carp, sing
cavaburd, thick snowfall
cay, jackdaw
chittering, trembling
clanjamfree, a company of people
coom, comb
cornskriech, corncrake
coup, upset
courage-bag, scrotum
couthie, affable
crammasy, crimson
cratur, creature
cray, a pig pen
crine, to shrivel
croon, crown
cull, testicle
cullage, genitals
cundy, a gutter
cwa', come away

daffing, playing
daidle, dandle
deid, dead
deil, devil
dern, secret
din, done
dok, duck

doup, buttock
dour, sullen
dozent, stupid
dree, endure
dumfouner, dumfounder
dwine, pine away

eeel-ark, breeding ground for eels
eemis, insecure, tottering
eident, industrious
eisening, yearning
elbuck, elbow
ettle, to intend

fankle, to tangle, or
    become tangled
fash, fret
faurer, further
feck, large amount
fegs, indeed
fidge, to move restlessly
fleg, to frighten
foch, to shift, turn
fog-theekit, fog-thatched (of a beard)
forekent, to know beforehand
forenicht, between twilight and night
forfochen, worn-out
fou', drunk
foudrie, lightning
freaths, froth
fremt, strange
fug, moss

gangrel, wanderer
gantree, barrel-stand
gar, compel
gaw, to catch
geylies, pretty well
gleid, spark
glit, slime
goloch, earwig
gorlin', fledgling
gawd, gold
greet, weep
grue, revulsion
gudeman, husband
guissay, pig
gundy, greedy, voracious

haill, whole
haik, hoist
hairst, harvest
harns, brains
harth, lean
haud, hold
haw, hollow
hazelraw, lichen
heels-owre-gowdy, head over heels
heich, high, height
hoo, dog-fish
houk, hulk
how'd, shorn down
how-dum-deid, dead of night
howe, a hollow
howff, a tavern

ingangs, intestines
ingles, hearths

jing-bang, crowd
jouk, dodge

keckle, cluck
keeth, to become manifest
kelter, undulate
ken, know
kink, bend
kip, bed ; [*coll.*] brothel
kittle, ticklish
knool, peg
kyth (as keeth)

laich, low
laroch, ruins
lauch, laugh
laverock, lark
licht, light
lift, sky
loon, boy
loup, leap
lourd, heavy (of the sky)
lown, hush
lowse, unyoke, loosen
lozen, window pane
lug, ear

mapamound, world map

meissle, nibble
mense, honour
mawse, joke
muckle, huge
Muckle Toon, big town (Langholm)
munk, swing away
mutchkin, measure of liquor

neist, next
nesh, tender

ocht, anything
on-ding, downpour
owre, over

peerie, top
peerie-weerie, pianissimo

quither, quaver
quhair, where

rax, to stretch
reek, smoking fire
reenge, to flush
rouchled, ruffled
row'd, wrapped up
routh, abundance

sclaffering, slovenly
scunnersome, repulsive
seil o' yer face, fortune favour your face
seilful, blissful
send, bride's escort
sentrice, scaffolding
sheckle, wrist
sinnen, sinew
skimmering, glimmering
skinlan', shining
skirl-i'-the-pan, fried outmeal
slee, sly
sliggy, cunning
slotter, slobber
slounge, sharp fall
soom, swim
sough, sigh (of wind)
souple, supple
spatril, a musical note

spauld, shoulder
speir, ask
sperk, spark
spiel, climb
splairging, spluttering
stap, fill up
starnies, stars
sta'tree, tethering pole
steek, to shut
stegh, to cram
stickit, failed
stramash, hubbub
stawns, chains
swaw, ripple
swelth, a whirlpool
syne, afterwards, then

taet, taste
thole, put up with
thocht, thought
thrum, thread end
thunner, thunder
tine, lose
tint, lost
tousie, rumpled
tweel, tweed cloth
tyauve, to tire out, struggle

unco, very strange

waesucks, alas
wallop, thump
wame, belly
watergaw, vague rainbow
weet, wet
weird, fate
wheesht, hush
whiles, at times
whuds, dashes
whummle, upset
whuram, crochet, quaver
wrocht, wrought
wud, wood
wunds, winds

yabbling, gabbling
yalla, yellow
yett, gate

yill, ale
yirdit, buried

yowdendrift, snowfall
yow-trummle, ewe-tremble
(after shearing)

INDEX TO WORKS BY MACDIARMID

(**Bold Face** indicates detailed treatment)

213